AN A TO Z OF THE OCCULT

AN A TO Z OF
THE OCCULT

SIMON COX
AND MARK FOSTER

with additional material by
Ed Davies, Susan Davies, Jacqueline Harvey and Ian Robertson

MAINSTREAM
PUBLISHING

EDINBURGH AND LONDON

First published in Great Britain in 2007 by
MAINSTREAM PUBLISHING COMPANY (EDINBURGH) LTD
7 Albany Street
Edinburgh EH1 3UG

ISBN 9781845961572

A catalogue record for this book is available from the British Library

Typeset in Apollo and Hamilton

Printed in the UK by CPI William Clowes
Beccles NR34 7TL

ACKNOWLEDGEMENTS

So here we are, at the section of every book that is pretty much bypassed by everyone unless they think they're in it! If I have accidentally missed you out, please accept my deepest apologies and know that all help and encouragement in the creation of this tome was greatly appreciated and absolutely needed.

Thanks first and foremost, for her incredible energy and drive, and her ability to kick serious butt, to Susan Davies, the project manager of sheer brilliance without whom . . . A deep and heartfelt thank you goes out to all the contributors: Ed Davies, who was, as per usual, impeccable in his research and absolutely on time every time; Ian Robertson, a guardian of secrets and fount of knowledge from a bygone era; and Jacqueline Harvey, whose diligent and superb research leaves me in awe.

My co-author, Mark Foster – another great job, my friend. Let's do some more! Many thanks to Dawn Allynn for a breathtaking cover image.

Great friends Neil, Alison, Joe and Imogen; Jane and Alexander; Marcus Davies – remember Antwerp! Mark Oxbrow and Jill – looking forward to meeting Oxbrow junior – great job finding the grail. In the United States, Jennifer Clymer, thrice brilliant once again! M.J. Miller, who still knows it's all about me, me, me. Caroline Davies, a great photographer. Michael Paige and Charlotte Danielsen for your friendship – have a wonderful life together. Joel and Lynne Schroeder; Mark and Tina Finnell; Michael Kowall; Edgar Pablos; Garth Frederick; Judith Cummings; Michael Juris; Milt Hoffman and the crew at MPTF Channel 22. Elizabeth and Earl Clymer, my B&N spies! Plasma on its way!

A big thank you to my family: Mum and Dad in the sun on Gozo; Mark and Claire; the Welsh crew, Uncle Alan, Aunt Betty, David, Carol and Pauline. To David, Alison and Connor in Newtownards.

As always, my agent Robert Kirby has been a great friend and mentor. It's time for some more kofte lamb meatballs! Katie and all at PFD; Bill Campbell, Claire Rose, Fiona Brownlee, Ailsa Bathgate and all at Mainstream for getting the series out.

Richard Belfield at Fulcrum TV; Bill Locke and Max Shapira at Lion TV; Ahmed and Salah in Cairo, new business partners and wonderful friends; everyone who is helping to bring Henu Productions to life.

Andy Gough at Arcadia; Greg Taylor at TDG; everyone who has been so supportive on the Web about the books.

And finally, you. The buying public. See, you did make it in! Without your hard-earned cash being spent buying my books, I would be unable to continue, so my biggest thank you is to the readers. Feel free to contact me with any questions or suggestions for more investigations at coxinvestigates@mac.com

Simon Cox

My thanks go to Ali Russell for once again being a light in a dark place and for truly making my world a better place. My mother, Susan Foster, for the boundless love, support and encouragement. Simon Foster for being a friend as well as a brother – and for adventures in far-off places. Simon Cox, my co-author, for giving me the opportunity and for so much more, but most of all for being such a true friend throughout the years.

Andy Gough for countless days and nights of inspiration and for helping me to keep body and soul together at times. Keep steering your course. Greg Taylor for being a beacon of hope in the wilds of the Internet – and for maintaining our friendship across half the world. Craig Davies for continued inspiration – you are still a revelation. Jason Keane for the thought-provoking discussions and the laughs – watch out for the werewolves. Susan Davies for superhuman feats amid looming deadlines and for general all-round unflappability. Ahmed Abo el Ela and Salah Tawfik in Cairo for the hospitality, the discussions and the laughs. Victor Russell for being truly amazing and one of a kind. Pat Arnold for becoming one of the family. Sarah Kear for being an avid reader and a consummate critic.

Once again, thanks to everyone who has made it all possible: Kate and Paul Struys and the Girls, Adam Miller, Rich Cassaro, Ralph Ellis, Filip Coppens, Mark Oxbrow, Ian Robertson, Barry McCann and Geoff Webb.

Finally, a warm thank you to all at Mainstream, especially Emily Bland and Graeme Blaikie for smoothing the way.

Mark Foster

The extract from *Ta Chuan: The Great Treatise* (Carroll & Brown, 2000) by Stephen Karcher in 'I Ching' is reproduced by kind permission of Carrol & Brown.

The extract from *The Satanic Bible* (© Anton Szandor LaVey) and two from the website www.churchofsatan.com (© Church of Satan) in 'Satanism' are reproduced by kind permission of the Church of Satan.

The extract from Plato's *Timaeus* in 'Ouroboros' is taken from *Timaeus and Critias*, trans. Desmond Lee, advisory editor Betty Radice, Penguin, 1977, reproduced by permission of Penguin Books Ltd.

CONTENTS

INTRODUCTION

In this volume of Simon Cox's A to Z Series, we turn our attention to the mysterious and much maligned world of the occult. The occult is one of those subjects that conjures up controversy and is a topic that is often misunderstood and misinterpreted in the modern age. The word has attracted negative connotations over the centuries, and the occult is often viewed as something unsavoury, which involves anything and everything to do with black magic. This is certainly not the whole story, and while it is true that what we would term the 'dark arts' form a distinct part of the realm of the occult, there is much within it that is wholesome – esoteric and mysterious, yes, but certainly not exclusively dark.

An intriguing notion is that anything which cannot be explained by the rational discipline of science is considered to be part of the occult. Therefore, as science has progressed over the centuries, many 'occult' concepts have been explained and moved into the realm of the known and tangible; yet much remains outside the remit of science even today, and it is in this grey area that the occult thrives.

Furthermore, 'the occult' is also a loose term used to describe anything spiritual that does not come under the umbrella of the major religions. So, while examples of what some might be tempted to label occult phenomena are to be found within the canons of certain religious movements – such as the concept of Christ rising from his tomb, after death on the Cross, to speak with his disciples

– these events are not considered to exist within the realm of the occult simply because they are explained in terms of the beliefs of that particular religion.

So we are left with this somewhat vague definition of the occult, which has come to include anything which cannot be explained by the twin bastions of science and religion. This is probably why the occult has come to encompass subjects and studies that are seen by some as dark and shadowy, to be greatly feared and avoided. That is perhaps not surprising if the occult is defined as that which lies outside of the known – and comfortable – worlds of religion and science. If the occult inhabits a space outside of these realms, then at first glance it is indeed likely to seem a frightening and fearsome beast.

However, as we shall see, once the student of the occult overcomes this prejudice, there is in fact a lot of sacred and positive, life-affirming knowledge to be found. This isn't to say that the occult doesn't also contain unpleasant elements, because there is plenty of evidence to prove that this is the case; however, that is not the whole story, and, like everything in life, occult practices are nothing more than what is made of them. In itself, knowledge of the occult is neither benevolent nor wicked; it can be turned to good just as easily as it can be turned to evil, and it is only the intent and will of the student or practitioner that make it one or the other.

One of the first problems we had to overcome when composing this guide was the question of which subjects we should include. Our modern term 'the occult' comes from the Latin *occultus*, which literally means 'the knowledge of the hidden'. This inspired us to search far and wide for topics which could be defined by this phrase, and the more we looked the more subjects we felt should be included. You might therefore be surprised at some of the entries, but, on closer inspection, all involve hidden knowledge and esoteric elements. So, alongside the usual suspects such as alchemy and satanism, we have also included a look at such subjects as yoga, the I Ching, shamanism, Druidism and Kabbalah, all of which are ancient traditions with a long and illustrious history which easily fall into the category of the occult because of the arcane knowledge secreted at their roots.

As might be expected, occult practices and knowledge began in ancient times and have evolved over many centuries and passed through countless hands. Alchemy can be traced all the way back to Ancient Egypt, and although it came to be seen as a highly mystical and esoteric tradition, it is very likely that in the beginning it was nothing more than a scientific discipline, a way of understanding and interpreting the world. In time, as the knowledge of the ancient alchemists was lost, alchemy evolved into a very complex and arcane art, steeped in mystery and ripe with hints of the unknown and the unknowable.

So it was that alchemy and the occult flourished in the Middle Ages, and much of the imagery that we associate with the occult today comes from these times, a period when wizards experimented in their laboratories and devised devilishly complicated procedures whereby they tried to transmute one element into another, sometimes with the aid of summoned spirits and beings. Thus the medieval era could be seen as the apogee of studies into the occult, a time when science was not able to answer all of man's questions regarding the universe and the occult was therefore looked to as a way of understanding the world around us.

In recent years, the children's fiction of J.K. Rowling has done much to bring about a resurgence of interest in all things occult, albeit carefully and with a fair amount of humour. The world of Harry Potter is steeped in the occult, and the title of the first book, *Harry Potter and the Philosopher's Stone*, even references the ultimate aim of many alchemists: achieving the philosopher's stone, the creation of which was said to lead to immortal life. With the introduction of such concepts into mainstream fiction, a whole new generation has grown up hungry to learn more about magic and the occult. Our interest in these eternal subjects, far from dimming over time, becomes ever stronger.

Even today, when science professes to be able to explain much of what we see around us in the material world and religions seek to comfort us by allowing us to believe that the spiritual world and the fate of our eternal souls has been detailed and mapped out, many turn to belief systems and practices that fall within the realm of the occult. This might be surprising to many people, but in fact it only demonstrates that even in this day and age science and religion do not have all the answers. More and more people are looking to religions such as Wicca and Druidism, seeking knowledge of the future through the use of the Tarot, consulting the I Ching for divination, or practising yoga or shamanism – all because people, now as at any time in the past, are seeking answers that they cannot find anywhere else.

In this A to Z guide, we seek to explore many of the subjects that are labelled occult, and we will attempt to unlock the hidden knowledge at the heart of these disciplines, as well as documenting the stories of some of the most famous occultists, who spent their lives unravelling the timeless mysteries of the universe.

Simon Cox and Mark Foster
April 2007

ALCHEMY

Alchemy has its roots far back in human history. The word itself is derived from the ancient name for Egypt, '*kemet*', which means 'black land'. This was a reference to the dark, rich, fertile mud which was spread across the Nile Valley each year when the river began its annual flood. The black land was the inhabitable region of the country of Egypt, made possible by the life-giving mud that enabled the inhospitable desert region to be farmed. It was in contrast to the 'red land', the lifeless desert itself, which we still use the Ancient Egyptian word '*deshret*' to describe. Misunderstanding of the title 'black land' has often led to the assumption that alchemy is something to be feared, that it is a part of the so-called black arts. We also get the word 'chemistry' from 'kemet', which is not surprising, for the arts of alchemy and chemistry are closely related.

Why should Egypt lend its name to this most esoteric of sciences? Egypt was a source of great fascination for the classical world of the Romans and Greeks, and the Egyptians' knowledge of chemical processes was second to none. It seems that in Egypt metallurgy was held in high esteem and was not viewed as a merely practical discipline. The transformation of dull metallic ore into shiny, beautiful metal objects was considered to be a magical process, and was one that was venerated.

The Greeks tell us that alchemy flourished in Ancient Egypt, although we have no written records from the Egyptians themselves. One event in particular may have been responsible for this absence of historical documents providing proof for the birth of alchemy in Egypt: the Roman emperor Diocletian issued an edict against alchemy sometime in the third century AD. It was ordered that all books containing discourses on alchemy were to be burnt and destroyed. So it was that we have lost countless books once held at Alexandria and elsewhere that could have helped us to understand the true nature of the beginnings of alchemy in Egypt.

Diocletian's reasons for such drastic action against the art of alchemy were not esoteric in origin; rather, he feared that if alchemists succeeded in producing gold from other metals, this supply of cheap gold might cause a collapse in the already fragile economy of the Roman Empire. He also feared that if the Egyptians stumbled upon an endless supply of gold, it might enable them to rise up against Rome.

Clearly, alchemy has its roots in simple chemistry. To the ancients, however, such mastery over nature was an incredible and literally supernatural process. Those who could perform such miracles were viewed suspiciously and jealously by ordinary men and women who did not understand such practices, and so it was that alchemists were viewed as magicians – as sorcerers and wizards.

The alchemists themselves did nothing to shatter the illusion of this image and instead worked at developing their reputations as possessors of arcane secrets. They began to veil their working methods in obscure ways and added mysterious symbolism to their writings. For example, during the early days of alchemy there were seven known metals and also seven known heavenly bodies. Somewhere along the line, it was decided that it would be interesting to match each planet to a particular metal. So when alchemists discussed the chemical changes that occurred when alloys were formed, they were referred to in more mysterious, cosmological terms. Thus gold was equated with the sun, silver with the moon and so on. One throwback to this time in history is the metal still known today as mercury.

This mysticism, rather than being a temporary phase, held sway and became ever more convoluted, creating within the art of alchemy a mire of impenetrable meaning and interpretation that made comprehension almost impossible to an outsider.

Furthermore, the Egyptians believed that their god Thoth was responsible for all chemical interactions, and the Greeks saw in Thoth a mirror of their own god Hermes. Over time the two aspects were merged to become the great god of alchemy, Hermes Trismegistus, 'thrice-great Hermes'. He was said to have written 42 ancient books heavily featuring the art of alchemy. His symbol was the caduceus, the winged staff with twin snakes entwined around it, and this symbol was adopted by the alchemists. Incidentally, today it is also a symbol associated with the medical profession.

It is the alchemy of the Middle Ages with which we are probably all most familiar. The alchemist sorcerer in his stone-walled laboratory, surrounded by vials and potions as well as esoteric symbolism, is an image that is still resonant today and appears in popular culture, including the incredibly successful Harry Potter series.

In the Europe of the Middle Ages, we see a distinct change in the direction of alchemy. It was no longer associated only with metals and chemical elements. Spurred on by the pursuit of the legendary philosopher's stone (a substance, often described as a dry powder, that was purported to be able to create an elixir which would confer eternal youth on the person who consumed it), alchemy became ever more spiritual and concerned with more abstract and philosophical concepts. Eventually, it was considered that the transmutation of lead into gold was simply a metaphor for the transformation of base matter, in this case the human soul, into a much purer and higher state of being.

This concept was clearly inspired by the detailed knowledge of the alchemists concerning the material world. They had long known that it was possible to hide rarer elements such as gold inside other, baser materials, such as metal alloys, and that these rarer elements could be recovered later by certain chemical processes that could separate and isolate the hidden element. So it was that these higher, purer elements of man's soul could be thought of as hiding within the base material of the human body, and it was believed that, as with gold secreted inside an alloy, they could be released and refined if the correct methods were devised and followed.

This clear distinction between the different pursuits of alchemy was defined by the terms 'the Lesser Work', which was the laboratory-based, practical side of alchemy, and 'the Great Work' — what is known as internal alchemy.

Alchemy began to decline in the Western world when the discipline of modern science began to replace it. Science itself relies on rigorous experimentation and the practical proving of theories. Alchemy, with its reliance on ancient books and a certain amount of superstition, had no place in this new regime, and although its demise did not happen overnight, its fate was sealed nonetheless.

However, many famous alchemists from history would no doubt view many of our scientific advancements as alchemical in nature. It is also ironic that it is modern scientific methods that have finally managed to alter the elements themselves, including achieving the fabled transmutation of lead into gold. Modern particle accelerators transmute elements as a matter of course, bombarding atomic nuclei with electrically charged particles that are travelling at incredibly high speeds. In 1980, the scientist Glenn T. Seaborg successfully converted a few thousand lead atoms into gold by removing protons and neutrons from the lead atoms using the principles of nuclear physics. So the question has to be asked: where does alchemy end and modern science begin? Have we not merely succeeded where the early alchemists of over 2,000 years ago failed?

SEE ALSO: Dee, John; Philosopher's Stone

ANGELOLOGY

Angelology is that strand of theology and religion which deals specifically with angels and their ranks within heaven. Angels are found in many religions and cultures in one form or another. They feature heavily in Judaism and Christianity, as well as in Islam, where we are told that the prophet Muhammad received the text of the Koran directly from the archangel Gabriel. In Islam, angels are separate beings from the jinn, the chief of which, Iblis, fell from grace and is a figure similar to the fallen angels of Christianity. Jinn are creatures of free will in Islam and can choose to do good or evil, unlike angels, creatures solely of goodness and light, which can do only God's bidding and will never commit sin.

Many scholars believe that the religion of Zoroastrianism had a profound effect on the development of Judaism, and it seems especially to have influenced angelology within the Jewish tradition. Elements from Zoroastrianism crept into the Judaic canon after Jerusalem was sacked by the Babylonian ruler Nebuchadnezzar and the Jews themselves were taken in captivity to Babylon, where they came into contact with the Persian Empire. It was there that the Hebrew scribes were immersed in Zoroastrian concepts, and it was probably at this time that angels entered Jewish thought and texts.

In Zoroastrian angelology, we find that Ahura Mazda, the universal god, created six Amesha Spenta, 'bounteous immortals', and these would later be deemed archangels within the religion. Assisting the Amesha Spenta are lesser angels known as the Yazata, and together these formed the ranks of angels that would influence the conception of angels which appears in Jewish and subsequently Christian theology.

According to Christianity, the angels form several ranks, or orders, known as angelic choirs, and these are divided into three spheres. Chief amongst the first sphere are the seraphim, the highest order of angels. The word 'seraphim' is found in the Old Testament, and it simply means 'flame'. The jinn of Islam, of which Iblis is probably the best known to us, were said to have been created by God from smokeless fire, so the correspondence here with the meaning of the word seraphim is interesting, although inconclusive in linking the two. Below the seraphim are found the cherubim. These are not the cute figures we know from Renaissance art: the plump, winged infants often incorrectly referred to as cherubs are in fact putti, symbols of love. After the cherubim come the ophanin; these are found in the apocryphal text the Book of Enoch and are seen as vigilantly guarding the throne of God, never sleeping.

Below these three ranks of angels we find the second sphere, which comprises the dominions, the virtues and the powers. The role of these three ranks of angels was to take instruction from the seraphim, cherubim and ophanin, and to order the work of the lower angels. The angels of the second sphere hardly ever had contact with mankind; their duties kept them firmly fixed in heaven, away from mortal realms. However, the third and lowest sphere is probably the best known to humans, because it was these angels that acted as heavenly messengers, administering the wishes of God in relation to man, and they often appeared and spoke to humankind directly. The word 'angel' came to us through the Latin 'angelus', which in turn was derived from the Greek 'angelos', both of which mean 'messenger'. In the Christian and Judaic texts, angels are shown as divine emissaries, acting out God's will, interceding on his behalf and spreading his message to humankind. First amongst the third sphere are the principalities, which order and instruct the angels below them as well as acting as the guardian angels of nations. Next we find the archangels and, finally, the lowest rank, the angels themselves, which, while the most humble of all the angels, are most familiar to us through religious literature.

Today, the term angelology denotes not only the strict theological discipline but also a widespread belief in such concepts as guardian angels and spirit guides. Many people believe that there are angels watching over them, and the belief that every individual has their own angel watching over them can be traced back as far as Plato and other philosophers in Ancient Greece. The Romans also believed that spirits or minor gods were sent to watch over certain individuals, though not everyone was allocated their own tutelary spirit. Much later, Honorius of Autum, the twelfth-century Christian theologian, declared that every single human received a guardian angel as soon as the soul took up residence in its body. Today, the Catholic Church still adheres to this belief that guardian angels are with us and that even when we die our angel is not separated from us but accompanies the soul of the deceased into heaven.

Many people today call on their guardian angels or the angels of Christian, Judaic and Islamic tradition and send them specific prayers. We will leave this section on angelology with a prayer to the archangel Michael, one of the chief angels known to man and a figure which has a particular resonance for many because of the legend that he cast down Satan, defeating him in hand-to-hand combat and wounding him in the side:

> St Michael the archangel, defend us in battle. Be our protection against the wickedness and snares of the devil. May God rebuke him, we humbly pray; and do Thou, O Prince of the Heavenly Host — by the Divine Power of God — cast into hell Satan and all the evil spirits who roam throughout the world seeking the ruin of souls. Amen.

SEE ALSO: Fallen Angels

ANIMISM

The term 'animism', first used by the anthropologist Sir Edward Burnett Tylor in 1871, is derived from the Latin word for soul, '*anima*', and describes an ancient doctrine that asserts that all things in nature, such as animals, trees, mountains and rivers, are imbued with their own life forces, commonly referred to as spirits. These spirits are separate from the thing they energise, although they reside within the apparently inanimate objects and phenomena of nature.

It is believed by many that animism is the earliest, most primitive form of religion, although others consider it to be a philosophy developed by ancient man to try to make sense of the world by externalising the human condition, especially as some natural phenomena appear to be alive. It is also thought that animism sprang from the need to explain the nature of, and distinction between, sleep and wakefulness, life and death, and to account for the cause and meaning of dreams. As a philosophy, however, animism has developed among some cultures into a religious system – polytheism – and the belief in many gods associated with nature and natural objects.

Accordingly, the world is animated with objects that have spirits in the same manner as human beings. Bearing in mind that animism is an attempt to rationalise unseen powers of nature, it follows that these spirits will need to be appeased when animals are killed for food, plants and crops harvested, trees chopped down, volcanoes erupt or rain is required – in fact whenever humans interact with the natural world. Because of this and the respect that has, as a consequence, to be bestowed on all natural phenomena, Porphyry, the third-century philosopher, considered animism to be a huge handicap, stating:

> primitive man led an unhappy life, for their superstition did not stop at animals but extended even to plants. For why should the slaughter of an ox or a sheep be a greater wrong than the felling of a fir or an oak, seeing that a soul is implanted in these trees also?

In his great anthropological study *The Golden Bough*, James Frazer describes the animistic pantheon as 'departmental gods' because 'spirits are restricted in their operations to definite departments of nature'. Accordingly, throughout the world these spirits are named after the object they animate – corn mother, tree spirit and so on – and are not given more individual names; they do not move from one object to another (a tree spirit cannot become a corn spirit); and while they are often able to leave the objects they animate, they do not have individual personalities and associated life experiences.

In Europe in particular, tree spirits and tree worship were very important, which is not surprising considering the vast swathes of forest that at one time covered most of the continent. Sacred groves were a common feature in Teutonic Germany, where the worship of trees was taken so seriously that an old law demanded that anyone who peeled off the bark of a standing, living tree was to suffer a terrible punishment. This consisted of the perpetrator's navel being cut out and attached to the part of the tree that had been attacked; the person was then dragged around the tree until all his guts had been wound round its trunk. As James Frazer points out, 'the punishment clearly was to replace the dead bark by a living substitute . . . the life of a man for the life of a tree.' Vestiges of tree worship can still be found in European customs, in particular the maypole, traditionally cut from the may tree, or hawthorn. Maypoles are either erected outside homes or a larger pole is set up in the village, acting as a focal point for celebration, the idea being to obtain the blessing of the tree spirit in order to ensure fecundity and good luck for the spring and subsequent harvest.

As it is believed that even plants scream and cry out in pain when they are cut, trees have to be felled carefully and sensitively so as to cause the least hurt and avoid angering other tree spirits, which may attack the thoughtless or incompetent woodcutter. With this in mind, Austrian woodcutters would ask forgiveness of the tree before cutting it down, an action which has also been attested to elsewhere in the world. Among some Native American tribes, a woodcutter will inform the tree next to the one selected that it is to be cut down, in the belief that the chosen tree will faint at the thought of seeing its neighbour hurt and will therefore feel no pain when the axe falls on it. For some cultures, the desire not to anger the tree spirits even extends to after the tree is felled and cut into planks, as it is believed that the tree spirit continues to dwell within the wood. If, therefore, a house is built from wood, either a blood offering will be given to the tree spirit or a period of penance will be observed in recompense for the builders' actions. However, tree spirits are not always treated with due respect, with Frazer pointing out that in Malaysia, Japan and Bulgaria fruit-bearing trees were threatened with the chop if they did not bear fruit, being literally frightened into compliance.

Another widespread belief is that in corn spirits throughout Europe and the Americas and in rice spirits in the Far East. Again, it was thought necessary to appease these spirits, for to anger them meant failure of the crops. Accordingly, many rituals are attested to relating in particular to harvest time and the last ear of corn left standing in the field, which is cut, bound and sometimes made into a doll to be taken into the house for good luck. In some instances, the last sheaf of corn is fed to the cattle so that they will flourish, thrown into the river to ensure sufficient rain for the next year or scattered among the new crop to guarantee continued productiveness. However, some societies saw the last ear of corn as unlucky and in Pembrokeshire, Wales, the slowest reaper had the dubious task of cutting the last ear of corn, which was referred to as 'the hag' (in the sense of 'an old woman'). In some parts of Germany, the last ear of corn was beaten so that the corn mother would be driven away from the harvested field.

In the Far East, the rice spirit played a similar role to the corn spirit of Europe, with a great deal of respect given to the plant and its incumbent spirit through all the stages of cultivation to prevent the crop from withering. Even after the rice was harvested, it was thought necessary to capture the rice spirit in a bamboo box and to store it with the grains.

In many animistic cultures an important role as intermediary between physical and spirit worlds is fulfilled by a shaman figure, who performs rituals such as dances that imitate the movements of birds and animals in order to reach a trance-like state and enter the world of spirits. Once in this state, the shaman can contact the dwellers of the spirit world in order to find the answers to specific questions, such as the cause of illness or the failure of crops, acting as a go-between in order to connect the human world with the world of spirits. Shamans can also interpret dreams, considered to be journeys of the spirit.

With regard to humans, the absence of the spirit is thought to cause coma or death, and sickness is often believed to be the result of a temporary departure of the spirit. The spirit is understood by most animistic cultures to reside in the heart, although others believe the spirit dwells in the head. However, an object's shade or shadow is also associated with the spirit, and if its shadow falls on you, illness or death can result. For example, in some Arab countries it is believed that if a hyena steps on your shadow, you will lose the powers of motion and speech for a time. A trace of this idea can be seen in our phrase 'to cast a shadow' over someone. Whilst most such societies believe that humans have one spirit, some believe that they have more. In Ancient Egypt, a person was thought to consist of five aspects: the physical body, the *ka*, the *ba*, the name and the shadow. The ka was the life force that continued to live beyond physical death and thus had to be sustained by food and drink offerings to the deceased, whilst the ba was seen as the personality that gave an individual their uniqueness. At death, the ka and ba had to be reunited for the individual to become an *akh*-spirit – the 'blessed dead'.

According to animism, the spirit does not die with the body but merely leaves the physical and enters the world of spirits. Most cultures believe that the spirit goes on to a better life without pain or concerns, as in the Christian heaven, but others believe that the spirit remains on earth as a ghost. Such a concept existed in Ancient Mesopotamia, where the deceased were thought to be earthbound but in an astral form. To the Mesopotamians, the dead did not enjoy the benefits of an easy, work-free afterlife but merely continued as in their earthly life, though within the realm of the dead on earth. Accordingly, they considered their world to be filled with ghosts, with one text stating: 'A door cannot exclude them; a bolt cannot turn them back; they slither through the door like a snake; they blow by the hinge like the wind.'

Animism is still the belief system of choice for many today, especially neopagans, Wiccans and new-age followers, and as such it is considered to be the oldest surviving system of belief. For those who have faith in animism, humans are not superior to nature but are an integral part of the greater whole, as a hand is to a body. Because every natural thing has a spirit, animism stresses respect for all the elements of nature and our environment.

SEE ALSO: Shamanism; Wicca

ASTROLOGY

Despite its popularity, many people are dismissive of astrology, finding it hard to accept that the movement and relationship of the planets might have an effect on everyday life. Unfortunately, the only encounter the majority of people have with astrology is via horoscopes read in newspapers and magazines, which cover the daily trends of millions of people and take into account only sun signs, disregarding all the other pertinent factors that an astrologer utilises in order to produce a comprehensive horoscope.

Newspaper horoscope columns are not, however, truly representative of astrology, which is an ancient pseudo-science dating from early Mesopotamia (c. 3500 BC in its earliest form) and practised in Babylonia, Ancient Egypt, Greece, Rome and Arabia, as well as being studied in Mesoamerica, China and India, where a Sanskrit astrological text dating to 3000 BC and using the standard 12 signs has been discovered.

Early Mesopotamians first studied the night sky in search of portents and omens such as those found in the appearance of stars, eclipses or comets. The zodiac was developed for this reason at an early date, but there is no indication that at this time astrology was used as a regular means of forecasting. However, by the sixth century BC astrology in Mesopotamia had become a scientific study, with the ancient astrologers seeing the movement of the planets as representative of the deeds and events of their gods. It was thought that the actions of the gods would naturally reflect upon the plight or success of those living on earth.

By the fourth century AD, the practice of astrology was declining in the Christian world due to the anti-astrology views of the very influential St Augustine, Bishop of Hippo, who declared: 'Those who hold that stars manage our actions or our passions, good or ill, without God's appointment, are to be silenced and not to be heard.' Because of St Augustine's pronouncement, it was not until the twelfth century that astrology found favour in Europe once again.

So how does astrology work? The sky is divided into 12 sections of 30 degrees, each representing a sign of the zodiac. In addition to this there are 12 houses, each dealing with a particular facet of life. For example, the first house relates to personality, the second deals with wealth and the fifth with creativity. The planets, constellations and hence the signs of the zodiac move through these houses. Each sign is based on a Moon cycle, with each month marked by a particular constellation. The Babylonians identified these by giving them animal and human forms and names. Many of these signs are still used in astrology today, such as Aries the Ram and Taurus the Bull, although others have changed.

Since the Earth and other planets revolve around the Sun, the position of the constellations, and hence their relationship to the zodiac, also changes every day, and it is these movements and shifting relationships that the astrologer is interested in. Divining the future by use of astrology works by predicting where the planets will be at a given date and how they will be placed in relation to other planets. In addition to this, the planets rule certain signs: for example, the Sun rules Leo, the Moon governs Cancer, and Saturn reigns over Capricorn and Aquarius. When the planets are in their particular signs, it is thought that their influence is exceptionally powerful.

Most people are aware of their 'birth sign', the Sun sign, which is decided by the part of the zodiac the Sun was in at the time of birth; but also of importance is the rising sign (the sign that was rising on the eastern horizon at the moment of one's birth). The zodiac signs are subdivided into four elements: Air (Gemini, Aquarius, Libra), the qualities of which include compassion, intellect and refinement; Fire (Aries, Sagittarius, Leo), headstrong, enthusiastic, idealistic; Earth (Capricorn, Taurus, Virgo), organised, cautious, ambitious; and Water (Cancer, Pisces, Scorpio), emotional, sociable, sensitive.

Astrologers believe that the planets too have particular traits. For example, the Sun represents the individual's true nature and has characteristics of generosity and loyalty; the Moon corresponds to a person's subconscious and relates to emotion; Venus is grace and charm; and Jupiter is associated with generosity and success. The relative positions of the planets to one another are also taken into account by the astrologer. Known as 'aspects', these include conjunct (when two planets are next to each other in the zodiac), which strengthens each planet's characteristics; square (planets separated by 90 degrees), which reduces the effect of each planet; trine (separated by 120 degrees), which balances the effect of each planet and produces an easy transition; and sextile (opposite one another), which can cause difficulties and differences.

The relationship of the planets, signs, houses and aspects produces a multifaceted and comprehensive picture of the individual, which has been described as being as unique as a fingerprint. There are many types of horoscopes. The most common is the natal horoscope, which can be based on any point in time, a wedding or a new job, perhaps, but more usually a birth date. This predicts the personality, physical characteristics, possible development path and fate of the subject. It can also assess favourable dates for certain events. Horary charts are drawn up to answer a specific question, with the horoscope cast at the time the question is asked. Mundane astrology looks at groups, such as nations and organisations, rather than individuals, and event charts study the zodiac at the time of certain events to see what the future holds. One particular use of event charts is decumbiture, a means of medical diagnosis and prognosis, a horoscope cast from the time a person becomes ill in order to find out the cause of illness and how it will proceed. Many Western countries have placed legal limits on the use of decumbiture.

Electional astrology attempts to find out the best time to do something; this was popular with Ronald Reagan, who consulted astrologer Joan Quigley in order to determine the times and dates of meetings and journeys. Local-space astrology is similar in many ways to feng shui, as it gives the ideal location for rooms in a house, or directions from the house that will be best to find friendship or a successful career, for example.

Some believe, however, that astrologers are now using the wrong zodiac signs, because the effect of precession of the equinoxes caused by the Earth's shift in axis means that the Sun is now in a different part of the zodiac. Most astrologers calculate that the Sun enters Aries at the spring equinox, as it has done for thousands of years;

but currently the first day of spring actually occurs when the Sun is in Pisces. Therefore the Sun now enters each sign a month later than before, so that those born in the sign of Leo, for example, should now be Cancerians, while Scorpios are really Librans. In addition to this, the demotion of Pluto to a dwarf planet and the discovery in 2003 of UB313 in the outer reaches of our solar system mean that astrology is in the process of considering how this will affect the discipline. Most astrologers have no desire to lose Pluto, as, despite its small size and the fact that it is so far away, Pluto's influence is very important, presiding as it does over far-reaching changes and transformations.

In 1940, an engineer called John Nelson began a study of sunspot activity, which he noticed grew worse when planets were in certain positions. By the 1960s, he was able to use his research to predict acute cosmic storms by analysing the positions of the planets. So if planets aggravate magnetic storms on the sun, could they similarly have an influence on us? It is known that the moon has an effect on people; we have the concept of 'lunacy', a madness associated with the full moon, and it is recorded that more suicides, murders and hospital admissions occur when there is a new or full moon.

Interestingly, French statistician Michel Gauquelin set out in the 1950s to discredit astrology, but his study of 25,000 subjects found trends for those born at certain times. Gauquelin noted that of 576 prominent professors of medicine, a high proportion were born after the rising of Mars or Saturn; similarly, he found that Mars or Jupiter featured prominently in the horoscopes of the majority of distinguished soldiers. Other such astrological trends were discovered in relation to other sections of the community. Likewise, the American Edmund van Deusen examined 163,953 birth dates, while in the UK Joe Cooper and Dr Alan Smithers studied 35,000 birth dates, with both noting through statistical analysis that, even taking into account the monthly birth variations, a high proportion of soldiers are born in late summer and early autumn, and that in general bankers are Virgos, politicians are Aries and lawyers are Geminis.

All this suggests that the time of year a person is born may have an influence over their personality and evolution. In *Cult and Occult*, Peter Brookesmith points out that a market-research bureau noted that children born around noon in the first two weeks of August were healthier, strong, tall, kind-hearted and practical. He also asks whether we should be looking at the whole question of how astrology works from another angle: by studying people's characteristics over hundreds of years, the ancients noted that people born at certain times shared particular traits that could be associated with specific animals, gods or themes. As Brookesmith points out, the constellation of Leo does not look like a lion, but could it be that 'the experience of centuries showed that those born in . . . August tended to exhibit leonine characteristics'?

The Babylonians amassed their information over centuries so it is not unreasonable to suggest that they named the constellations of the zodiac after the general qualities of those born at certain times. Studies undertaken over the past 60 years support the astrological tenet that planets have an effect on us, or perhaps, rather, that past study of human activity in relation to the movement of planets was so thorough that astrologers can now assess possible future trends based on the experience of thousands of years.

This experience has enabled some astrologers to make surprising predictions. Writing in 1923, the German astrologer Elsbeth Ebertin stated in *A Glimpse into the Future*:

> A man of action born on April 20, 1889, with Sun in the 29th degree of Aries at the time of his birth . . . could very likely trigger off an uncontrollable crisis. His constellations show that this man is to be taken very seriously indeed. He is destined to play a 'Führer-role' in future battles.

Hitler, whose date of birth was 20 April 1889, was a great believer in astrology, and Karl Ernst Krafft, Hitler's private astrologer, predicted that between 7 and 10 November there would be an attempt on Hitler's life, which turned out to be an accurate prediction, as a bomb that was intended to kill him was found in a beer cellar. Believing that Hitler was using astrologers for advice, the British government used their own astrologers to determine what their German counterparts were telling Hitler.

The Establishment has not always looked favourably on astrologers. A prominent example is the arrest of the American astrologer Evangeline Adams in 1914 for fortune telling. In court, she gave the judge a detailed account of how she cast a horoscope and made predictions. She also offered to draw up a horoscope for anyone the judge wished to nominate, the person remaining anonymous to all apart from the judge. He chose his son and was so impressed with the accuracy of the horoscope that he stated: 'The defendant raises astrology to the dignity of an exact science.' As a result, Adams was released and was able to carry on as a successful astrologer, even predicting in 1931 that the USA would be at war in 1942.

Whilst daily newspaper horoscopes may be dismissed by many, the fact that the majority of publications run such columns is a testament to their success and our desire to know what the future may hold.

SEE ALSO: Divination

BLAKE, WILLIAM

William Blake is best remembered today as a painter and poet. While not greatly known or admired in his own lifetime, he left behind him an intricate and highly original body of work that inspired many who would follow him, and he has come to be considered an artistic genius. Much of his work involved a union of his visual art and his poems and they complemented each other perfectly to produce an end product that at the time was unique.

Blake was born in London in 1757, and his fascination for art began at an early age. When he was 10, he was producing engravings copied from drawings of Greek antiquities, encouraged and supported by his father. By the age of 14, he became an apprentice engraver under James Basire, becoming a professional engraver at 21.

In 1784, after his father's death, Blake opened a print shop with his brother and it was here that he became immersed in the worlds of literature, poetry and alternative thinking. He had published his first book of poems not long before, sometime in 1783, but at the print shop he began experimenting with new methods of engraving and was soon producing illuminated books such as *Jerusalem: The Emanation of the Giant Albion* and *Milton: A Poem* amongst others.

Blake had visions throughout his lifetime, and we know that he was experiencing these at just eight years old, when he saw a tree whose branches were inhabited by angels. In *The Stranger from Paradise: A Biography of William Blake*, G.E. Bentley quotes from Frederick Tatham's unpublished 'Life of Blake' (*c*.1832), which records that once 'his mother beat him for running in & saying that he saw the Prophet Ezekiel under a Tree in the Fields.' These visions played a large part in Blake's work and on one occasion in 1810 his wife, Catherine, is even said to have remarked: 'I have very little of Mr Blake's company. He is always in Paradise.'

Blake was also a deeply religious man; however, his views were far from conventional, and during his lifetime Blake would continue to push the boundaries of what was considered customary religious thought. In 1789, he became involved with a group called the Swedenborgians, a religious order based on the work and writing of Emanuel Swedenborg, a Swedish scientist-turned-mystic who prophesied that a new church would be born from his work; and so it turned out: the Church of the New Jerusalem was founded some 15 years after Swedenborg's death.

Swedenborg proclaimed that he had witnessed the Second Coming of Christ and that to him was bestowed the honour of witnessing Christ's Last Judgement. Swedenborgianism differs from other forms of Christianity in that it teaches that there is only one true God and that this is Jesus Christ himself.

Although Blake later became heavily involved with the Swedenborgians, it would seem that early on he was sceptical, and he wrote *The Marriage of Heaven and Hell* as a satirical take on Emanuel Swedenborg's best-known work, *Heaven and Hell*. However, Blake would grow to be deeply influenced by Swedenborg, particularly on the matter of marriage and sexual union. Blake saw marriage as an institution that could lead to the oppression of women, and both he and Catherine believed in sexual equality. However, when Blake at one point in the marriage suggested that he take on a concubine, his wife became so distressed that he dismissed the idea.

Robert Rix, writing in the journal *Esoterica*, reveals certain aspects of Swedenborgianism that we find echoed in Blake's work:

> Swedenborg's authorisation of concubinage must be seen within the larger context of his mystical theology of 'conjugal love.' Robert Southey, who had studied the Swedish prophet for his semi-autobiographical *Letters from England*, wrote that Swedenborg 'dilates with more pleasure' on conjugality, which is what 'flows from the Creator into all things; from the Creator it is received by the female, and transferred through her to the male . . . it finds its way through the breast into the

genital region.' As Southey is well informed, Swedenborg saw
the sexual union as a means for man to unify the portions of
his divinity separated in the fallen world.

This belief that spiritual fulfilment might be found through the
act of sexual union was not a new idea in Blake's time, though
it was rarely practised or preached within a group such as the
Swedenborgians that held Christian ideals. So it is evident that
prior to and during Blake's lifetime there was a coming together
of conventional Christian teachings and more esoteric ideas within
certain groups.

The Swedenborgians, along with other similar groups of the
late 1700s, were thought of as part of the Gnostic movement, and
their unconventional take on religion clearly influenced Blake, who
considered organised religion something akin to an affront to Jesus
Christ himself. Blake, although deeply inspired by the Bible, found
himself opposed to many of the teachings of the mainstream Christian
Church and abhorred many of its values:

> Remove away that black'ning church;
> Remove away that marriage hearse:
> Remove away that place of blood:
> You'll quite remove the ancient curse.

However, in 1804 Blake had a radical vision which prompted a
drastic change in his views on religion; he reverted somewhat to the
traditional view of Christ and after this event was found less in the
company of the more esoteric groups such as the Swedenborgians.
However, even in later life, when Blake had accepted Jesus as his
companion and deliverer, he wrote this in his poem 'The Everlasting
Gospel':

> The vision of Christ that thou dost see
> Is my vision's greatest enemy.
> . . .
> Seeing this False Christ, in fury and passion
> I made my voice heard all over the nation.
> What are those . . .
> I am sure this Jesus will not do,
> Either for Englishman or Jew.

We see in this that while he believed in the divinity of Jesus, he still abhorred the organised religion of the Christian Church.

Blake inspired the Pre-Raphaelites, including Dante Gabriel Rossetti and William Morris, and many of his themes can be seen in their work. Towards the end of his life, he attempted what might have been his greatest work if only it had been completed, an illustrated version of Dante's *Divine Comedy*. Blake died, however, in the early stages of its creation, and we only have a few watercolours left to indicate what the finished project would have looked like. He is said to have died filled with the joy of the life to come. One of his friends wrote that: 'His Countenance became fair. His eyes Brighten'd and He burst out into Singing of the things he saw in Heaven.'

William Blake's most famous poem is perhaps 'And Did Those Feet in Ancient Time', inspired by the tale that Jesus had come to England accompanied by Joseph of Arimathea. It was written merely as part of the preface to his epic poem *Milton*, and Blake even omitted it from later editions, yet it has assumed a life of its own since his death and has become Blake's signature work. It has been set to music as the hymn 'Jerusalem', but the original poem is just as powerful without the music, and Blake's intention in writing this poem still intrigues and puzzles scholars and laymen alike.

> And did those feet in ancient time
> Walk upon England's mountains green?
> And was the holy Lamb of God
> On England's pleasant pastures seen?
> . . .
> I will not cease from Mental Fight
> Nor shall my Sword sleep in my hand,
> Till we have built Jerusalem,
> In England's green and pleasant Land.

Appreciating fully the mind that produced such a unique body of work is probably impossible today, and the meaning of his work and his true message are probably known only to Blake himself. Yet we can glimpse in his paintings and verses a remarkable imagination and a truly inimitable style, and the fact that he is still influencing people today, nearly two centuries after his death, speaks more about his genius than anything else. In letters written to Reverend John Trusler in 1799, he gives us an insight into the way his visionary experience of the world informed his art:

> I feel that a man may be happy in This World. And I know that This World is a World of Imagination & Vision. I see Every thing I paint in This world, but Every body does not see alike. To the Eyes of a Miser a Guinea is far more beautiful than the Sun, & a bag worn with the use of Money has more beautiful proportions than a Vine filled with Grapes. The tree which moves some to tears of joy is in the Eyes of others only a Green thing which stands in the way. Some see Nature all Ridicule & Deformity, and by these I shall not regulate my proportions; & some scarce see Nature at all. But to the Eyes of the Man of Imagination, Nature is Imagination itself. As a man is, so he sees. As the Eye is formed, such are its Powers . . .

And then this telling paragraph: 'Why is the Bible more Entertaining & Instructive than any other Book? Is it not because it is addressed to the Imagination, which is spiritual sensation . . .?'

SEE ALSO: Gnosticism

CHYMICAL WEDDING, THE

The Chymical Wedding of Christian Rosenkreutz is an alchemical text first published in the seventeenth century, in 1616 to be precise. The Christian Rosenkreutz of the title is the legendary founder of the Rosicrucians, a mysterious order the existence of which came to light in the early seventeenth century when it published a trio of esoteric pamphlets known as the Rosicrucian Manifestos, which intrigued and mystified European intellectuals, leading to a fascination with their ideas, which included the pursuit of an idealised European civilisation that would be founded on hermetic as well as Christian principles. *The Chymical Wedding* was the third of these manifestos.

In the text, Rosenkreutz travels to the castle of a king, where he is asked to oversee the wedding of the king and his bride. The story takes place over the course of seven days; it has been suggested that each day represents a stage in a ritual transformation, and that the marriage of the king and his bride is an allegory for a very complex alchemical process. During the first few days, Rosenkreutz has to undergo certain tests and initiations, as if the wedding of the story were the 'Great Work' itself, the ultimate aim which the alchemist hoped to achieve through the spiritual, questing aspect of the discipline.

The seven days during which the events of *The Chymical Wedding* take place may be the key to this allegory. The alchemists knew of seven planets, and certain metals were identified with these planets. Furthermore, author Adam McLean, who has written many books on alchemy, such as *The Alchemical Mandala*, has demonstrated that the most prized alchemical works, including the creation of the philosopher's stone, involved a sevenfold transmutation process – the same process that is being described allegorically in the seven days of *The Chymical Wedding*. 'This archetypal sevenfold pattern is, in fact, one of the secrets of Alchemy, one of the skeleton frameworks upon which the alchemists hung their symbols.'

The text hints that the royal wedding is the 'sacred marriage', a concept with which many alchemists became obsessed. This was the union of the individual's divine spirit with first the soul and then the physical body. The achievement of such was the Great Work of alchemists. This sacred marriage was seen as a coming together of opposites – of the spirit and the physical. Alchemists often dealt in opposed elements (for example, describing physical matter by way of paradox, such as 'fiery water') and they believed that the coming together of the spirit and the body was achievable.

The Gnostic Gospel of Thomas also alludes to the concept of the sacred marriage:

> Jesus said to them, 'When you make the two one, and when you make the inside like the outside and the outside like the inside, and the above like the below, and when you make the male and the female one and the same, so that the male not be male nor the female female; and when you fashion eyes in the place of an eye, and a hand in place of a hand, and a foot in place of a foot, and a likeness in place of a likeness; then will you enter the kingdom.'

So the sacred marriage in *The Chymical Wedding* is alluded to in terms of the royal wedding of the king and queen because, just as in the sacred marriage of the spirit and the body, when the king and queen are finally married they are no longer two halves of the equation, male and female; they are suddenly one, unified.

We see evidence of the mystical nature of the marriage in *The Chymical Wedding*; the king and queen are executed just after they are married, but they come back to life with the aid of Rosenkreutz and others present, through what can only be described as an alchemical process. So not only is there a sacred union, but we also have death and resurrection present in the text.

The text is full of riddles and simply bristles with symbolism;

someone could probably spend their whole life studying the text and still not find all of the possible connotations and meanings hidden within it. Here is a very short extract from the chapter titled 'The First Day', in which Rosenkreutz receives the invitation from the king:

> In so unlooked for an adventure I was at a loss, how either to advise, or assist my poor self, and therefore fell upon my Knees, and besought my Creator to permit nothing contrary to my Eternal Happiness to befall me; whereupon with fear and trembling, I went to the Letter, which was now so heavy, as had it been meet Gold, it could hardly have been so weighty. Now as I was diligently viewing it, I found a little Seal, whereupon a curious Cross with this Inscription, In Hoc Signo Vinces, was ingraven.
>
> As soon as I espied this sign I was the more comforted, as not being ignorant that such a seal was little acceptable, and much less useful to the Devil. Whereupon I tenderly opened the Letter, and within it, in an Azure Field, in Golden Letters, found the following Verses written:

> This day, this day, this, this
> The Royal Wedding is.
> Art thou thereto by birth inclined,
> And unto joy of God designed?
> Then mayest thou to the mountain tend,
> Whereon three stately Temples stand,
> And there see all from end to end.
> Keep watch, and ward,
> Thy self regard;
> Unless with diligence thou bathe,
> The Wedding can't thee harmless save;
> He will damage that here delays;
> Let him beware too light that weighs.

Underneath stood Sponsus and Sponsa.

The true author of *The Chymical Wedding* is not known. Johann Valentin Andreae (1586–1654) claimed he had written the text; this has never been proven, although today it is more often than not attributed to him. What casts doubt on his authorship of the work is the fact that Andreae actually mocks the science of alchemy in several of his writings. It is worth noting that the occult and religious writer Manly P. Hall, author of *The Secret Teachings of All Ages*, believed that Andreae was actually none other than Francis Bacon; in his view, Bacon had faked his death and moved to Germany, where he adopted the persona of Andreae.

The truth is that there is no firm evidence that he did or didn't write *The Chymical Wedding*, and while the Rosicrucian Order was certainly formed during his lifetime, whether he was involved with it is not known for sure. So this mysterious text remains just that – a small but intriguing part of the Rosicrucian canon, a text that came into existence at a time when the Rosicrucian Order, amongst others, was bringing about a change in alchemy and taking steps to turn it into what we know today as rational science.

SEE ALSO: Alchemy; Philosopher's Stone; Rosicrucianism

CROWLEY, ALEISTER

So great is the notoriety that surrounds Aleister Crowley that even the mere mention of his name is enough to provoke outbursts from some quarters. Crowley was once called 'the Wickedest man in the World' and he himself did nothing to contradict this description. In 1934, a London judge addressed the jury in a libel case brought by Crowley in the following way during his summing-up:

> I thought that I knew of every conceivable form of wickedness, I thought that everything which was vicious and bad had been produced at one time or another before me. I have learned in this case that we can always learn something more . . . I have never heard such dreadful, horrible, blasphemous and abominable stuff as that which has been produced by the man who describes himself to you as the greatest living poet.

One of his favourite titles for himself was even 'The Beast whose number is 666'.

So who was this man who could inspire such outrage and indignation? Crowley was born in Royal Leamington Spa in Warwickshire in 1875, the son of a successful retired brewer. Although he had a strict Christian upbringing, Crowley never accepted the faith of his parents, who were both Plymouth Brethren. His mother was so distraught at his rebellious ways that she used to call him 'The Beast', taking this name from the Book of Revelation in the Bible. It was a title that Crowley would use until his death.

His childhood was a very unhappy one, and, after his father died in 1887, he was sent away to live with his maternal uncle, where he attended a school of the Plymouth Brethren. However, happier times lay ahead. Crowley went to Cambridge in 1895, and the following year he came of age and inherited his father's fortune, at last free of his family.

It was in 1896 that Crowley took his first steps towards what would become a lifetime devoted to the occult. He immersed himself in books on magic and alchemy and by 1898 he had been initiated into the Hermetic Order of the Golden Dawn, an esoteric society that had such luminaries as W.B. Yeats and Dion Fortune amongst its members. Crowley was not popular within the Golden Dawn, and after only a couple of years he was expelled from the order, after which he took part in what have been described as magical and psychic battles with the chief of the order, Samuel Liddell MacGregor Mathers.

This was far from the end of Crowley's occult studies, and he soon set up his own temple within a house on the shores of Loch Ness in Scotland, where he created his own magical formulae and developed some of the techniques he had acquired from the Golden Dawn.

Far from dabbling in Magick merely to summon demons, Crowley saw it as a way of reaching God. In *Magick in Theory and Practice*, he stated:

> There is a single main definition of the object of all magical Ritual. It is the uniting of the Microcosm with the Macrocosm. The Supreme and Complete Ritual is therefore the Invocation of the Holy Guardian Angel; or, in the language of Mysticism, Union with God.

Crowley used the spelling 'Magick' to differentiate what he saw as sacred magic – any act which brought about change in the universe through the application of the individual's will – from lesser forms of magic such as that practised by conjurors.

It is always supposed that Crowley was a black magician and guilty of all the evils that such a title implies. However, the truth is that there is no evidence that this was the case. While a lot of what Crowley wrote was distasteful and shocking at the time it was published, he was actually strongly opposed to the practice of black magic. In his own words from a newspaper article of 1933:

> To practice black magic you have to violate every principle of
> science, decency and intelligence. You must be obsessed with
> an insane idea of the importance of the petty object of your
> wretched and selfish desires.
>
> I have been accused of being a 'black magician'. No more
> foolish statement was ever made about me. I despise the thing
> to such an extent that I can hardly believe in the existence of
> people so debased and idiotic as to practice it.

Some of Crowley's most lasting works were his studies into Thelema,
his complex philosophy concerning the application of human free
will in the world, and these could be seen as a treatise against black
magic; in fact, the laws that Crowley penned and by which he lived
his life forbade the practice of black magic.

Crowley came to discover the Law of Thelema while he was in
Cairo on honeymoon. His wife, Rose, had a series of visions that led
to her telling Crowley that over the course of three days he was to
write down what he was told by a spirit guide in the form of Aiwass,
a messenger of the Egyptian god Horus. The result was *The Book of
the Law*, or *Liber Al vel Legis*, which contains three chapters, each
dictated during one of those three days in Cairo by Aiwass, a spirit
that Crowley would later identify as his Holy Guardian Angel, his
spirit guide. Crowley believed that connection with this guide was
an extremely important matter, and he wrote:

> It should never be forgotten for a single moment that the
> central and essential work of the Magician is the attainment
> of the Knowledge and Conversation of the Holy Guardian
> Angel. Once he has achieved this he must of course be left
> entirely in the hands of that Angel, who can be invariably
> and inevitably relied upon to lead him to the further great
> step – crossing of the Abyss and the attainment of the grade
> of Master of the Temple.

The famous quote from *The Book of the Law* which is often used to
illustrate Crowley's Law of Thelema is, in full:

> The word of the Law is Thelema. Who calls us Thelemites will
> do no wrong, if he look but close into the word. For there are

therein Three Grades, the Hermit, and the Lover, and the man
of Earth. Do what thou wilt shall be the whole of the Law.

The message, essentially, was that each of us is free to live our life and
exercise our will as we see fit. However, this has been misconstrued at
times and does not, as some have suggested, mean that we are free to
run riot and act without responsibility. Crowley proposed that before
we exercise this free will, we must first look within ourselves and
through long study come to know ourselves and work out the true
nature of our will before implementing it. Therefore this free will is
to be interpreted as the individual's destiny or purpose in life, and,
in effect, with this freedom also comes great responsibility and self-
discipline.

Another aspect of Crowley's life that shocked and offended
society was his engagement in sex magic. He would routinely take
part in magic rituals that involved sex with both male and female
participants. Crowley was open about his bisexuality, and although
some historians claim that Crowley only had sexual relations with
men during his rituals and that all of his romantic encounters were
with women, there is evidence that he had at least one significant
relationship with a man, Herbert Pollitt, while at Cambridge. It must
be remembered that Crowley came of age during one of the most
repressed periods of British history, the Victorian era, and many of
Crowley's activities were shocking to the majority of the population.
Crowley, though, felt that much of this indignation was not genuine.
In *The Confessions of Aleister Crowley*, he noted that: 'Part of the
public horror of sexual irregularity so-called is due to the fact that
everyone knows himself essentially guilty.'

Crowley's experiments in the world of Magick continued, and in
1907 he formed his own occult society, known as the Argentinum
Astrum, or the Order of the Silver Star. Later, in 1912, he became the
chief of the British Ordo Templi Orientis, and later still, in 1924, he
went on to become the head of the order after its founder, Theodor
Reuss, died.

During his lifetime, Crowley explored many different facets of the
occult: he developed the Magickal ideas he had been introduced to at
a young age; studied the I Ching and Eastern philosophy; developed
his own version of the Book of Thoth; and practised yoga extensively
in later life. Alchemy was also a great interest of Crowley's, and he
claimed on more than one occasion that he had successfully created

an elixir of life, similar to the magical substances said to have been created by the alchemists of medieval Europe, the secret to eternal youth.

> I made it first when I was forty. It was done hastily and with imperfect knowledge. I took seven doses, as the first two or three had no apparent effect. The consequences were extremely violent.
>
> One day, without warning, I woke up to find that I had lost all my maturity. I became mentally and physically a stupid stripling. The only thing I could think of doing was to cut down trees! . . .
>
> . . . Six years later I experimented again with the elixir, taking precautions to avoid such drastic results. The result was that at 47 I was as powerful an athlete as any man of 30.

Crowley left a vast amount of work behind him, and today his books and publications sell for large amounts of money and are highly collectible. The largest collection of Crowley's work in private hands is said to be owned by Jimmy Page, guitarist with Led Zeppelin, and Page even owned Boleskine House, Crowley's home on the shores of Loch Ness, for a time. The Warburg Institute of the University of London now houses the large collection that once belonged to Gerald Yorke, a close associate of Crowley.

It would seem that as well as a magician, Crowley was also a philosopher, and much of his work could easily fall into the realm of philosophy, such as his discourse on the system of Thelema. As well as his serious studies, we are also left with the unshakeable image of Crowley as a mischievous child, hell-bent on constantly shocking and prodding at the soft underbelly of society, pushing boundaries to see how much he can get away with, always testing the limits of what is seen to be acceptable. Perhaps the role Crowley assumed is a vital one in any society, and for such a position he was willing to be demonised in most people's eyes.

Critics, on the other hand, propose that Crowley made much of his reputation and deliberately set out to capitalise on his standing as the most evil man in the world simply to try to make money, releasing revelatory and scandalous books such as *The Confessions of Aleister Crowley* and *Diary of a Drug Fiend* to cash in on his infamy. Indeed, Crowley squandered his inheritance on a hedonistic lifestyle and was made bankrupt later in life, so it is possible that he sought to make the most of his besmirched name.

Crowley's final years were those of a man worn out by a lifetime of excess and hedonism. He suffered from asthma and bronchitis and as a consequence had become addicted to heroin (this was a common prescription for asthma at the time). He finally died in 1947, aged 72, in Hastings in southern England.

His colourful funeral took place in Brighton. His erotic poem 'Hymn to Pan' was read out over his coffin by a devotee, and the whole scene was so unconventional that the chairman of Brighton's crematorium, where the service had taken place, declared to newspapers: 'We shall take all necessary steps to prevent such an incident occurring again.' When we review the text of this poem, we can understand why this brought about such a harsh reaction in 1947 and that even in death Crowley did nothing to dim his reputation as 'the wickedest man in the world'.

> I am Pan! Io Pan! Io Pan Pan! Pan!
> I am thy mate, I am thy man,
> Goat of thy flock, I am gold, I am god,
> Flesh to thy bone, flower to thy rod.
> With hoofs of steel I race on the rocks
> Through solstice stubborn to equinox.
> And I rave; and I rape and I rip and I rend
> Everlasting, world without end.
> Mannikin, maiden, maenad, man,
> In the might of Pan.
> Io Pan! Io Pan Pan! Pan! Io Pan!

SEE ALSO: Alchemy; Fortune, Dion; Hermetic Order of the Golden Dawn; I Ching; Ordo Templi Orientis; Yoga

CURSES

Ritual cursing has a long history within many cultures and religious traditions. The main purpose of a curse is to cause harm, evil or destruction, whether by illness, bad fortune, injury or death, and it is usually undertaken in order to exact revenge, for protection or out of jealousy. In *Aspects of Ancient Egyptian Curses and Blessings*, Katarina Nordh, discussing the effectiveness ascribed to curses by the Egyptians, refers to them as 'target-guided missiles'. Anyone can lay a curse, but it is generally thought that a curse is more potent if the person placing it is spiritually or physically more authoritative than the victim, so that the curse becomes 'clothed in power'.

In *The Republic*, Plato states that: 'If anyone wishes to injure an enemy, for a small fee they [sorcerers] will bring harm on good or bad alike, binding the gods to serve their purposes by spells and curses.' Calling on the power of God or gods, ghosts or demons was thought to give the curse more potency. One might also call on historical precedent to amplify the power of a curse. For example, in Ancient Egypt curses against scorpions were associated with the goddess Isis, who, according to tradition, had killed many scorpions. This connection with an ancient power was thought to enhance the strength of the curse as used by ordinary people.

In Egypt, where a wide range of cursing methods was available for both personal and official use, curses often utilised the dead in order to ensure the curse was enacted and to increase its potency. This can be seen in the letters to the dead, written pleas and requests, usually inscribed on bowls, placed within a tomb to ask the deceased to intervene on behalf of the living, for example to right a perceived wrong. These letters highlight the malevolent nature of the dead, who were considered to be the source of all life's ills, their anger and truculence the result of unresolved disputes or perceived omissions in their burial rituals, or because they felt they were no longer receiving the appropriate sustenance to nourish them in death. Curses were routinely left in tombs and cemeteries so that the resident ghosts would be obliged to carry them out.

These traditions continued through to the Christian Egyptian period, and were later incorporated into Egyptian Islamic practices; similar rituals were found in ancient Greece and Rome. Within Jewish and Christian traditions, curses are not proscribed but actively employed. In Genesis 3:14–19, God uses curses as punishment for the eating of the forbidden fruit: snakes are cursed for the serpent's duplicity; women are to suffer great pain in labour; and man is to suffer daily toil and sweat. Hence, according to the Old Testament, the reason for the very first curse was revenge and anger.

In Jeremiah 11:3, God threatens 'a curse on the man who does not observe the terms of this covenant', and in Deuteronomy 11:26–8 a curse is placed on those who do not obey the Ten Commandments. In these instances, the curse gives added force to proclamations and threats. The New Testament also contains curses, with Jesus instructing the apostles to curse disbelieving towns (Luke 10:10–15) and cursing a fig tree (Mark 11:14 and 20).

Marvin Meyer and Richard Smith relate in *Ancient Christian Magic* a number of early Egyptian Christian curses, which include a widow's curse against a man who was oppressing her in some way, asking to 'bring upon him fear and chill and jaundice'. Another incantation, against perjurers, asks for 'their eyes to fog and come out'.

Jealousy plays a large role in these curses, for example Mary's curse against Martha marrying a particular man, or sexual curses to make a man impotent so that he is unable to have intercourse with a specific, named woman. Such curses, of which there are a number, contain an almost identical formulaic structure and content, and state: 'May you dry it [the male organ] up like wood and make it like a rag upon the manure pile. His penis must not become hard, it must not have an erection, he must not have intercourse.' The standard wordings of curses illustrate some of the concerns people had and the reasons why they were using spells.

There are many forms of curses. Probably one of the simplest, but no less effective for it, is the spoken curse, such as a death-bed curse, which is believed to be particularly potent, as the dying person's very life force enters the curse with their last breath. It is believed that when a curse is spoken the words take on a force of their own, becoming a very effective and active agent. The word is particularly effective when a person's name is stated to enable the curse to reach the correct objective. The idea of the potency of the verbal curse can be seen in Jesus's curse of the fig tree, which was found to have withered and died from the roots up. In Ireland, there is a history of using cursing stones, whereby a curse is recited as the stone is turned three times to the left. Also well known are verbal Gypsy curses that invariably afflict the victim with a homeless, wandering life full of discomfort and unease.

Another form is the written curse, which was widely used in Ancient Egypt. One important motivation for such curses was the protection of a tomb and its owner. These curses were written at the tomb's entrance and were considered to be an effective weapon against desecration, both physical and by evil thoughts. Curses were therefore used to threaten anyone entering the tomb using all the force, fear and potency that the deceased owner could call upon. Accordingly, the deceased would threaten the violators, their home, family and 'assuredly their descendants' with destruction. Written Egyptian curses are also found in the Execration Texts, official state curses against the enemies of Egypt.

Since ancient times, effigies have been used for curses. Effigies are used throughout Africa, Europe, India and the Middle East to represent the victim, either being painted to look like the individual, named after them or containing some of their hair or nail clippings. Made of wax, wood, clay or cloth, the effigy of the intended victim is thought to enhance by its resemblance to him or her the connection with the target. The harming of the effigy is believed to produce, by a process known as sympathetic magic, a similar effect on the victim, so that wax effigies are melted, clay smashed, dolls stuck with pins and other sharp objects. With regard to wax and clay effigies, King James VI of Scotland wrote in his *Daemonologie* of 1597 that 'by roasting thereof, the persons that they beare the name of, may be continually melted or die away'. It is now commonly, although erroneously, thought that the cursing of dolls plays a prominent part in voodoo ritual.

CURSES

Some curses are not on a specific person but are carried with an object that brings disaster in various forms on whoever has the misfortune to own it. The Hope Diamond is believed to hold a curse, as is the burial equipment of Tutankhamun, which is said to be the cause of a number of unfortunate events that befell four of the RAF crew who transported it to London for exhibition in 1972. In *The Paranormal: An Illustrated Encyclopedia*, Stuart Gordon relates the story of the curse attached to a Hawaiian volcano and on anyone taking the stones, which is said to anger Pele, the volcano goddess. Gordon records that in 1977 the Loffert family from Buffalo, New York, took some stones, and on their return one of their sons broke his wrist, had knee surgery and appendicitis; another sprained his ankle and broke an arm; a third developed an eye infection; and the daughter fell and knocked out teeth. In July 1978, the desperate family sent the stones back to Hawaii, but the problems still continued until one of the boys confessed that he had kept three of the stones; when these were returned, the problems ceased.

Curses can be intended for immediate action, but they can also be enacted on future generations for a hurt inflicted by one of their ancestors, like the curse of Fyvie Castle in Scotland. The curse was put on the owners of the castle by a medieval prophet of doom called Thomas the Rhymer, who, unable to gain entry to the castle on a particularly stormy night, cursed three stones and hid them in the oldest tower, the lady's bower and the watergate. The curse stated that whilst the stones remained the laird of the castle would die an agonising death and his wife become blind, and the eldest son would never survive long enough to inherit the estate. Only one of the stones has been found, and this is kept in a chest placed in a locked chamber that no one is allowed to enter for fear of the curse.

It is generally thought that a curse is more potent if the victim believes in such magic and is aware that it has been placed on them. However, evidence suggests otherwise, as in the case of the writer David St Clair, highlighted by Colin Wilson in *Beyond the Occult*. In the 1960s, St Clair had lived in Brazil for eight years and did not believe in witchcraft or curses. However, his scepticism was to be turned on its head when he made plans to leave Brazil. From the time that St Clair gave his maid, Edna, six months' notice that he was departing, he experienced a number of difficulties and setbacks, financial, social and medical. A friend suggested that his awful run of luck was because someone had placed a curse on him and thought that Edna might be the culprit. St Clair was persuaded to approach Edna and ask her to take him to an *umbanda* religious ritual to see if there was a curse and whether it could be lifted. The priestess told St Clair that Edna had put the curse on him because she wanted to keep him in Brazil so that he could either marry her or buy her a house. The priestess ordered Edna to leave the ritual, which continued until the curse had been lifted. After that, St Clair's bad luck began to change: his finances improved, his job prospects and social life were back on track, and his health returned. Unfortunately, Edna did not fare so well, as she became very ill with a stomach growth, which an *umbanda* priest claimed was the result of the curse she had put on St Clair coming back to her – she would not improve until she accepted what she had done and repented.

Whilst it is more likely that people who live in cultures that are very aware of a curse's malevolence will succumb to one, some argue that such a spell will be more effective if the recipient does not know that they have been cursed because if they are aware, they can easily go to a sorcerer to reverse its effectiveness – at a price. According to this point of view, a curse becomes imprinted on a person and is effective whether or not the victim is a believer and even if they are unaware that a curse has been placed on them. However, an undeserved curse will be ineffective and indeed will return to the person who sent it.

SEE ALSO: Voodoo

DEE, JOHN

John Dee was a famous magician and alchemist who became adviser to Queen Elizabeth I of England. He was a mathematician of renown and also had great influence in the spheres of geography, navigation, astronomy and astrology – but it is as grand magician and alchemist that he is now remembered.

Dee was born in 1527 in London and spent the first half of his life concerned with conventional studies, travelling throughout Europe to increase his knowledge. Following the coronation of Elizabeth I, Dee became her scientific adviser and aided her greatly in forming Britain's Empire; in fact, he is credited with inventing the phrase 'British Empire'. Dee believed that the colonisation of North America and other parts of the world was Britain's entitlement, and he was instrumental in pushing for such colonisation. In his book *The Limits of the British Empire*, he explains that it is Queen Elizabeth's right to introduce these foreign lands into the Empire and to occupy those lands that were discovered by Britain's navy and were not in the possession of a Christian monarch.

Much later, when Dee was in his 50s, he began to experiment with scrying – using a reflective surface such as a pool of water or a crystal ball to try to discern the future or contact spirits. In Dee's case, he was attempting to contact angels with whom he could converse and attempt to gain knowledge.

The most well-known work in which Dee figures is *A true and faithful relation of what passed for many years between Dr. John*

Dee and some spirits, which was published by the scholar Meric Casaubon 50 years after Dee's death and in which we see the results of his experiments into scrying. What is interesting is how the book coloured the perception of Dee in the mind of the general public. Before this account was published, there was not widespread knowledge of Dee's supernatural work, and the book became very popular. Dee had been known mainly for his work as an adviser to the Crown and as a scientist. Although he had written the very cryptic *Monas Hieroglyphica*, a study into the whole of creation expressed through a single symbol that he had devised, his occult activity had not been much publicised. Casaubon's publication of *A true and faithful relation* changed forever the way in which Dee was perceived, bringing his more esoteric activities plainly to the fore.

Casaubon wrote a preface to the book in which he insinuates that Dee had been the unwitting tool of evil spirits who had contacted him under the pretence of being angels:

> What is here presented unto thee (Christian Reader) being a True and Faithful Relation (as the Title beareth, and will be further cleared by this Preface) though by the carriage of it, in some respects, and by the Nature at it too, it might be deemed and termed, A Work of Darknesse: Yet it is no other then what with great tendernesse and circumspection, was tendered to men of highest Dignity in Europe, Kings and Princes, and by all (England excepted) listened unto for a while with good respect. By some gladly embraced and entertained for a long time; the Fame whereof being carryed unto Rome, it made the Pope to bestir himself, not knowing what the event of it might be, and how much it might concern him. And indeed, filled all men, Learned and Unlearned in most places with great wonder and astonishment.

Dee's partner in his scrying experiments was Edward Kelley. Before meeting Dee, Kelley had lived in Lancaster, and it was rumoured that he had raised spirits of the dead in a churchyard at Walton-le-Dale. He was an alchemist and claimed to be able to turn base metals such as copper into gold. It was Kelley who approached Dee in 1582, and Dee was excited at the prospect of having Kelley's help with his scrying because he claimed to have had great success with the method. The two of them would work closely on their supernatural experiments for the next five years, and this work would take them all over Europe.

Kelley claimed to have 'received' via the scrying ball the language of angels referred to today as Enochian. This alphabet was recorded by Dee and Kelley and used in their spiritual work. The name Enochian was never actually used by Dee and Kelley. Dee refers to the alphabet in his journals as 'Angelical' or 'Adamical' (he believed the language was used by Adam in the Garden of Eden). It has become known as Enochian because Dee wrote that Enoch, the descendant of Adam and himself a biblical patriarch, was the last man to use the language. According to Dee, Enoch wrote a book in Enochian to preserve the language as well as other sacred knowledge, but this book was lost in the Great Flood. Dee and Kelley would use this lost language at the heart of a set of rituals that would come to be known as Enochian magic, which they used to summon and converse with angels and other spirits. Aleister Crowley was a student of this system of magic. He wrote about it and publicised its practice, and this in turn has contributed to its continued use in modern times.

An excerpt from *A true and faithful relation* demonstrates what occurred when Dee and Kelley were visited by spirits during their scrying experiments. The text, according to the publisher, came directly from Dee's own diaries:

> Spirit Voice: Pride is rewarded as sin, Ergo the first offender was damned. What say you Sir? [speaking to Kelley] What difference is between your mind and Pride?
>
> Kelley: Wherein am I proud?
>
> Spirit Voice: In the same wherein the Devil was first proud.
>
> Who glorified the Devil?
>
> Kelley: God.
>
> Dee: God glorified not the Devil, but before he became a Devil he was in glory.
>
> Spirit Voice: The abusing of his Glorification made him a Devil: so the abusing of the goodnesse of God toward this man, may make him a Devil.
>
> The works of the Spirit quicken; the doings of the Flesh lead unto distraction. Art thou offended to be called a Devil? Then extol not thy self above thy Election . . .
>
> By true understanding you learn, first to know your selves what you are: of whom you are, and to what end you are.

This understanding causeth no self-love, but a spiritual
selfe-love.
This understanding teacheth no Blasphemy.
This understanding teacheth no fury.

Kelley is a controversial figure, and many scholars claim that he
was a fraud and a charlatan. It has even been proposed that it was
Kelley who wrote the contentious Voynich Manuscript, a mysterious
illustrated text that is still an impenetrable work although some of
the world's top code-breakers, including the greatest cryptographers
of the Second World War, have worked on deciphering its pages. It
has been suggested that either Kelley deceived Dee into believing the
book was genuine, an ancient document which would reveal great
secrets and mysteries if it could only be decoded, or the two of them
were accomplices in trying to pass off the counterfeit document as
the real thing. The author most often cited as having written the
manuscript is Roger Bacon, the famous thirteenth-century Franciscan
friar. It is known that Dee had a large collection of Bacon's work, so
one theory goes that Kelley might have fabricated the text knowing
that it would have gained plausibility by association with Dee's
library. Some researchers claim that Dee himself fabricated it.

Dee and Kelley travelled all over Central Europe attempting to find
patronage for their work. All the while, they continued their pursuits
into alchemy and scrying. They settled for a time in Bohemia under
the patronage of Count Vilem Rozmberk. However, it was here that
Dee and Kelley were to split. Kelley apparently told Dee that he had
been instructed by the angels that the two of them should share each
other's wives. Dee was appalled at the idea but reluctantly agreed.
After a time, Dee became so distressed at the demands of the angels
that he abandoned the scrying sessions and eventually returned to
England, in 1589, never to see Kelley again.

Some scholars have suggested that Kelley in fact made up the
angelic orders to engineer such a split, the motive being that Dee was
surplus to requirements because it was Kelley who was in demand
by the wealthy Count Rozmberk on account of his claims to be able
to transmute lesser metals into gold. Whatever the reason, Kelley
came to a sticky end, dying in Bohemia after, it is claimed, he tried
to escape from the castle where he was imprisoned for failing in his
attempts to transmute copper into gold.

Dee lived in Manchester for a while, given the position of warden of Christ's College, where he continued his studies into the occult. However, he returned to London to end his final years amidst the vast library of books he had amassed. When Queen Mary had been alive, he had tried to persuade her to found a national library, but after this project was rejected, he instead spent his life building up his own personal library until it became the greatest private collection of books in England, surpassed only by those of the universities. Dee was to spend his last few years in poverty, unable to interest King James in his ideas and proposals, and he died in either 1608 or 1609 (the exact records are lost), having had to sell items from his library and collection of artefacts to survive – an ignominious end for someone who had contributed so much to the advancement of the occult and studies into magic.

SEE ALSO: Alchemy; Crowley, Aleister

DIVINATION

The enormous advantages of being able to predict accurately the future or the direction of the fickle finger of fate seem obvious. Fortunes could be made if one could be sure of the winner of a horse race tomorrow, the rise and fall of the stock market over the next year or the result of a hotly contested election. Yet would the gift invariably have entirely happy results? Would we wish to know that a loved one was due to die soon, that we ourselves were fated to catch a dreadful and lingering disease or that World War Three would bring destruction and chaos to us all in the near future? It might be argued that if we knew what the future held, we could take steps to avoid the consequences; but, logically, if we could do something to alter what destiny had in store, the prediction must, by definition, be false.

The beautiful Trojan princess Cassandra, daughter of King Priam, has for long been famous as the prophetess whose predictions were invariably correct. She was cursed, however, by the fact that no one would believe her. She had been courted by the god Apollo, one version of the story runs, who had promised to grant her a wish if she would give herself to him. She agreed, asking for the power to see into the future, but once the wish was granted, she refused to keep her part of the bargain. In revenge, Apollo ensured that the Trojans regarded her as mad when she cautioned them against actions which she knew would bring disaster at the hands of their Greek enemies. However, if the Trojans had heeded her and the future had been altered as a result, Cassandra's gift/curse would have been flawed: her forecast would not have been accurate.

There is a tradition that the English King Henry IV was told that his death would occur in Jerusalem. It was probably supposed that this would happen if he went on crusade to attempt to wrest control of the Holy Land from the Muslims. He decided that he would never go to Jerusalem, but, inevitably, of course, he died despite his caution. In 1513, he was taken ill while praying at the shrine of St Edward in Westminster Abbey and drew his last breath in the abbot's chamber. Some say that this room was known as the Jerusalem Chamber before the king's death and that as a result people were willing to believe that the prophecy had been fulfilled. The other possibility is that the abbot's room acquired the name in consequence of the event.

Henry was not the first King of England to be the subject of an unwelcome prophecy. During the reign of John, a seer named Peter of Pomfret, who makes a brief appearance in Shakespeare's *King John*, forecast that the king would lose his crown in 1213. This poor man and his son were taken from a dungeon at Corfe Castle, Dorset, and dragged five miles to Wareham, where they were executed as traitors. The irony is that John was indeed forced to resign his lands to the papal legate in that year; technically, he became the Pope's vassal. Peter had spoken nothing but the truth. Even correct predictions can have terrible consequences for those with 'the gift'.

Looking back even further in time, the future Roman emperor Tiberius (reigned AD 14–37), having met a Greek philosopher and astrologer during an extended stay on the island of Rhodes, became interested in the possibilities engendered by having foreknowledge of what is to come. The wise man, named Tiberius Claudius Thrasyllus, a native of Alexandria, became hugely influential as adviser to the emperor, and he was to see his granddaughter married to the prefect of the Praetorian Guard. He was also to become an ally of Tiberius's scheming nephew Caligula, on whose behalf he convinced the old emperor that he would reign for another decade about a year before he died, thus allowing Caligula to step up to the succession more easily. Belief in Thrasyllus's black arts – astrological predictions, magic rituals and dream analysis – so influenced Tiberius that many powerful Romans died as a result of treason trials prompted by Thrasyllus's prophecies. The historian Tacitus reports the first such victim as Marcus Scribonius Libo Drusus, who committed suicide before condemnation.

Only a little later, emperors such as Otho firmly believed in the ability to see the future, and the normally level-headed Vespasian took advantage of omens forecasting his succession, advertising them as propaganda, though we can never know whether he actually believed them himself. Graeco-Roman society generally was convinced that the future could be accurately predicted, an idea which tied in with their religious beliefs.

The Romans thought that the will of the gods was indicated to mortals through a variety of signs. If Jupiter threw his thunderbolts, it indicated that he was not pleased, which was easy enough to understand; more occult divine messages, however, required greater skills. There were augurs who read the signs before any decisions affecting state policy were taken, haruspices who peered at the entrails of the animals which had been the victims of public sacrifices, and sages who interpreted the words of oracles, as well as ordinary people who believed that they could access the will of the gods at a personal or family level. Thus an oddly shaped or strangely coloured piece of bird's liver or gall bladder, or a missing ox kidney, could affect military decisions and make or break treaties, or simply cause a family not to travel to see Aunt Livia today – it might be safer to go tomorrow.

Much of what we know of Roman soothsaying comes from Cicero's *On Divination*, which he wrote in 45 BC. Generals sometimes had the flight of wild birds interpreted before a battle in order to divine whether the day was auspicious or not. An alternative was to have a number of sacred chickens to hand and observe how they ate food offered to them. The analysis of this could indicate whether the impending conflict was likely to have a successful outcome. The Romans also believed that dreams could be interpreted to reveal the future, just as the Jews had done for generations. We read in the Bible, in Genesis 40 and 41, how Joseph interpreted the dreams of Pharaoh's butler and baker and then of Pharaoh himself. Other methods of divination used by the Romans included drawing lots, taking words randomly from poems, observing the taste or colour of wine, and throwing dice.

In the hard-headed modern world, it might be expected that most people would have little time for attempts to look into the future, to see what God or Fortune has in store, and yet popular astrology columns are included in most daily newspapers, while some people read tea leaves, turn playing cards or go to have their palms read.

They are willing to pay to find out what is awaiting them, so it must be presumed that they believe there is something to it.

A more sinister aspect of divination is necromancy. Since ancient times, people have attempted to conjure up the spirits of the dead in order to discover the secrets of the future. Since the emperor Theodosius issued an edict against it in AD 391, necromancy has traditionally been regarded in Christian societies as an evil aspect of witchcraft. Yet in Renaissance times, necromancers were still attempting to raise the spirits of the dead to enhance their own powers and knowledge. Many of us are familiar with the story of Dr Faustus, who sold his soul to the Devil in exchange for such power, from Christopher Marlowe's play, Goethe's work or the music of Berlioz or Gounod.

What is perhaps less known is that there was at least one real-life prototype for Faustus, a soothsayer, alchemist, astrologer and sorcerer. The historical Faustus or Faust was a German magician, a traveller with a bad reputation as a charlatan, who died around the year 1540. Although the Reformers Luther and Melancthon appear to have taken him seriously, many intellectuals of the day were totally unimpressed by his trickery. He lived around the same time as the famous occultists Nostradamus and Paracelsus, and it may be that some of their reputations became conflated with Faust's own, while stories of other widely recognised 'wizards' from previous ages, such as Merlin and Roger Bacon, may also have fuelled belief that powers such as those ascribed to Faust were genuine.

SEE ALSO: Astrology; I Ching; Necromancy

DOWSING

'**D**owsing' is the term used to describe the process by which water, metals, minerals such as oil, or other objects present beneath the ground are searched for and found using non-invasive methods. Traditionally, this is achieved using a special twig in the shape of a Y, divining rods or a pendulum; however, some dowsers use no equipment at all and claim that they still receive the same signals and obtain the same results as people who use implements. Dowsers claim that the equipment they use only amplifies their natural sensitivity to the material they are searching for.

Dowsing has been called 'divining' and also 'water witching' over the years, while the implements of the dowser have been given names including dowsing or divining stick, divining rods and doodlebug. The origins of dowsing go back as far as history will allow us, and there are accounts of it in China, where its use is mentioned by Confucius; in Ancient Egypt, Greece, Rome and India; and Herodotus mentions the practice of dowsing in Persia.

It is a controversial subject, and sceptics claim that what these diviners find is simply down to chance and that dowsing does not work at all. However, there are many accounts of occasions when dowsing has been successful, or at least, whether through dowsing or chance alone, the dowser has found the material or object that he was searching for.

One of the most hotly debated forms of dowsing does not involve walking the landscape at all; instead, the dowser uses a map and, with the aid of a pendulum or the traditional twig or rods, attempts to identify locations on the map where what is being searched for may be found.

Originally, the term referred specifically to divining water. When the dowser encountered water underground, the stick he used would either twitch or bend downwards towards the ground. If a pair of divining rods were used, they would cross when the dowser passed over water. Each practitioner develops his own technique, and some dowsers use completely different methods to those described above, though these are the most common.

Dowsers, together with researchers who have studied the matter and believe in the technique's effectiveness, suggest that there are unseen force fields that, as yet, science knows nothing about. It is these invisible force fields, produced either by bodies of water underground, by minerals or by deposits of oil, that are said to be 'felt' by the dowsers, and the twig or other instrument that they use simply amplifies the presence of such a force field and tells the dowser when he has encountered this phenomenon.

Paracelsus, the sixteenth-century alchemist and occultist, whose real name was Philippus Theophrastus Bombastus von Hohenheim, was a firm believer in many unorthodox practices, yet he had his warnings for those who would practise dowsing:

> Therefore care is to be sedulously taken that ye suffer not yourselves to be seduced by the divination of uncertain arts. For they are vain and frivolous, especially the Divinitory Rods, which have deceived many miners. For if they show anything rightly, they on the contrary deceive ten times.

This message is still true, and experiments carried out to try to prove once and for all whether dowsing really works have produced results that prove Paracelsus was right. In closely monitored studies, such as that carried out in Munich in the late 1980s, involving over 500 dowsers in what was probably the most exhaustive test of its kind, it has been found that while in certain cases dowsing can be very effective and produce results, often a positive reading can produce absolutely nothing at all, so a dowser could pick up a sign that there is guaranteed water below his feet only to dig a dry hole. Furthermore, as Paracelsus indicates, there are generally many more failures than there are successes when conducting these tests. Sceptics take these results as proof positive that dowsing does not work, suggesting that the positives are no more than what we would expect to find through chance alone, while dowsers themselves put the high numbers of failures down to the delicate nature of the process and the fact that the so-called force fields of energy that they dowse are so complex that false results can be obtained.

Dowsing has come to mean more than water divining or searching for minerals in the ground and now refers also to the process of using a pendulum, made from crystal or other material, to answer specific questions posed by the seeker. Traditionally, the dowser holds the pendulum and establishes which direction means 'yes' and which 'no', and then questions are asked. The way the pendulum moves after a certain question is posed indicates the answer. If the pendulum moves from side to side, this is taken to mean that either the question is not understood or there is no clear answer.

Finally, it is worth suggesting that the magician's wand may have its origins in dowsing and water witching. Dowsing has been believed to be a strong form of magic for thousands of years, and the dowser with his twitching twig can be seen as a precursor of the modern image we have of a magician with his wand, cut from a stick of wood. Dowsers would have been seen as sorcerers in times past, with their ability to find water – a very powerful gift in the ancient world, when villages were not connected to the water supplies generally available today – and so the magician's wand may very well have developed from the dowser's twig and the idea of the magical powers the dowser seemed to possess.

SEE ALSO: Alchemy; Magic

DRUIDS

The Druidic tradition can be traced back thousands of years. Druids were part of the Celtic cultures of Northern Europe, and within Celtic communities they were considered the wisest and most respected members of society.

The word 'Druid' comes to us from Latin, but there are also other forms from other languages. The Latin form *'druidae'* comes from the Gaulish word *'druides'*, which in turn derives from *'dru'* ('tree', with particular emphasis on an oak tree) and *'wid'* which means 'to know'. This might be loosely translated as 'those who have visions of the oak tree', this particular tree being sacred to the Druids. Other forms of the word include the Old Irish *'dru'* and the Gaelic *'druadh'* both of which mean 'magician' or 'sorcerer'.

The Druids operated within Celtic society rather like a social class of educated, elite high priests, preserving much of the wisdom of the Celts as well as ancient laws and customs. It was through the Druids that the Celtic people connected with their gods, but they were much more than just priests and also performed the roles of teacher, judge, healer, philosopher and scientist. The Druids maintained an oral tradition, passing down all their customs, rituals and knowledge to the next generation, and contemporary accounts tell us that this knowledge was disseminated amongst the initiates by having them learn a great mass of verses that could take up to 20 years in total to commit to memory. Because of this verbal tradition, very little of their beliefs or customs has survived to the present day. In fact, we don't have a single line of Druidic writing to scrutinise, and most of what we know about the Druids comes from the reports of other cultures that came into contact with them, primarily the Romans.

The most comprehensive account of the Druids is by the hand of Julius Caesar, and we find descriptions of them and their lifestyle in his *Commentarii de Bello Gallico* (*Commentaries on the Gallic War*). Written sometime between 50 and 40 BC, the book covers the nine-year war that Caesar waged against the Gauls, during which he and his forces often came into contact with Druids.

The Druids worshipped many gods, and these seem to have varied depending on where the particular tribe was based. Scholars believe that many of the deities present in the pantheon of Irish gods known as the Tuatha de Danaan were sacred to the Druids. These include Brigid (some of whose mythology became associated with the Christian St Bridget), Dagda the Good, and Lugh, who seems to be based on the pan-Celtic god Lugus. As well as these deities, the Druids also worshipped forces and objects found in nature, such as the sun and moon, trees like the oak, sacred plants including mistletoe, as well as rivers, streams and hills, amongst many others. The Druids also believed in an afterlife, and Caesar describes this in his writings:

> They wish to inculcate this as one of their leading tenets, that souls do not become extinct, but pass after death from one body to another, and they think that men by this tenet are in a great degree excited to valour, the fear of death being disregarded.

It is also through Caesar that we know that the Druids were astronomers, studying the stars and other heavenly bodies:

> They likewise discuss and impart to the youth many things respecting the stars and their motion, respecting the extent of the world and of our earth, respecting the nature of things, respecting the power and the majesty of the immortal gods.

Caesar records that the Druids, as well as acting as the guardians of Celtic society, could also be harsh arbiters of law. The Druids, acting as judges and magistrates, would punish those who transgressed, and often the harshest punishment that could be handed out was deemed to be excommunication. According to Caesar's report:

. . . and if any crime has been perpetrated, if murder has been committed, if there be any dispute about an inheritance, if any about boundaries, these same persons decide it; they decree rewards and punishments; if any one, either in a private or public capacity, has not submitted to their decision, they interdict him from the sacrifices. This among them is the most heavy punishment. Those who have been thus interdicted are esteemed in the number of the impious and the criminal: all shun them, and avoid their society and conversation, lest they receive some evil from their contact; nor is justice administered to them when seeking it, nor is any dignity bestowed on them.

However, this was not the only penalty, and the Druids punished some criminals in more bizarre, ritualistic ways:

The nation of all the Gauls is extremely devoted to superstitious rites; and on that account they who are troubled with unusually severe diseases, and they who are engaged in battles and dangers, either sacrifice men as victims, or vow that they will sacrifice them, and employ the Druids as the performers of those sacrifices . . . Others have figures of vast size, the limbs of which formed of osiers they fill with living men, which being set on fire, the men perish enveloped in the flames. They consider that the oblation of such as have been taken in theft, or in robbery, or any other offence, is more acceptable to the immortal gods; but when a supply of that class is wanting, they have recourse to the oblation of even the innocent.

The heart of the Druidic world seems to be have been the island of Anglesey, now part of Wales. We know very little about why this place was so important, but we do know that Druids came from all over Europe to this centre of learning, and here they studied the ancient wisdom and secrets of their priesthood. There were sacred oak groves on the island of Anglesey. This tree was revered by the Druids, and they always used it in their rituals, according to Pliny the Elder, who tells us that: 'They choose the oak to form groves, and they do not perform any religious rites without its foliage.' In the Celtic world which the Druids inhabited, the oak was a very special tree indeed and stood as a doorway to the Otherworld, the Celtic realm of the dead. Because it was used in rituals at the summer solstice, it was also seen as the gateway between the light and the dark, summer and winter. Furthermore, it was also often home to mistletoe, a sacred plant to the Druids and one that represented fertility and potency. So perhaps the groves of oak on Anglesey were the reason why the island was so sacred; we will never know for certain, however, because the heart of the Druid order was cut out brutally by the Romans.

Tacitus, the Roman senator and historian, calls Anglesey 'Mona', and he tells us in his book *Annals* that Gaius Suetonius Paulinus attacked this sacred isle in AD 61 during his campaign to subjugate the British Isles. In *Annals*, Tacitus reveals that Paulinus sent a force of legionnaires to Anglesey specifically to destroy this centre of Druidic learning. Not only did he kill the Druids he found there, but he also cut down and destroyed the sacred groves of trees. No explanation of why Paulinus did such a thing is given, but it must be surmised that if these trees were central to the Druids' belief system, then destroying them would be seen as a way of neutralising the power of the Druids' religion. The account of the final battle is wonderful in that it offers a tantalising glimpse into the world of the Druids that we know so very little about:

> On the shore stood the opposing army with its dense array of armed warriors while between the ranks dashed women, in black attire like the Furies, with hair dishevelled, waving brands. All around, the Druids, lifting up their hands to heaven, and pouring forth dreadful imprecations, scared our soldiers by the unfamiliar sight, so that, as if their limbs were paralysed, they stood motionless, and exposed to wounds. Then urged by their general's appeals and mutual encouragements not to quail before a troop of frenzied women, they bore the standards onwards, smote down all resistance, and wrapped the foe in the flames of his own brands. A force was next set over the conquered, and their groves, devoted to inhuman superstitions, were destroyed. They deemed it indeed a duty to cover their altars with the blood of captives and to consult their deities through human entrails.

Later accounts of the Druids come to us through Irish manuscripts of the twelfth century, in works such as the Ulster Cycle and the

Mythological Cycle. Here again we see accounts of the Druids as magical priests who occupied privileged roles in society, often as magicians and advisers.

Antiquarians such as William Stukeley inspired a revival of interest in Druidism in the 1700s, and in 1717 John Toland, a writer and freethinker from Ireland, founded the Ancient Druid Order in London. There is evidence that William Blake was also heavily involved in the revival, and the Ancient Druid Order claimed that he had borne the title of their Chosen Chief between the years 1799 and 1827.

Today, Druidism is growing and the number of Druids in the UK is increasing. In 1989, the Council of British Druid Orders was formed, prompted by the closure of Stonehenge during the summer solstice. Although some Druid orders chose to break away from the Council in 1995, there are still 16 orders which belong to the Council, including the Mystic Order of Druids, the British Order of Free Druids, the Druids of Albion and the Secular Order of Druids.

Druids have become an accepted part of British culture, although the general public does not know much more about them than the familiar scenes of their ceremonies at Stonehenge each June. Whether or not the rituals that these Druids carry out are authentic or not, it is fascinating that after thousands of years the spirit of Druidism is still alive in Great Britain.

SEE ALSO: Blake, William

EVIL EYE

Whilst not as prevalent as it once was, belief in the evil eye is still a widespread superstition in the Mediterranean, the Middle East, South Asia and South America. The idea behind the evil eye, known as 'overlooking' in Old English, 'eye of envy' in Arabic and 'eye of Satan' in Turkish, is that an envious look, or even praise by someone in respect of another's good fortune, can result in a jinx on the recipient, leading to illness and misfortune.

What is interesting about evil-eye folklore is that in the majority of cases the person with this power is believed to have no control over it and no idea that they are affecting people or things adversely. Indeed, in medieval society there were theological discussions concerning certain elements of magic, including the evil eye, and whether or not they came under the auspices of demonic magic – considered immoral – or natural magic, which was not caused by spell or ritual but more the result of unspoken desire. As Richard Kieckhefer notes in *Magic in the Middle Ages*, the consensus of opinion was that the evil eye was actually a natural phenomenon caused by one person's soul influencing another person.

In fact, most societies consider it to be an unconscious and unintentional curse, for the individual casting the evil eye does not usually mean harm towards the recipient or have any perception that they are the cause of the curse. In his book *Witchcraft*, Eric Maple mentions a case documented in seventeenth-century England that highlights this point. It concerns a certain Christian Malford who unconsciously affected his children, farm animals and crops in a negative manner because of his evil-eye affliction. In more modern times, Pope Pius IX (r. 1846–78) was believed to be an unwilling possessor of the evil eye because it was noted that misfortune often affected areas and people he had visited and blessed. On Sicily and in southern Italy, where the superstition is particularly widespread, it is thought that the evil eye can be intentionally and knowingly cast on individuals and things, although it is also thought that those who have this ability (*jettatores* or 'projectors') do not necessarily mean to be malicious.

The evil-eye superstition is an ancient one, and, according to Professor Alan Dundes, in his 1981 study *The Evil Eye: A Folklore Casebook*, it appears to have its origins in the fourth millennium BC in Sumer (modern-day Iraq). His theory is based on the geographical position of the ancient land in the very heart of the area where the superstition is common, suggesting that the belief spread abroad from Sumer, eventually dispersing as far westwards as Spain and Portugal, and northwards towards England, Scotland and Ireland, where it had a particular resonance with the Celts. In the seventeenth century, the belief reached South America with European occupation and immigration.

The Ancient Egyptians certainly believed in the adverse power of the evil eye, which they called *iret benet*. Spells and amulets were employed to counter its malign effect. In *The Mechanics of Ancient Egyptian Magical Practice*, the Egyptologist Robert Ritner points out that the wall carvings in the chapel at Denderah contain spells for averting the evil eye in order to protect the temple, whilst an amulet from the Egyptian Roman period portrays an eye pierced with spears and arrows. However, it cannot be stated with any degree of certainty whether or not the archetypal evil-eye concept was known during the Egyptian pharaonic period or came to Egypt via foreign influences, as evidence for belief dates to the later, Graeco-Roman period (332 BC–AD 337). There are a number of references to the evil eye in the Bible, such as in the Book of Proverbs 23:6, which states: 'Do not eat bread belonging to him who has the evil eye.' In the New Testament, Mark 7:21–2 indicates that Jesus considered the evil eye to be a human sin, placing it within a list that included adultery, murder and blasphemy.

Professor Dundes reached the conclusion that the consequences of the evil eye relate to desiccation and dryness, with dryness and drought bringing death, whilst the cure is moisture, as water brings life. Accordingly, the consequence of the evil eye in children is vomiting and diarrhoea, and in nursing mothers and livestock it is the drying up of milk; fruit and crops wilt, whilst men become impotent. Although beliefs about the evil eye appear similar throughout diverse areas, the cures and protection employed to counter its effects are varied.

All societies that believe in the evil eye agree that those most at risk are babies and children, because their delightful and endearing appearance draws strangers to them who invariably stare, smile and coo over them and comment on how beautiful they are. Accordingly, in some regions a parent may immediately say something derogatory about their child in order to negate the praise and offset an attack by the evil eye. Elsewhere, the way to counter praise and/or envy is to immediately spit before the person receiving adulation or, in South America, to touch the person praised. Other regions take the view that the best way to prevent an evil-eye attack is to remove the cause of envy. To this effect, mothers try to make their children look imperfect by daubing their faces with dust or, as in Bangladesh, drawing black dots on the child's forehead.

Protection against the evil eye is taken very seriously and is found in the form of amulets and hand gestures. The most popular talisman is a blue amulet with a depiction of an eye in the middle, thought to reflect evil back onto the instigator. In Greece and Turkey, where this amulet is especially widely used, it is believed that blue-eyed people have the evil eye, probably because this colouring is unusual in those parts and people are naturally wary of strangers. In the Middle East and India, hand-shaped amulets, sometimes decorated with blue eyes, are common. Alternatively, some hand amulets have fish on them, which are thought to be immune from the drying effect of the evil eye because of their association with water.

The use of the colour blue in a protective talisman against the evil eye is a popular feature found not only in amulets but also in bead talismans, as in the Mediterranean region and the Middle East, where animals are bedecked with blue beads, and in India, where babies wear a cord necklace of blue beads. When the cord breaks, it is considered a sign that the child no longer has to fear the evil eye. Because of their eye-like shape, cowrie shells are hung on cots for protection in some Mediterranean fishing communities; these shells were also widely used in Ancient Egypt as a general form of protection.

In Italy, hand gestures are the form of protection used by men, who are particularly threatened by the evil eye reducing their potency. To prevent such an attack the *mano cornuta* or 'horned hand' gesture is employed, where a fist is made with the little and index fingers extended like horns. Another popular protective gesture is the *mano fica* or 'fig', a sexual gesture whereby a fist is formed with the thumb placed between the index and middle finger, representing sexual intercourse, which Dundes believes embodies the desire to guarantee wetness and hence counter the effect of the evil eye. Interestingly, an ancient Roman protective amulet was a phallus.

In seventeenth-century England, one way of countering the effect of the evil eye was to heat some of the victim's hair, nail clippings, urine and blood over a fire at midnight. Eric Maple states that this was believed to neutralise the evil eye's malevolent effect and return it back to the perpetrator. However, most cures for the effects of the evil eye involve offsetting the drying-up symptoms by utilising wetness. Liquid of some kind is therefore often used, particularly eggs, as they are representative of life, rebirth and moisture. In a folklore study carried out among Mexican Americans in Texas in 1949, Soledad Perez spoke to the local population about their belief in the evil eye. Perez's research, which was used in *The Healer of Los Olmas and Other Mexican Lore*, stated that one of the many cures for the evil eye consisted of holding a raw egg in front of the victim's face, rotating it around their face, cracking the egg into a saucer and finally placing it under their bed.

Elsewhere, cures include drinking holy water or lemon juice, sticking a lemon with nails or, bizarrely, drinking water that contains the spittle of the person who cast the evil eye. In India, a method used that does not revolve around moisture concerns fumigation by lighting a flame on a plate that is held in front of the victim's face and moved in a circular motion. Similarly, in Afghanistan and Pakistan aspand seeds are burned, causing them to pop and emit an aromatic smoke. The smoke is then fanned around the face of the afflicted person as prayers are said.

Whilst to many the evil eye is a worthless superstition, there is, nevertheless, a significant number of people who believe in its potency and harmful consequences. Even when it is believed to be an involuntary result of envy or praise, the effects on those who fear the evil eye's influence are real and formidable.

SEE ALSO: Curses

FALLEN ANGELS

Fallen angels feature in many studies into occult lore, and sorcerers traditionally called upon them in their rituals and ceremonies because they were seen as very powerful entities which could be summoned to do the bidding of the magician. We find them in many grimoires, books that detailed magical practice and how to conjure such beings. Fallen angels are found in all the Abrahamic religions – that is, those religions which trace their ancestry to Abraham, including Christianity, Islam and Judaism.

It is in the Book of Enoch, an apocryphal text, that we first find the story of how a group of angels known as the Grigori (also called the Watchers) rebelled against God and left heaven, after which they descended, or 'fell', to earth, where they married mortal women and had children who were giants on the earth. The Book of Enoch describes how this first came about:

> And it came to pass when the children of men had multiplied that in those days were born unto them beautiful and comely daughters. And the angels, the children of the heaven, saw and lusted after them, and said to one another: 'Come, let us choose us wives from among the children of men and beget us children.' And Semjâzâ, who was their leader, said unto them: 'I fear ye will not indeed agree to do this deed, and I alone shall have to pay the penalty of a great sin.' And they all answered him and said: 'Let us all swear an oath, and all bind ourselves by mutual imprecations not to abandon this

plan but to do this thing.' Then sware they all together and
bound themselves by mutual imprecations upon it. And they
were in all two hundred; who descended in the days of Jared
on the summit of Mount Hermon.

These children of the angels and mankind, these giants, were
called the Nephilim, a word that comes from Hebrew and is usually
translated in the Bible literally as 'giant'. However, modern versions
of the Bible have not made this translation, and the word is simply
left as Nephilim. It is interesting to note that the word seems to come
from the Hebrew root *'naphal'* which actually means 'to fall'. When
the Greek version of the Old Testament, the Septuagint, was created,
sometime between the third and first centuries BC, the word they used
in place of 'Nephilim' was *'gegenes'*, and this actually means 'earth-
born'; the same term was applied to the Greek Titans, other giants
who were said to be half celestial and half earthly creatures.

According to the Book of Enoch, the Nephilim, being much larger
and stronger than men, began to turn on humankind and sought to
acquire all the kingdoms and possessions of man, as well as turning
to every kind of imaginable sin, until there was such bloodletting
and chaos on the earth that the angels in heaven were moved to do
something about the appalling scenes they were witnessing. Some of
God's loyal angels, Michael, Uriel, Raphael and Gabriel, were dismayed
at these events, and they brought the news to God himself:

Thou hast made all things, and power over all things hast
Thou . . . Thou seest what Azâzêl hath done, who hath taught
all unrighteousness on earth and revealed the eternal secrets
which were preserved in heaven, which men were striving
to learn: And Semjâzâ, to whom Thou hast given authority
to bear rule over his associates. And they have gone to the
daughters of men upon the earth, and have slept with the
women, and have defiled themselves, and revealed to them
all kinds of sins. And the women have borne giants, and
the whole earth has thereby been filled with blood and
unrighteousness. And now, behold, the souls of those who
have died are crying and making their suit to the gates of
heaven, and their lamentations have ascended: and cannot
cease because of the lawless deeds which are wrought on the
earth.

God did not fail to act. He told Uriel to take this message to earth:

> Go to Noah and tell him in my name 'Hide thyself!' and reveal
> to him the end that is approaching: that the whole earth will
> be destroyed, and a deluge is about to come upon the whole
> earth, and will destroy all that is on it. And now instruct him
> that he may escape and his seed may be preserved for all the
> generations of the world.

So it was that the Great Flood was unleashed and, apart from Noah
and his kin, all humankind, together with the offspring of the Grigori,
the Nephilim, perished in the great destruction that followed.

God had other plans for the fallen angels themselves, and he
ordered before the flood arrived that his angels should apprehend
their leader:

> Bind Azâzêl hand and foot, and cast him into the darkness:
> and make an opening in the desert, which is in Dûdâêl, and
> cast him therein. And place upon him rough and jagged
> rocks, and cover him with darkness, and let him abide there
> for ever, and cover his face that he may not see light. And
> on the day of the great judgement he shall be cast into the
> fire. And heal the earth which the angels have corrupted,
> and proclaim the healing of the earth, that they may heal
> the plague, and that all the children of men may not perish
> through all the secret things that the Watchers have disclosed
> and have taught their sons.

So it was that the era of the fallen angels ended and, as is told elsewhere
in the texts of the Bible, the flood subsided, Noah's ark restored life to
the earth and humankind began again.

The Book of Enoch is not the only place where we find reference
to this story of the fall of the angels. In the King James Version of the
Bible, the Epistle of Jude from the New Testament alludes to the story:
'And the angels which kept not their first estate, but left their own
habitation, he hath reserved in everlasting chains under darkness unto
the judgment of the great day.' There are other mentions of the story
elsewhere, including a strange reference in I Corinthians implying that
women should cover their heads so as not to tempt the angels:

> But every woman that prayeth or prophesieth with her head
> uncovered dishonoureth her head: for that is even all one as if
> she were shaven . . . For this cause ought the woman to have
> power on her head because of the angels.

Is the blame here for the fall of the angels, and the destruction of mankind that followed, being placed on the women with whom the angels slept? It seems entirely possible, though the question is not answered satisfactorily in the text. If this is the judgement that is being made, then it seems a very harsh one to lay on the shoulders of women.

There are other fallen angels apart from the Grigori. The best known is probably Lucifer. In a complex and unfortunate set of circumstances that scholars do not wholly understand, Lucifer went from being a benign figure to one synonymous with the Devil himself. The name Lucifer originally meant 'to bear light' or 'to bring light', and it was associated with the planet Venus and represented the morning star.

Lucifer was not originally a fallen angel, and quite how he came to be regarded as such is not entirely clear. It is thought that a mistranslation in the King James Bible could have initiated this change in perception. In the Old Testament, the Book of Isaiah says: 'How art thou fallen from heaven, O Lucifer, son of the morning! How art thou cut down to the ground, which didst weaken the nations!' Some more recent translations, such as the New English Bible, state this as: 'How you have fallen from heaven, bright morning star.' The reference to Lucifer has disappeared in this new translation, and we get the sense that the text relates to the morning star, Venus, rather than to a fallen angel, which is likely to be more in keeping with the intent of the original author.

This idea that Lucifer was not an agent of darkness but rather one of light is borne out by the fact that Lucifer Calaritanus, who was the Bishop of Cagliari, still retains a feast day in the Catholic Church's calendar, which suggests that the name Lucifer was not always associated with that of Satan.

As we mentioned, all of the three major Abrahamic religions refer to fallen angels, and in Islam we have the story of Iblis. According to the Koran, Iblis was created by Allah as a jinn, a creature of pure, smokeless fire. However, Iblis disobeyed God by not bowing down to Adam, and so he was sent from heaven and damned to Jahannam, the Islamic equivalent of hell. However, Iblis suggested to Allah that if he were to walk the earth instead, he would attempt to bring down humankind, acting as both accuser and devil, whispering in the ears of all men. Allah decided to allow Iblis this role in order to test humankind, and so it was that Iblis came to earth.

Fallen angels seem to function as an allegory for the sins of pride and lust, and in the biblical and other apocryphal texts, we can see them as a lesson for humankind: that even the great, the angels, born of God himself, can falter and succumb to temptation, that such a fall from grace is not above even the highest and mightiest.

SEE ALSO: Angelology; Goetia; Grimoires

FLAMEL, NICHOLAS

Nicholas Flamel is known to millions of readers today as a character in J.K. Rowling's bestselling children's novel *Harry Potter and the Philosopher's Stone*. What most of these readers may not be aware of is that this name actually belonged to a real person who is acknowledged to have been one of Europe's most famous alchemists. He is rumoured to have succeeded in achieving the ultimate goals of alchemy: turning base metals into gold and discovering the elixir of life, through which he achieved immortality (although adepts of 'the Great Work' would argue that spiritual perfection is the true aim of alchemical study, and this too may have been his prize). An alchemical work known as *Le Livre des Figures Hiéroglyphiques* was published in Paris in 1612, and is said to be based on a work written by Flamel himself. It purports to contain amongst its pages Flamel's autobiography. It is on this work that most histories of his life are based. Because of the fantastic legends about the alchemist that have arisen from this work, many historians question the authenticity of this 'autobiography', believing the text to have been written after Flamel's death.

Born at Pontoise, outside Paris, in 1330, Nicholas grew up in a poor family. Despite this, his parents managed to provide him with a good education, allowing him to achieve, amongst other things, a working knowledge of Latin. Based on this education, and as an adult, he moved to the city of Paris to pursue a professional career as a scribe and bookseller. Once there, he secured lodgings and set up a shop near to the church of St-Jacques-la-Boucherie. His choice of profession proved fortuitous in that it gave him the opportunity to access the occult wisdom that would shape his life. From around 1350 onwards, numerous alchemical works and grimoires, or books of magic, were being discovered, translated and transcribed across Europe, and it is known that Nicholas stumbled across at least one of these great works.

In the early days, his choice of career did not make him a wealthy man. Indeed he often went hungry, and life was not particularly easy. His earliest attempts to supplement his earnings included writing poetry and painting. Sadly, he was not particularly accomplished at either of these pursuits and failed to improve his circumstances by these means.

His first real success came with what appears to have been his first venture into the occult arts. He took up fortune telling, which he excelled at, and soon developed a reputation that attracted many fee-paying customers. Now experiencing a more comfortable lifestyle, he married a girl named Perenelle. She was to be his life's companion, with whom he shared his occult pursuits over the following decades. Their ultimate goal at this point was to seek out and master the secrets of alchemy and the enigmatic philosopher's stone.

The mastery of alchemy could take a lifetime to achieve, if one succeeded at all, so it is not surprising that it took Flamel until 1378 before any significant developments materialised. In this year, he is said to have had a dream about an occult book, 21 pages long, bound in metal and filled with strange diagrams. He is said to have subsequently discovered the book in real life and bought it from a fellow bookseller. This strange episode was ascribed to an angel named Bath-Kol, who appeared in his dream and told him that the discovery and study of this book was to be his life's work.

It was written in Hebrew, and he succeeded in deciphering it with the aid of a Jewish scholar whom he travelled to Spain to find. It was a Kabbalistic text written by Abre-Melin the Mage (a work later translated into English by S.L. MacGregor Mathers of Golden Dawn fame). The book was a magical treatise written by a father for his son, a sorcerer for his apprentice.

Studying the work apparently allowed Nicholas, with the assistance of his wife, to achieve the Great Work itself in January 1382. He first managed to transmute mercury into silver; then, a few months later, with hard work and diligence, he successfully produced gold. News of this work was said to have reached King Charles VI of France, who sent an envoy to discover the secret of the philosopher's stone. By all accounts, the envoy returned empty-handed.

Whether any of the accounts of his alchemical success are true or not, the fact remains that Nicholas Flamel did amass a great fortune, some of which he and his wife expended on the charitable work of building hospitals and chapels and the adornment of churches. One of their building projects still stands today at 51 rue de Montmorency in Paris. Built in 1407, it has now been converted into a restaurant.

Inevitably with such a character, a great deal of mythology has grown up around his life and death. In 1410, at the age of 80, he designed his own tomb, covered with alchemical symbols, diagrams of which were published in a book in 1610. In 1418, he died, although some say that, having discovered the secrets of the philosopher's stone and immortality, he staged his death.

For 100 years after the death of Flamel, many adepts (students of alchemical wisdom considered to have special knowledge) believed that he was still alive and that he would live for upwards of 600 years. The house he formerly occupied, at the corner of the rue de Marivaux, has often been bought by people interested in his wealth and ransacked from top to bottom in the hopes that gold might be found. In about 1816, it was reported in Paris that tenants of the house had discovered several jars in the cellars filled with a heavy, dark-coloured substance, but no sign of gold was ever found.

As late as the eighteenth century, Paul Lucas, archaeologist to Louis XIV, wrote that he had met a Sufi who had recently met Flamel. Another eighteenth-century account, by the writer Amans-Alexis Monteil in his *Histoire des Français des divers États*, claims that Flamel had been discovered still carrying out the Great Work in his laboratory. A traditional tale also exists telling that a robber went to the home of the departed alchemist to seek his gold. Not finding anything at the house, he went to his tomb and broke into it only to discover that there was no gold and no Nicholas Flamel either.

SEE ALSO: Alchemy; Grimoires; Kabbalah; Philosopher's Stone

FORTUNE, DION

Dion Fortune was one of Britain's most famous and respected occult practitioners and writers. She was born in 1890 as Violet Mary Firth, and she took the name by which she would forever be known from the Latin phrase '*Deo, non fortuna*' (by God, not by chance), which was her family's motto.

Her parents owned a seaside hotel and spa in Llandudno in Wales, and it was here that Fortune grew up. As a young girl, she was introduced to Christian Science, which was practised by her family. Christian Scientists believe that spiritual healing is more important than conventional medicine, and they attempt to heal the sick and ill through prayer alone, believing that this was how Jesus himself operated.

At 21, Fortune enrolled at Studley College in Warwickshire, where she studied horticulture. She was to leave after just two years following what she claimed in later life had been a psychic attack by the warden of the college, Dr Hamilton. This attack left Fortune exhausted, and she experienced a nervous breakdown. In order to heal her damaged mind, she became interested in psychology and began a course at the Medico-Psychological Clinic in London.

There, in London, Fortune joined the Theosophical Society, and while attending a lecture on telepathy, she began to discover her own psychic powers. Working with an Irish occultist called Theodore Moriarty, who would become her esoteric teacher, she began to experiment with her newfound talents. She was also initiated into a group known as Alpha et Omega – a society that was associated with the Hermetic Order of the Golden Dawn.

In time, Fortune became disillusioned with the progress she was making within these institutions and so decided to set up her own esoteric group, in Glastonbury, said to have had as its meeting place an old officers' mess hut in a dramatic setting just below the enigmatic Glastonbury Tor. This group she called the Fraternity of the Inner Light, which later became the Society of the Inner Light. Not long after this, Fortune fell out with the leader of the Alpha et Omega Order, Moina Mathers, wife of MacGregor Mathers, one of the leading lights of the Golden Dawn, and was expelled from Alpha et Omega, leaving her free to devote her time to her own group and to her writing.

Many of Fortune's ideas on magic found expression through her fiction, which contains detailed magical information and knowledge. In her novels, she puts forward the idea that Christianity is not sufficient to sate the spiritual needs of the modern seeker of divinity and truth. This is a common theme in her work, and in *The Winged Bull* she has one of the characters, Murchison, say:

> And the trouble with Christianity was that it was so darned lop-sided. Good, and jolly good, as far as it went, but you couldn't stretch it clean round the circle of experience because it just wouldn't go. What it was originally, nobody knew, save that it must have been something mighty potent. All we knew of it was what was left after those two crusty old bachelors, Paul and Augustine, had finished with it.
>
> And then came the heresy hunters and gave it a final curry-combing, taking infinite pains to get rid of everything that it had inherited from older faiths. And they had been like the modern miller, who refines all the vitamins out of the bread and gives half the population rickets. That was what was the matter with civilisation, it had spiritual rickets because its spiritual food was too refined. Man can't get on without a dash of paganism, and for the most part, he doesn't try to.

Chas S. Clifton, in his article 'A Goddess Arrives', which appeared in the journal *Gnosis* in 1988, puts forward the idea that Fortune played a large part in influencing Gardnerian witchcraft, that brand of witchcraft developed by Gerald Gardner in the 1950s, which represented a modern revival and formed the foundations of the religion of Wicca. Clifton argues that Gardner used some of her work in formulating his rituals and incantations. Because so much of modern witchcraft bears an uncanny resemblance to the ideas found in Fortune's books, it is even suggested that rather than Wicca being based on a long history of witchcraft in Britain, the very ideas upon which it was founded actually began with Fortune and are no older than her. Certainly, as Clifton points out, her ideas concerning a Western tradition of magic, which include the worship of a dominant Goddess, are so close to Wicca that the two seem almost indivisible.

One of the most direct pieces of evidence we have that Gardner was inspired by Fortune can be seen in the ritual that he created called 'Drawing Down the Moon'. In it, the Goddess is summoned though the physical being of the priestess. It has been suggested that this ritual was based on one described in detail in Fortune's novel *The Sea Priestess*, which she self-published in 1938.

Today, Fortune is known particularly for her work in bringing the Kabbalah to the fore and generating popular interest in Britain in this esoteric tradition. She explains some of the roots of this tradition in *The Mystical Qabala*, considered to be not only her finest work, but possibly the best treatise on magic ever to have been written:

> It may be asked why it is that the Western nations should go to the Hebrew culture for their mystical tradition? The answer to this question will be readily understood by those who are acquainted with the esoteric theory concerning races and sub-races. Everything must have a source. Cultures do not spring out of nothing. The seed-bearers of each new phase of culture must of necessity arise within the preceding Culture. No one can deny that Judaism was the matrix of the European spiritual culture when they recall the fact that Jesus and Paul were both Jews. No race except the Jewish race could possibly have served as the stock upon which the new dispensation was to be grafted because no other race was monotheistic. Pantheism and polytheism had had their day and a new and more spiritual culture was due. The Christian races owe their religion to the Jewish culture as surely as the Buddhist races of the East owe theirs to the Hindu culture.

She also offered practical help in books such as *Psychic Self-Defence*, and a famous quotation comes from this book in which she outlines in some detail what psychic attacks are and how everyone can protect themselves from such attacks:

> It is not the inherent nature of atoms which causes them to arrange themselves in the complex patterns of living tissues. The driving forces of the universe, the framework upon which it is built up in all its parts, belong to another phase of manifestation than our physical plane, having other dimensions than the three to which we are habituated, and perceived by other modes of consciousness than those to which we are accustomed.
>
> We live in the midst of invisible forces whose effects alone we perceive. We move among invisible forms whose actions we very often do not perceive at all, though we may be profoundly affected by them.

Towards the end of her life, Dion Fortune had much contact with Aleister Crowley while he was living in Hastings, though, sadly, the correspondence between them and what exactly they discussed has been lost to us. He is said to have been a great admirer of her work and even attended her lectures.

In 1946, at the age of 55, Fortune died in London of leukaemia. Despite her early death, her legacy was assured: the Society of the Inner Light continued to practise as an initiatory school for students of the Western esoteric tradition and still operates to this day. Furthermore, Dion Fortune's books are still popular and continue to serve as a good introduction to the various schools of mystery and magic with which she was fascinated from an early age.

SEE ALSO: Crowley, Aleister; Hermetic Order of the Golden Dawn; Kabbalah; Wicca

FULCANELLI

Of all the great alchemists of whom we have knowledge, Fulcanelli is perhaps the most enigmatic and elusive of them all. He may have been one of the greatest people who ever lived or he may not have existed at all. If the latter is true, then an individual somewhere, or a group, is behind one of the biggest and most elaborate hoaxes ever. The question, however, is, if he was a hoax, what end did the great deception serve? These are puzzles that may never be answered in a satisfactory way.

If we believe that he did indeed exist, then Fulcanelli is the pseudonym of a great alchemist. Translated, it means 'little Vulcan', presumably chosen in reference to the Roman god of fire and volcanoes. Certainly, fire is one of the most important of the elements used in the alchemist's art, and intrinsic to discovering the philosopher's stone.

We first hear of Fulcanelli in the early twentieth century, when a strange book attributed to him was published in Paris in 1926. This work, *The Mystery of the Cathedrals*, explains that the greatest secrets of alchemy were carved in full display into the fabric of many Gothic churches of the Middle Ages. The book includes examples, with illustrations from the cathedrals of Bourges, Amiens and Notre-Dame in Paris. One example describes how the steps to discovering the philosopher's stone are inscribed on the façade of Notre-Dame.

The book, hailed as a masterpiece of esoteric literature, was obviously written by an adept, as no one has successfully disproved the claims. The work has captivated occultists around the globe since its appearance, and although for many years it was only available in its native French, it was published in English in 1984. The manner of the presentation to the world of this work has of itself generated many of the Fulcanelli legends. His pupil Eugène Canseliet claimed that Fulcanelli mysteriously appeared to him one day and took him as his apprentice. In 1926, he left instructions with Canseliet that his magnum opus, which he entrusted to his pupil, should be published – and then he disappeared.

The Mystery of the Cathedrals was followed around 1930 by another publication, also claimed to be by Fulcanelli, entitled *Dwellings of the Philosophers*. This too was embraced by occultists as the acknowledged work of an adept. A third book from Fulcanelli, to have been called *End of World's Glory*, was promised and much anticipated; but Fulcanelli decided that the world was not yet ready for this, and at his instruction to Canseliet, it was withdrawn. Later, a book did in fact appear in print with this title, purporting to have been authored by Fulcanelli, but this was later proved to have been an inferior work written by an opportunist.

By all accounts, the only person who really knew the man behind the pseudonym was Eugène Canseliet, Fulcanelli's disciple and the man behind the publication of *The Mystery of the Cathedrals*. Whatever the truth behind the great alchemist is, Canseliet took the secret of his master's true identity to his grave. He did, however, leave behind a number of anecdotal stories about his time with the alchemist. These have become the stuff of modern legend.

Canseliet related that, under the guidance and direction of his master, he actually accomplished the transmutation of lead into gold at a location near Sarcelles, on the outskirts of Paris. This was apparently accomplished using a powder produced from the philosopher's stone of the great adept himself. It is claimed that others witnessed the event, but, of course, whether the transformation took place cannot be scientifically proven.

Another fascinating story tells of a man who, claiming to be Fulcanelli, walked into the secure laboratory of the physicist Andre Helbronner in the late 1930s. Speaking to Helbronner's assistant, Jacques Bergier, the mysterious man claimed that he was an alchemist and had come to warn the physicist of the dangers of atomic research. This was eight years before the Allied Forces had produced the atom bombs that brought about the annihilation of Hiroshima and Nagasaki. The inference the scientist drew from the alchemist's words was that he already knew the secrets of their quest as well as the terrible consequences that would result from their discovery. Apparently, this encounter led to a security alert that had the forerunners of the American CIA searching for Fulcanelli. To date, by all accounts, they have not yet found him!

Canseliet claimed that his final meeting with his master took place in the 1950s in Spain, where he travelled to see him one last time. He claimed Fulcanelli would have been over 110 (by his own account) at this time but that he still looked no older than 50.

For the sceptical amongst us who believe that perhaps a number of contemporary twentieth-century characters might account for the myth of Fulcanelli, here are some of the 'prime suspects' whom various researchers of the Fulcanelli phenomenon have suggested. Some speculate that he was none other than Canseliet himself, and certainly if it was a hoax, he must have been in on it and, for whatever reason, have lied to numerous people over the years. Canseliet aside, the prime candidate most often cited is Jean-Julien Champagne, the painter who illustrated *The Mystery of the Cathedrals*. René Schwaller de Lubicz, a notable individual in occult circles, has also been suggested. He is famous for his in-depth 15-year study of the temples of Egypt, described in his book *The Temple of Man*. Members of the Martinist Order, including Jean Bricaud, Papus and latterly Robert Amadou and Robert Ambelain, may also have known something. These individuals were active at the heart of the French occult revival after the influential magician Eliphas Lévi, and each may have wanted to make his own mark on the esoteric history of the West. Throughout the twentieth century, these men were the custodians of many esoteric secrets in France. Another contender is Pierre Dujols, a bookseller who specialised in hermetic literature.

If we forget the sceptics for a moment and presume that perhaps immortals do walk amongst us, we can entertain the suggestion, made by some, that Fulcanelli was Nicholas Flamel. If this were the case, *The Mystery of the Cathedrals* would have been published when he was in his 596th year! The Count of St Germain, who has supposedly been spotted regularly since the eighteenth century, has also been proposed as the real Fulcanelli. Like Fulcanelli, the Count of St Germain is said still to have the appearance of a man no older than 50.

In some ways, many people hope that there is something behind these tales, perhaps a real, living result of what can happen if one discovers the great secrets of alchemy. In any case, Fulcanelli is still very much alive and amongst us today – in books, on the Web and even on British television. In 2006, the BBC's supernatural series *Sea of Souls* had Paul McGann playing a character suspected of being our elusive alchemist. In keeping with the tradition of Fulcanelli, by the end of the programme we were left wondering how much was fact and how much fiction.

SEE ALSO: Alchemy; Flamel, Nicholas; Lévi, Eliphas; Martinism; Philosopher's Stone; St Germain, Count of

GNOSTICISM

The term 'Gnosticism' is generally applied to heretical teachings popular at the time of the early Christian Church, although in a wider sense it is not limited solely to Christianity but also includes other religious and spiritual teachings that stress the importance of obtaining sacred hidden knowledge. Gnosticism, which comes from the Greek *gnosis*, meaning 'knowledge', is a mix of Egyptian, Persian, Jewish, pre-Christian Hellenistic and Greek philosophical and religious thinking, mysticism, self-discipline and astrology. These all combined to produce Gnosticism which, ultimately, was about the pursuit of salvation.

The central premises of Gnosticism are the belief that redemption and union with God can be obtained only through secret knowledge of the divine; that God is separate from matter; and that man possesses a spark of divinity enabling him to be saved from the world of matter and his lowly position within it. Philip Gardiner relates in his book *Gnosis* that the Gnostic Gospel of Thomas quotes Jesus as saying: 'For whoever does not know self, does not know anything, but whoever knows self, already has aquired knowledge about the depth of the universe.' Accordingly, in Gnosticism the obtaining of mystical and esoteric knowledge and enlightenment through inner visions and self-awareness was the means by which humankind could be saved and become divine once more.

This central tenet had a direct and adverse effect upon Gnosticism's relationship with the Church, as it opposed the Church's every doctrine and dogma. As Gnostics believed it should be the goal of all to attain salvation through a personal, spiritual quest for knowledge, it followed that there was no need for priests to act as intermediaries between man and God, for Gnosticism stressed that only through personal inner visions could spiritual enlightenment and secret, esoteric knowledge of the divine be obtained. As Elaine Pagels states in *The Gnostic Gospels*, 'Gnostic teaching . . . claimed to offer to every initiate a means of direct access to God of which the priests and bishops themselves might be ignorant.' As Christopher Knight and Robert Lomas point out in *The Hiram Key*, this would mean that anyone practising Gnosticism could be on a par with, or even exceed, the apostles and their successors in spiritual and arcane knowledge, thus threatening the authority of the Church.

Gnosticism taught that God resided in the highest realm – the world of light – whereas the earth, the lowest realm, is the world of matter. It was thus man's lot to be confined within a physical body, but his redeeming feature was that he possessed a divine spark. It was therefore the duty of humankind to strive to become reunited with God. This obligation to achieve personal enlightenment also applied to women, which meant that women were considered an integral and essential part of the equation. As such, women could and did take an active and equal role within Gnosticism. In addition to this, the divine spark that existed within humankind precluded the idea of original sin and the concept that humankind is inherently evil, for the spark suggested that humans were once divine themselves.

Gnostics also had different views from the Church regarding resurrection, for Gnosticism states that it is not essential to die in order to be resurrected, with the resurrection being the moment of enlightenment that enables an individual to escape spiritual death and instead to obtain spiritual life. Accordingly, the Gnostic Gospel of Philip states: 'those who say they will die first and then rise are in error; they must receive the resurrection while they live.'

Also at odds with the Church were the Gnostic beliefs that Creation was a mistake, that the Old Testament was redundant and that the historicity of the New Testament accounts of the ministry, death and resurrection of Jesus was questionable. Moreover, whilst great importance was placed on Jesus and his teachings, Gnostics did not consider Jesus to be divine. Understandably, the early Christian Church was fearful of Gnosticism, as its beliefs endangered the Church's authority. Not surprisingly, Gnosticism was suppressed although it continued as an underground movement, having major centres at Alexandria in Egypt and Edessa in Mesopotamia.

Timothy Freke and Peter Gandy, writing in *Jesus and the Goddess*, consider that the Gnostic teachings go far beyond the traditions, myths and stories of the Bible and extend 'to the mystical experience of the ineffable Mystery' so that none of these 'outer trappings' of religion should be taken as factual. Instead it is the 'inner essence' of the writings that are important. Freke and Gandy believe that the story of Jesus and his ministry was a Gnostic creation developed over time, thus 'fashioning a progressively more complex allegory in the form of an ever more colourful and emotive story'. The aim of this story was to help to steer people through a spiritual journey of illumination. However, for political reasons, the Jesus story was taken over and modified by others, who stripped it of its Gnostic origins. To underline this theory, Freke and Gandy highlight the differences and discrepancies contained within the Gospels, stating that if they were a historical account, this should not occur. However, such discrepancies are irrelevant if the Gospels are Gnostic 'initiation allegories', which Gnostics would have adapted 'to suit their own particular requirements'.

Some hints of Gnostic belief can be found in the New Testament, such as the Gospel of John and the association of God with the Word, or *logos*: 'In the beginning was the Word; and the Word was with God, and the Word was God'. Interestingly, the commentator Philo Judaeus (25 BC–AD 50) incorporates the idea of *logos* in his writings, which he describes as 'the Guide on the path which leads to Sophia [wisdom] and her Gnosis'. According to A.F. Walls in *The New Bible Dictionary*, Paul's letters to the Corinthians also 'reflect terms and concepts developed in Gnosticism'. This included their appreciation of *gnosis* and wisdom (1 Corinthians 8:1), their liberal sexual practices (1 Corinthians 6:12–20; 1 Corinthians 7) and the denial of the resurrection (1 Corinthians 15:12).

However, it is principally in the texts which have become known as the Gnostic gospels that the beliefs of the Gnostics can be uncovered. In 1945, a cache of 52 ancient scrolls was discovered at Nag Hammadi in southern Egypt. These contained the Gnostic gospels, which were excluded from the canonical corpus established by the Council of Nicaea in AD 325 as they were considered heretical and were therefore banned. Most of the texts date to AD 350–400, but they are considered to be copies of much older works. Included within these are the

Gospel of Truth, which examines the Christian message, the Gospel of Thomas, containing 114 sayings ascribed to Jesus, and the Gospel of Philip, which includes many references to Jesus and Sophia/wisdom, describing their offspring as gnosis. The Gospel of Philip mentions five rites: baptism, anointing, the Eucharist, redemption and the bridal chamber. The last and most important rite, the bridal chamber, suggests that sexual union between man and woman was considered to be of great significance, impelling all to 'understand what great power undefiled intercourse possesses', although sexual union was to be conducted behind closed doors so as not to be 'degraded through being seen by the multitude'. Another Gnostic gospel, the Pista Sophia, recounts the closeness between Jesus and Mary Magdalene, which is echoed in some of the other Gnostic gospels, including the Gospel of Mary, in which Mary Magdalene is depicted as the leading disciple, a role usually accorded to Peter.

In the face of continued persecution and prohibition by the early Church, Gnosticism gradually died out, yielding to the greater power of the Catholic Church. However, it may well be that a remnant of Gnosticism can still be found today among the Mandaeans who live in small areas of Iraq and Iran. Lynn Picknett and Clive Prince, in *The Templar Revelation*, put forward the theory that the Mandaeans are the only surviving Gnostics, explaining that 'their ideas concerning the universe, the act of Creation and the gods are familiar Gnostic beliefs'.

SEE ALSO: Blake, William

GOETIA

Goetia is a form of magic that concentrates exclusively on the calling forth of demons. Because of this, it is considered to be a lower form of magic as opposed to the pure, divine magic of theurgy. Thus goetia is the work of the sorcerer whereas higher magic is the work of the magus. Goetia is more commonly known as profane or black magic because it invokes demons and entities and is used in order to command these beings to do the sorcerer's bidding, usually for his own benefit and not for the common good. In relation to goetia, occultist Aleister Crowley stated in his book *The Goetia: The Lesser Key of Solomon the King* that 'its spirits offer a means of improving one's lot in life, addressing the entire spectrum of human concerns, from preferment and wealth to sex and knowledge'.

The term 'goetia' derives from the Greek word for sorcery and is also closely connected with the word that translates as 'howler' or 'wailer', in reference to the screeching out of invocations to call up the spirits. These invocations Julianus called the 'barbarous names of evocation', as related in *The Chaldaean Oracles*. Julianus is thought to have been a Chaldaean priest of the second century AD who came to Rome during the time of Marcus Aurelius, bringing with him the beliefs and wisdom of the Chaldaeans, a semi-nomadic people who ruled Babylon and were famed for their knowledge of astronomy and philosophy. In his *Oracles*, he is stated to have warned 'never to change barbarous names' into different languages because the names have 'an unspeakable power in Divine Rites' and to translate these into spoken languages was to bring forward dreadful powers.

Similarly, the nineteenth-century occult writer and practitioner Eliphas Lévi stated in relation to the invoking of spirits that he regarded 'the practice as destructive and dangerous'. For him, this was borne out by personal experience, because on three consecutive days he had used goetia to call up Apollonius of Tyana, a first-century philosopher. Preparations for this involved three weeks of meticulous planning, with Lévi later declaring that the practice of goetia was ultimately to the detriment of the sorcerer, as the 'result is intense exhaustion, and frequently a shock sufficient to occasion illness'.

According to Crowley, goetia (or ceremonial magic, as he referred to it) consists of six elements: sight, sound, smell, taste, touch and the mind. Crowley believed that it was the first five of these elements that together produced an unusual effect on a person's mind because 'the spirits of the *Goetia* are portions of the human brain'. As Crowley saw it, the practice of goetia serves to 'stimulate and develop' the brain and allows the sorcerer to see the demons and entities that are invoked.

Whilst there are other books of magic dating from the medieval period that contain instructions on the practice of goetia and list demons, their characteristics, seals, or symbols, to summon them by, sacrifices required and other paraphernalia, the best known such volume forms the first part of *The Lesser Key of Solomon*, made famous by Crowley, who edited *The Goetia: The Lesser Key of Solomon* along with S.L. MacGregor Mathers. *The Lesser Key* is a manual of Solomonic sorcery compiled from medieval and later grimoires (books of magic). It consists of four, sometimes five, parts: 'The Goetia', 'The Theurgia-Goetia', 'The Pauline Art', 'The Almadel of Solomon' and 'The Notary Art'. MacGregor Mathers also prepared an edition of the earlier *Greater Key of Solomon*, a book of ritual magic attributed to King Solomon, although it is generally thought that it probably dates to the twelfth century AD when the invocation of spirits became a popular form of magic.

The Lesser Key of Solomon includes a list of 72 demons, 'mighty kings and princes which King Solomon commanded into a vessel of brass, together with their legions'. The book states that God gave Solomon power over the lesser spirits, which he held captive within a brass vessel that was held shut by magical symbols. The king was able to command the demons, imprisoned in this way, to do his bidding. The first-century *Testament of Solomon* relates how he built his temple in Jerusalem by use of magic and by the evocation and commanding of demons. These legends are the basis of the Arabian tales of *The Thousand and One Nights* and the genie in the bottle.

The Lesser Key of Solomon contains detailed and comprehensive directions for the convoluted and meticulous ceremony and ritual essential for the safety and protection of the sorcerer when invoking one of the seventy-two entities supposedly imprisoned by King Solomon. The book also relates how to make the demons obedient once they have been called up. To aid the sorcerer, the character, rank, appearance and special talent of each of the entities are given in detail. For example:

> The Forty-ninth Spirit is Crocell or Crokel. He appeareth in
> the Form of an Angel. He is a Duke Great and Strong, speaking
> something Mystically of Hidden Things. He teacheth the Art
> of Geometry and the Liberal Sciences. He, at the Command
> of the Exorcist, will produce Great Noises like the Rushings
> of many Waters, although there be none . . . he governeth 48
> Legions of Spirits . . .

The Goetia notes that the 72 demons are made up of 36 day demons and 36 night demons, with each demon having a specific time at which it can be conjured up and bound. Kings are to be summoned between 9 a.m. and noon; marquises between 3 p.m. and 9 p.m., and 9 p.m. to sunrise; dukes from sunrise until noon in clear weather; prelates can be invoked at any hour of the day; knights from dawn until sunrise or 4 p.m. to sunset; presidents any time except twilight or at night; counts and earls can be called at any time, but only in woods or where no one lives, or where there is no noise.

In the actual ceremony, the sorcerer is to stand in a magical circle, within which he or she has to stay to ensure protection. Around the circle are to be placed signs symbolic of the names of the demons, known as their seals and detailed in the description of each demon. Within the magical circle are placed hexagrams to ensure the sorcerer's protection and to keep the demon out. Outside the circle are placed four pentagrams, and above the circle is the magical triangle of Solomon, which is where the demon is commanded to appear. Thus confined, the demon is compelled to obey.

Other requirements for the correct and safe practice of goetia include special robes for the sorcerer, decorated with the hexagram of Solomon, to ensure the demon takes on human form and does the required bidding. The pentagram of Solomon is also to be worn for protection and to command the demons, with the magic ring of Solomon being worn 'to preserve him from the stinking sulphurous fumes and flaming breath of the Evil Spirits'. To complete the ritual requirements, the sorcerer must have a sceptre, sword, mitre, cap, a lion-skinned girdle on which is written magical names, perfumes, charcoal, oil and water. With the sorcerer standing within the circle, certain words relevant to the particular demon required are said by way of purification and conjuration. These words can be said as many times as is desired. If this fails to raise the demon, a second conjuration is to be said, but if this fails 'The Constraint' is to be uttered. The failure of this to raise the demon indicates that it is unavailable, probably because it is in chains in Hell. If, despite all this, the sorcerer still wants this particular demon to be raised, 'The General Curse, Called the Spirits' Chain, Against All Spirits that Rebel' is to be pronounced. If this still fails, 'The Conjuration of the Fire' is required and then, finally, 'The Greater Curse'.

As an ultimate measure, the demon's seal is put on a parchment, placed in a black box and put in the fire. This will ensure that the spirit will come, and once the sorcerer shows the demon the pentagram of Solomon and recites 'The Address unto the Spirit upon his Coming', it will be obedient. Still within the circle, the sorcerer stretches out his arms and makes his requests. When he wants the demon to leave, 'The Licence to Depart' is to be said, and once the demon has gone, prayers of thanks are spoken to God for safely delivering the sorcerer 'from all the malice of the enemy the devil'. It is at this point that the sorcerer can leave the circle.

Goetia is highly ritualistic because of the inherent danger in its use. By their nature, the demons are more powerful than the sorcerer, and because of this they need to be constrained and ordered. The sorcerer must be in total command and control of the demon throughout the ceremony to make certain that it is his will, and not the demon's, that is adhered to. In this way, the sorcerer remains protected throughout.

SEE ALSO: Crowley, Aleister; Grimoires; Lévi, Eliphas; Pentagram

GRIMOIRES

Despite the great age and mystery associated with these books, most grimoires were actually written sometime between the Middle Ages and the eighteenth century. The word 'grimoire' is derived from the Old French *gramaire* which meant 'learning', particularly in relation to Latin and philology. This in turn came from the Latin *grammatica*, and a 'grammar' was the word for a book that taught Latin, a manual of the Latin language. The implication is clear: if grammars were books that enabled the reader to unlock the Latin language, then grimoires were instruction manuals that enabled the devotee to unlock the language of the magical arts.

Although on the surface many grimoires look like no more than lists of magical spells and incantations, the true mystery of these books was often hidden deep within their pages, and the magicians and authors who composed them concealed secrets and complex codes amongst the ritual instructions.

The most well known of all the grimoires is probably *The Greater Key of Solomon*, which was attributed to King Solomon himself but which was in fact first written down in the Middle Ages, probably in the twelfth century. Most surviving examples of the manuscript date from the sixteenth and seventeenth centuries. This grimoire probably inspired another famous, but later, work known as *The Lesser Key of Solomon*, or the *Lemegeton*. This book appeared in the seventeenth century and grew to become a very popular title; a famous version was produced in the twentieth century by Aleister Crowley.

A recurrent and often dominant theme of the grimoires is the subject of demons, and many texts detail the names of all the demons in existence, as well as containing explicit instructions on how to summon them and other entities (the practice of goetia). *The Lesser Key of Solomon* is one of these works, and a typical example of such a summons from this grimoire reads as follows:

> O Thou great, powerful, and mighty King Amaimon, who bearest rule by the power of the Supreme God El over all spirits both superior and inferior of the Infernal Orders in the Dominion of the East; I do invoke and command thee by the especial and true name of God; and by that God that Thou Worshippest; and by the Seal of thy creation; and by the most mighty and powerful name of God, Iehovah Tetragrammaton who cast thee out of heaven with all other infernal spirits . . .

Grimoires have been the subject of furious debate for centuries, and their content is taken extremely seriously. The man who translated and compiled the first publicly available version of *The Greater Key of Solomon* in 1888, the famous occultist Samuel Liddell MacGregor Mathers, had this to say in the introduction about some of the material and its potential to cause harm:

> There are, however, two works on *Black Magic*, the '*Grimorium Verum*,' and the '*Clavicola di Salomone ridolta*,' which have been attributed to Solomon, and which have been in some cases especially mixed up with the present work; but which have nothing really to do therewith; they are full of evil magic, and I cannot caution the practical student too strongly against them . . .
>
> In editing this *Volume* I have omitted one or two experiments partaking largely of *Black Magic*, and which had evidently been derived from the two *Goetic* works mentioned above; I must further caution the practical worker against the use of blood; the prayer, the *Pentacle*, and the perfumes . . . rightly used, are sufficient as the former verges dangerously on the evil path. Let him who, in spite of the warnings of this *Volume* determines to work evil, be assured that evil will recoil on himself and that he will be struck by the reflex current.

Mathers' warnings were not merely theatrical in nature, and it is clear that the original manuscripts do contain highly provocative material, for example, instructions on how to cause harm to befall others. Some of *The Greater Key of Solomon* was, and still is, considered extremely controversial. However, the original texts themselves are very explicit when they state that the person performing any of the included rituals must be cleansed and purified before attempting any of the procedures, and, even more importantly, that this includes being free of any evil intent whatsoever before commencing. There were dire warnings included with the incantations, so Mathers was only echoing their message. This, for example, is what it says in *The Greater Key of Solomon*:

> Thou mayest then, by the use of their seals and characters, render [the demons] familiar unto thee, provided that thou abusest not this privilege by demanding from them things which are contrary to their nature; for accursed be he who will take the Name of God in vain, and who will employ for evil purposes the knowledge and good wherewith He hath enriched us.

As well as the grimoires attributed to Solomon mentioned above, other well-known manuscripts include *Le Dragon Rouge*, *The Grand Grimoire*, *La Poule Noire*, *The Book of the Sacred Magic of Abramelin the Mage*, *The Books of Moses* and *The Grimoire of Honorius*, amongst many others.

It has been suggested that grimoires have their origins in the books of magical spells and incantations found in Ancient Egypt, works such as the Book of Coming Forth by Day. These funerary books dealt with the realm of the dead and instructed the deceased on how to navigate the underworld, including how to avoid some of the fierce spirits that dwelt there – material that we can certainly see might influence the content of the grimoires.

Grimoires are certainly not all about black magic, and many contain themes consistent with Judaism or Christianity. Indeed, *The Grimoire of Honorius* is said to have been written by none other than Pope Honorius III sometime in the early thirteenth century, and the text contains a list of fallen angels and how to summon them.

However, it is the grimoires that deal with black magic that have given them their often dark and grisly reputation, and it is these that most people think of when referring to the magical books. What must be remembered is that grimoires were written and gained their popularity at a time when science was still not understood by the general populace, so much store was set by magical texts and magicians who claimed they could perform miracles, whether it was summoning demons or bringing rain to quench a drought.

SEE ALSO: Crowley, Aleister; Goetia

HERMETIC ORDER OF THE GOLDEN DAWN

Claims exist that an ancient, secret magical tradition dating back centuries surfaced in England in the closing years of the nineteenth century. Some, however, contend that this so-called ancient heritage was only newly invented, a deception designed to attract gullible recruits. Whatever the case, the Hermetic Order of the Golden Dawn is the best-known and most influential modern magical order in the English-speaking world. Founded in 1888 by three esoterically inclined Freemasons, it imploded after just a decade, amidst personality clashes and power struggles. Its legacy, however, brought about the magical revival of the twentieth century in Britain and created offshoot orders and groups, many of which still survive today.

The founders, Dr William Robert Woodman (1828–91), Dr William Wynn Westcott (1848–1925) and Samuel Liddell MacGregor Mathers (1854–1918), were all members of the Masonic Rosicrucian body Societas Rosicruciana in Anglia (SRIA). These three men were already fairly accomplished students of the occult before the foundation of the Golden Dawn. There are varying accounts of how the order originally came into existence, but all acknowledge Westcott as the pivotal person behind its establishment. He apparently received a manuscript in 1887 encrypted with a secret cipher attributed to the fifteenth-century occultist Johannes Trithemius, who was the magical mentor to both Heinrich Cornelius Agrippa and Paracelsus.

One version claims that prior to this the manuscript had belonged to Kenneth Mackenzie, author of the famous *Royal Masonic Cyclopaedia*. He, so the story goes, had received these papers from the 'Secret Chiefs' of an ancient esoteric Rosicrucian tradition based on the Continent. Mackenzie was alleged to have been a member of this group, having been initiated by a Count Apponyi of Hungary. Mackenzie gave these papers to Reverend A.F.A. Woodford, who, unable to decipher them himself, and being a friend of Westcott and also a Freemason and member of the SRIA, passed them on to Westcott.

A slight variation on this account is that Woodford found the manuscript by chance on a London bookstall and, failing to understand the strange writings, he sent the papers to Westcott, who had more success. After arduous study, we are led to believe, Westcott successfully deciphered the code, uncovering rituals and teachings of an ancient magical order in five progressive grades of study. Topics included Kabbalah, tarot, ceremonial magic, meditation, astrology and alchemy. The document supposedly also revealed the name of an order chief, Anna Sprengel, who was based in Hanover.

Westcott shared these discoveries with Mathers and Woodman. Mathers then helped Westcott adapt the documents into a working ceremonial. Correspondence was immediately entered into with the mysterious Anna Sprengel. She conferred the title of Exempt Adept on all three and authorised the foundation of a branch of the order in England. And so it was that on 1 March 1888 the Golden Dawn was formed, with its three chiefs in charge of its destiny. Over the next eight years, working with the five-grade system, over three hundred people were initiated into their order.

There was a great deal of interest in the occult and esotericism in Victorian England. Spiritualism, the Theosophical Society and Freemasonry were attracting thousands of students to their respective folds. The Golden Dawn, with its unique mixture of Egyptian paganism and Christian mysticism, must have offered an attractive range of topics to interest intellectuals. Members were drawn from all aspects of society and included artists, poets, writers, actors, doctors and church ministers. The more famous of these included Arnold Bennett, William Butler Yeats, artist Pamela Colman Smith and A.E. Waite (the creators of the famous Rider-Waite tarot deck), and the infamous occultist Aleister Crowley.

As time went by, it was apparently discovered that the five grades of their order were merely the preparatory studies of an outer order designed to develop members in readiness for their reception into the inner order. Correspondence with Anna Sprengel had by this time stopped. It was presumed that she was either dead or had been told to break contact. In 1893, Mathers claimed to have made contact with the Secret Chiefs in Paris. He said that they had shared new cipher documents with him that contained the secret teachings necessary to establish the second order of the Golden Dawn. Back in England, the members who had completed initiations in the five grades and completed the necessary study formed this 'inner order' and began work.

Eventually, a third order was established and this amounted to the full magical Golden Dawn system that has been handed down. The grades, based on the Kabbalistic tree of life, with its ten spheres, closely resembled the grade system of the SRIA, which has led many to suggest that the three founders had created the order by borrowing teachings from other groups, rather than discovering its tenets on an encrypted manuscript.

In 1896, the original driving force, Westcott, resigned, claiming that he had been let down by certain members of the group, MacGregor Mathers in particular. He worked as a coroner, and his magical practices had come to the attention of the authorities. He was forced to choose between his 'respectable' career and his passion for magic, which many regarded either as nonsense or sacrilege. In 1897, Florence Farr, a famous stage actress of her day, assumed control of the London temple. By 1899, serious power struggles had erupted within the order, ultimately leading to its collapse in 1903.

Many of the members were becoming disillusioned with Mathers in particular and wanted to deal directly with the Secret Chiefs. Aleister Crowley had joined the Golden Dawn, and by 1899 he had worked his way through the grades and studies of the first order. When he demanded admission into the second order in London, Florence Farr refused. Mathers then caused more anger amongst the membership by advancing Crowley into the second order at his temple in Paris.

Splinter groups quickly formed, and by 1903 the original Golden Dawn as it had been was no more. Parts of the system were published by Crowley in occult periodical *The Equinox*, much to the dismay of many. Later, between 1937 and 1940, Crowley's secretary, Israel Regardie, published the complete system in four volumes. This opening up of the secrets has preserved the workings of the Golden Dawn to this day, and many have added their own innovations to the seeds planted by Westcott, Mathers and Woodman.

SEE ALSO: Alchemy; Crowley, Aleister; Kabbalah; Rosicrucianism; Tarot

HERMETICISM

The word 'hermeticism' is taken from the god Hermes Trismegistus, who is said to have written the texts that form the basis of the belief system known as hermeticism. Hermes Trismegistus is a complex character, an amalgamation of the Egyptian god Thoth with the Greek divinity Hermes. They shared similar characteristics, and so sometime between the first and third centuries AD the two gods merged to become one entity. However, not everyone in the Greek world recognised this new creation and most still revered Hermes, so the two were distinct and separate deities, hence the use of the name Hermes Trismegistus, which means 'thrice-great Hermes', to differentiate this new god from the old Hermes.

The writings that are ascribed to the hand of Hermes Trismegistus are known as the Hermetica, thought to have been composed sometime between the first and third centuries AD, and these sacred texts form the backbone of hermeticism.

During the Middle Ages, the works of the Hermetica passed out of knowledge in Europe, and they were not discovered again until the fifteenth century, when Italian printers made the texts popular, reprinting in 1463 a volume that had been collected together by the Byzantines. This group of ancient texts is not the whole of the Hermetica, and many texts have been lost entirely, so today this body of Hermetic texts is termed the Corpus Hermeticum and comprises all the books that are known to have survived.

Sections of the Corpus Hermeticum were found amongst the hoard of ancient codices discovered at Nag Hammadi in Egypt in 1945, the collection of manuscripts also known as the Gnostic Gospels. While many of the Gnostic texts that form the Nag Hammadi Library deal with Judaeo-Christian themes, the Hermetica does not. While it speaks of the singularity of God, or at least of 'the All', it also describes many pagan practices such as the worship of physical objects. It also explains that there are many entities in the universe: gods, angels and humans, amongst many others. In the world of hermeticism, everything in creation is a part of the All, and furthermore, everything and everyone is connected within that unity. Even though the ideas that are found in the Corpus Hermeticum appear to have been formulated around the same time, and share the same birthplace, as Christianity, we can clearly see that the discipline of hermeticism took a unique path.

Most of the Hermetica takes the form of a narrative told by Hermes Trismegistus himself. It begins with him giving an account of a revelation that he experienced in the presence of what can only be described as the cosmic mind of the universe, perhaps the one true god, known as Poemandres, or 'Man-Shepherd'.

> It chanced once on a time my mind was meditating on the things that are, my thought was raised to a great height, the senses of my body being held back — just as men who are weighed down with sleep after a fill of food, or from fatigue of body.
>
> Methought a Being more than vast, in size beyond all bounds, called out my name and saith: What wouldst thou hear and see, and what hast thou in mind to learn and know?
>
> And I do say: Who art thou?
>
> He saith: I am Man-Shepherd (Poemandres), Mind of all-masterhood; I know what thou desirest and I'm with thee everywhere.
>
> I reply: I long to learn the things that are, and comprehend their nature, and know God. This is, I said, what I desire to hear.
>
> He answered back to me: Hold in thy mind all thou wouldst know, and I will teach thee.

Alchemists of the Renaissance are said to have been steeped in the hidden knowledge that they believed lay at the heart of the Hermetica.

A work that sits outside the Corpus Hermeticum, but which also purports to be by the hand of Hermes Trismegistus is the 'Emerald Tablet'. Over the centuries it has been claimed that it contains detailed alchemical knowledge. It is only a short work, but it was prized by alchemists and lies at the heart of hermeticism, containing as it does the now famous quotation: 'That which is above is as that which is below,' which today is often shortened to the more popular 'As above, so below.'

The line sums up the idea that what happens in the macrocosm also happens in the microcosm. An example of this is that in many plants the shapes formed by the leaves and roots can be seen mirrored in structures found at the cellular level. In other words, what happens on one level reflects what occurs on another. A more literal interpretation of the phrase is found in astrology, where what happens in the celestial realms, 'above', is seen as being intrinsically linked to events that befall individuals on the earth, 'below'. It is also interesting to note that this hermetic concept became firmly implanted in Christian worship, where we find it today in the Lord's Prayer, in the line 'On Earth as it is in Heaven.'

A translation of the Emerald Tablet text was found in Isaac Newton's notebooks:

> And as all things have been & arose from one by ye
>> mediation of one: so all things have their birth from
>> this one thing by adaptation.
> The Sun is its father, the moon its mother,
> The wind hath carried it in its belly, the earth its nurse.
> The father of all perfection in ye whole world is here.
> Its force or power is entire if it be converted into earth.
> Separate thou ye earth from ye fire, ye subtle from the
>> gross sweetly with great industry.
> It ascends from ye earth to ye heaven & again it descends
>> to ye earth and receives ye force of things superior &
>> inferior.
> By this means you shall have ye glory of ye whole world
>> & thereby all obscurity shall fly from you.

Newton's version of the text emphasises the use of alchemical language and philosophy, for example the instruction to separate distinct strands of matter from one another, and especially the 'subtle from the gross', an idea that is at the heart of alchemy.

While today most people believe that the Hermetica dates to somewhere between the first and third centuries AD, during the Renaissance it was thought that the texts dated back to Ancient Egypt, and some schools of thought still maintain that this is the case. The publication of the Corpus Hermeticum in the fifteenth century was an event that galvanised large sections of the population, and its potential was electrifying. It was seen as a possible catalyst for reintroducing magic into Christian Europe. At the time, church leaders were quoting from the Corpus Hermeticum, and hermeticism was viewed as an acceptable and very profound philosophy. Many believed that it would bring about a radical shift in the Christian West and it certainly led to an upsurge in the practice of alchemy and magic. However, the final outcome was very far from this ideal of a future based on hermeticism; the Protestant Reformation and the Catholic Counter-Reformation of the sixteenth century, rather than embracing magic, turned it into a heresy, and hermeticists were burned at the stake. Hermeticism did not die out, but its new shoots of growth were seriously trampled, and it was forced underground, though thankfully we still have the Corpus Hermiticum to consult today, and hopefully, as in the case of the Nag Hammadi Library find, we will discover more lost fragments from the fascinating world of hermetic thought.

SEE ALSO: Alchemy; Gnosticism

HYPNOTISM

For most people, their only contact with hypnotism will be either watching a hypnotic stage act or listening to one of the various self-help tapes that use hypnosis to aid weight loss, beat stress or help with stopping smoking. But these are just the tip of the iceberg and are not completely representative of hypnotism, which has a mixed history of scientific study and application, sometimes considered a matter worthy of serious consideration and sometimes ridiculed. Similarly, public interest in the practice has fluctuated between intense fascination and near indifference.

A British doctor, James Braid, first used the term 'hypnotism', in 1843, although the Marquis Chastenet de Puységur discovered the phenomenon in 1784. Puységur, a follower of Franz Anton Mesmer, had unintentionally put one of his patients into a deep trance when attempting to mesmerise him (a process involving the use of magnets to heal and restore the body's harmony). Unlike the subjects of mesmerism, however, who often suffered strong spasms, those who Puységur hypnotised fell into a trance-like state. Furthermore, Puységur noted that his subjects were able to respond to him telepathically, for even when their backs were turned they reacted to his actions. Despite the differences, Puységur still believed that his version was akin to mesmerism and that it worked by utilising the force of 'animal magnetism'. However, a certain amount of uncertainty surrounded mesmerism, which was accused of being linked in some way to witchcraft, with Mesmer denounced as a fraud. As a consequence, hypnotism was largely ignored and actively derided.

In 1842, even an English surgeon who routinely and successfully used hypnotism for pain relief when operating on patients, including during amputations, was lampooned and accused of making his patients *pretend* not to feel any pain. However, in 1843 James Braid published his study on the subject, concluding that hypnotism worked by suppressing the nervous system and other subsystems. Unlike those which had come before, his study was taken seriously, perhaps in part due to Braid's dissociation from mesmerism and the use for the first time of the term 'hypnotism'. However, it was not until the 1930s that the psychologist Clark Hull brought hypnotism once more into the limelight, undertaking in-depth experimentation.

What exactly is hypnotism? Hypnotism is often explained as an 'altered state of consciousness' – an accurate description but one that tells us little about how or why hypnosis works. This altered state can be achieved either by a lengthy use of relaxation techniques and an induction process or relatively quickly by simple suggestion; either way, visual and auditory methods are incorporated in order to induce such a state. In this condition, an individual becomes extremely focused, blocking out all external stimuli apart from the hypnotist's voice. People can also train themselves to be hypnotised at will by using a prompt, such as pulling on their ear to attain a state of hypnosis.

Other forms of hypnotism include walking hypnosis, where the action of doing something monotonous produces a trance-like state so that a person is no longer aware that they are doing the task – such as driving – but even so goes through the process, arriving, for example, at their destination without being aware of the journey. Waking hypnotism is when someone can change another's behaviour simply by suggestion and without inducing a trance, convincing someone, say, that a non-alcoholic drink is intoxicating so that they show symptoms of drunkenness. Mass hypnosis can also be induced, usually by a charismatic leader who is able to rouse their followers into an altered state; the effects that Hitler was able to produce on the crowds at the Nuremberg rallies are often held to be a prime example of this effect.

Experienced practitioners say that anyone can be hypnotised, even those with strong willpower, although those who are more suggestible are easier to induce. However, a person cannot be hypnotised against their will. The theory is that the subject becomes very receptive to suggestion because of the intensity of focus, which is amplified and enhanced by the continued suggestion of the hypnotist, with the subject accepting what the practitioner says. Psychologists Nicholas Spanos and John Chaves, in *Hypnosis: The Cognitive-Behavioral Perspective*, put forward the theory that social compliance and expectation play a large part in the process, with the subject thinking that they are hypnotised and so acting in a way that they believe a hypnotised person should – the way the hypnotist wants them to behave. They believe that the hypnotist achieves this by both suggesting and informing, in statements such as 'relax your eyes . . . your eyes are heavy and you are feeling sleepy'.

However, it has been found that subjects will not do anything that is against their moral or religious code, which indicates that while suggestibility is part of the process of hypnotism, coercion is not, as the hypnotised subjects are able to wake up if asked to do something that is not in their nature. This seems to be contradicted by the antics of stage hypnotists who are able to persuade people that they are animals or to perform silly acts, but it has to be borne in mind that people who volunteer to take part in this form of entertainment have chosen to do so willingly and know that they will be asked to do odd things.

Handled properly, hypnotism can be an amazing tool that provides the key to unlock the subconscious mind. In *Beyond the Occult*, Colin Wilson relates that in the 1880s a Professor Carpenter of Boston held a demonstration in which a graduate was hypnotised and told that Socrates was in the room and could be asked any question. This led to a two-hour discussion between the graduate and Socrates during which the philosopher's answers were conveyed to Professor Carpenter by the graduate – answers that, according to Thomson Jay Hudson, a watching newspaper editor and author, were 'so brilliant and plausible that some of the audience began to wonder whether there really *was* an invisible spirit in the room'.

The same thing happened when other philosophers were 'introduced' to the hypnotised graduate, who once again expounded a 'wonderful system of spiritual philosophy'. To help dispel the audience's belief that spirit entities were being channelled, Professor Carpenter told the graduate that the next philosopher was a pig, and even this creature spoke profoundly about reincarnation. Hudson later described the philosophy expounded by the hypnotised subject as one that 'formed one of the grandest and most coherent systems of spiritual philosophy ever conceived by the brain of men'. This begs the question of where such information comes from. The obvious answer is that it came from the graduate's own subconscious.

Hudson believed that we possess a subjective and an objective mind: the subjective mind is responsible for memories and intuition, and the objective mind governs the more practical concerns of everyday life. In his book *The Law of Psychic Phenomena*, published in 1893, Hudson concluded that the subjective mind is incredibly powerful, able to access deep-seated memories and call on enormous and exceptional reserves of energy and bodily control. Hudson believed that the only inhibiting factor to this energy was the objective mind, with hypnotism a way of bypassing this obstructive force. Such an idea is borne out by the Russian physician Dr Vladimir L. Raikov, who in the early 1960s noted in his article 'Artificial Reincarnation through Hypnosis' that a hypnotised individual can display an excellence in a subject (for example, painting) of which they have no knowledge.

Although the effects of hypnosis are tangible, the reason why or how it works is not so apparent. Opinion on its nature varies, and indeed it is difficult to understand how it works bearing in mind that people can have different experiences of it. Whilst some subjects go into a deep trance, cannot remember what has occurred and feel that they have entered some form of altered state, others remain highly aware of what is happening throughout their experience but feel content to follow the suggestions of the hypnotist.

It was hoped that a greater insight into hypnotism could be gained from the study of brain activity. Unfortunately, brain scans have been inconclusive, although they do show increased neural activity, and in those cases where auditory phenomena are experienced, scans illustrate that the brain reacts as if it is actually hearing something, which does not occur in subjects who are merely daydreaming.

In *Experimental Psychology*, written in 1957, Ivan Pavlov described hypnosis as a 'partial sleep' (as suggested by the etymology of the term, from the Greek *hypnos* for sleep), as once hypnosis is induced the subject falls into a relaxed, restful state with eyes closed. However, Pavlov points out that whilst the subject is in a hypnotic state the blood level and reflexes suggest a state of wakefulness, a conclusion upheld by physiochemical and EEG (electroencephalograph) studies. Therefore, whilst some changes in brainwave activity can be discerned, they do not help us to understand how hypnotism works or where our minds fit in to all this. In his book *More Lives Than One?*, Jeffrey Iverson quotes the words of Dr Dafydd Huws who notes: 'we can define [the mind] only by describing what it does or by discussing the mechanism of the brain – which is like discussing a scene from a film in terms of the projector.'

There are many diverse uses for hypnotism, including hypnotherapy, which is used to help the subject achieve an aim, such as stopping smoking, losing weight or easing stress and anxiety; as a means of controlling or easing pain in childbirth, for cancer sufferers and those with other chronic conditions; and to enhance sporting performance, especially in the area of confidence. Recovered memories acquired by hypnosis are sometimes used by police forces to help the witness remember specific details of a crime or crime scene, although this evidence is not always acceptable in court.

Regression in order to explore and cure a deep-seated problem or phobia is also a well-known use of hypnotism. However, some repressed memories, such as of sexual abuse in childhood, must be approached with caution and concern, as such accounts can actually be false memories caused by the hypnotist asking leading questions of a highly suggestible subject. Related to regression is hypnosis to recall past-life experiences. One of the best-known examples of this is the case of Virginia Tighe, a Colorado housewife regressed by Morey Bernstein in the 1950s to a nineteenth-century Irish girl called Bridey Murphy. Under hypnosis, she gave a detailed account of her life and death, which Bernstein published in 1956 in his book *The Search for Bridey Murphy*. However, the authenticity of Bridey Murphy has subsequently been discredited, as it transpires that as a child Virginia Tighe was told tales of nineteenth-century Ireland by an old lady of the same name.

The veracity of past-life regression is very hard to ascertain, as the historical detail may be known consciously or subconsciously, perhaps from a novel, history book or film which is no longer consciously remembered. Because of the vast array of information we have been bombarded with since birth, and bearing in mind the depth of the subconscious that can be unlocked by hypnotism, some believe that regressions are nothing more than cryptomnesia – stories based on long-forgotten knowledge. Dr Ian Stevenson, a reincarnation researcher and one-time director of the Division of Parapsychology of the Department of Psychiatry at the University of Virginia, stated in his 1974 work *Twenty Cases Suggestive of Reincarnation* that:

The subconscious parts of the mind are released from ordinary inhibitions, and they may then present in dramatic form a new 'personality'. If the person has been instructed by the hypnotist – explicitly or implicitly – to 'go back to another place and time' or given some similar guidance, the new 'personality' may be extremely plausible both to the person and to others watching him or her.

In *More Lives Than One?*, Jeffrey Iverson related the studies undertaken in the 1970s by hypnotherapist Arnall Bloxham, who hypnotised hundreds of people and taped their experiences. The most famous of Bloxham's subjects is Jane Evans, whose accounts have been described as 'impressively accurate'. In particular, she recounts her life as a Jewish woman in twelfth-century York during the time of a massacre of the Jews. Evans, as the Jewish woman Rebecca, described fleeing York Castle, where they had initially sought refuge, with her husband and two children to the crypt of a small church close by. At first, this was thought to indicate the inaccuracy of her account, as the only medieval church in York with a crypt is York Minster – obviously not a small church. However, renovation of the church thought to be the one described – St Mary's, Castlegate – unearthed an unknown crypt. Iverson pointed out that Evans' account is not a 'straightforward rewording of history-book versions of the massacre' and concludes that if she was making it up, it is strange that she did not relate the best-known events of the massacre. In addition, Iverson stated that Evans displayed an impressive knowledge of the political entities of the time as well as details of York in the medieval period, a town she had never visited.

However, subsequent investigations by Melvin Harris, the results of which were published in 1986 in his book *Sorry, You've Been Duped!*, cast doubt on the credibility of Jane Evans' past lives, as not only was Harris able to prove that some of the information given was incorrect, he also noted that some past-life 'memories' had sprung from historical novels rather than reality. Therefore, although Evans may have been recalling long-forgotten memories, they were not 'real' memories. From their studies of supposed past-life regression, Nicholas Spanos, Cheryl Burgess and Melissa Burgess concluded in their 1994 article 'Past-life identities, UFO abductions, and Satanic ritual abuse: The social construction of memories' that those who recall past lives are not deliberately deceiving the hypnotist but are extremely imaginative individuals retrieving from the subconscious hidden memories of, for example, historical novels that the conscious mind has forgotten.

Taking the idea of recalling lives through hypnosis one stage further, Dr Chet B. Snow and Dr Helen Wambach even suggested in their 1993 book *Mass Dreams of the Future* that future lives can be accessed by hypnotic progression. Accounts of supposed alien abductions have also been extracted by hypnosis, but whether these tales are true or fall under the umbrella of cryptomnesia is hard to discern.

Despite the number of studies undertaken, the nature of hypnosis is still not fully understood. While it is know that hypnotism allows subjects to be more open to suggestion and that it can unlock hidden levels of the subconscious, how this happens or why is difficult to identify. Even if we do not know why it works, we cannot deny its versatility and ability to recover information that might otherwise not be retrievable. As Iverson notes, hypnotism is 'clearly a doorway to the secret world of a strange and powerful altered state of consciousness'.

I CHING

The I Ching is one of China's oldest texts. In its current form, it is at least 3,000 years old, and it is thought to have existed long before this in alternative forms. It is a method of divination that has survived for so long simply because it is a very effective and useful oracle and one that has been revered and trusted throughout the ages. Today, the I Ching is known worldwide, and its use is probably more widespread than at any other time in its long history.

It is also known as 'the Book of Changes', because of the nature of the wisdom contained within it. Essentially, the I Ching works on the assumption that the universe and all that happens within it is the result of the interaction between yin and yang: the interplay between masculine and feminine, positive and negative, active and passive.

An important consideration impressed upon people consulting the I Ching is that the texts were not composed with worldly goods or material gain in mind, and the book was developed specifically with the individual's spiritual needs in mind. Furthermore, it is said that the I Ching does not tell the future, rather it assists the person seeking its help to decide how best to act in the present so that the path to the future is as smooth and auspicious as possible.

While the I Ching that we possess today was developed by King Wen during the twelfth century BC, the trigrams that are at the heart of the Book of Changes are said to have been invented by a legendary figure known as Fu Hsi, a sage who united the people of China and became the first emperor. Like some of the world's other mythical heroes, such as Egypt's Osiris and South America's Quetzalcoatl, Fu Hsi is cast as a civiliser and educator, teaching mankind how to cook, hunt and domesticate animals. Like Osiris, Fu Hsi married his sister, Nuwa, and is also credited with introducing laws to the Chinese people. Who exactly this mythical figure really was, we will never know, but he stands at the birth of Chinese culture and is said to have handed the Chinese the beginnings of what would become the I Ching.

Legend has it that Fu Hsi discovered the eight trigrams, the foundations of the whole of the I Ching, upon the shells of turtles and other animals. The trigrams are made up of three horizontal lines, either solid or broken, and the set of eight contains all of the possible permutations of these two types of line. To each of the trigrams were attributed very specific yet multiple meanings; for example, a trigram might represent mountains, creative energy and inflexibility. According to the Ta Chuan, an ancient appendix to the I Ching, written sometime between the fifth and third centuries BC, this is how Fu Hsi developed the system of the trigrams. The translation is by Stephen Karcher in *Ta Chuan: The Great Treatise*:

> In antiquity Fu Hsi ruled the world we live in.
> He looked up and saw the symbols hanging down from
>   Heaven.
> He looked down and saw the patterns on the Earth.
> He saw markings on birds and animals
> and the places where they lived on the Earth.
> He drew on what was near within his body.
> He drew on what was far.
> He spontaneously brought forth the Eight Diagrams
> to connect with the bright spirits
> and to categorize the natures of the myriad things.
> He was the first to use Change to help the people.

It was a historical figure, King Wen, the founder of the Zhou Dynasty, who went on to expand the legendary trigrams of Fu Hsi into the I Ching as we know it. He is said to have developed the I Ching while in prison, where he could devote all his time to the mystery of the trigrams and their meaning. He took the trigrams and built from them the hexagrams we see in the I Ching today. It was also King Wen who left us his 'Judgements' on the meaning of the hexagrams, and these survive in the Book of Changes to this day and form a vital component when making a reading.

At the heart of the I Ching today are the sixty-four hexagrams devised by King Wen – figures comprised of two trigrams placed one on top of the other, making six lines in total. The sixty-four hexagrams comprise all of the possible combinations that can be derived from the arrangement of the two types of line, solid and broken. Each of these hexagrams has its own specific name and meaning. Each of the trigrams also has its own name and meaning; however, when combined, they form the more elaborate hexagram and a new meaning develops, based on the relationship of the composite trigrams.

The sixth hexagram of the I Ching, the Sung Hexagram

In China, the traditional method for consulting the I Ching is to use dried yarrow stalks. Yarrow is a herb used for medicinal purposes in China and many other countries, and the I Ching is sometimes known as 'the Yarrow Stalk Oracle'. Yarrow itself has acquired the name 'herb of divination' because of its association with the I Ching. It is interesting to note that studies into the effects of yarrow tea have shown it to be a mild psychotropic, and drinking yarrow tea is said to produce a change in how colours are perceived as well as a slight shift in perception. It is not known if originally yarrow tea was drunk at the same time as the dried stalks were used to begin the divination process, but it is interesting to speculate whether this was once the case, and it could explain why yarrow in particular is used.

Today, especially in the West, a far quicker method of consulting the I Ching is used: three coins are tossed to ascertain how the Book of Changes is to be read. However, the original and much more time-consuming yarrow-stalk method still carries with it a sense of mystery, and it is said that the length of time it takes to complete allows the person seeking divination to meditate on the question they would like answered.

When using the yarrow-stalk method, fifty such dried stalks are chosen. One is laid aside and the resulting forty-nine are used to decide which hexagram is chosen for the purpose of divination. After a fairly complex procedure, in which the stalks are divided and held in the left hand again and again, the sticks are finally sorted into smaller bundles. The numbers of these are used to decide which line will make up the first line of the hexagram. It can be either a solid or a broken line, yang or yin, and furthermore it can also be 'old' or 'young', resulting in a total of four different types of line. The first line is the bottom line – the foundation of the hexagram – and subsequent lines are added above it. The process of dividing the yarrow stalks is repeated until a total of six lines have been decided upon.

The end result is that one of sixty-four hexagrams is arrived at, and this symbol acts as the device by which the divination is offered. Each hexagram imparts its own message of wisdom and enlightenment. The advice is couched in terms that can be interpreted by the reader. Sometimes this wisdom is obvious, other times it is hidden beneath veils of meaning. Depending on how the lines fell and whether the hexagram contained any old lines, the so-called 'moving' lines, there may be further, more in-depth information imparted, and often it is these final, more precise comments that answer the specific questions of the person seeking divination.

Each of the sixty-four hexagrams has its own name as well as a very precise meaning: for example, the first hexagram (which contains six solid, or yang, lines) is the Ch'ien Hexagram and is called the Symbol of Creativity. These titles are not merely arbitrary descriptions; they are very precise and bear a direct relationship to the hexagrams themselves, serving to explain and sum up the meaning inherent in the lines that make up the hexagram.

As well as the names of the hexagrams, the I Ching also gives a more detailed description of the meaning of each hexagram. Here is an extract from the description of the Ch'ien Hexagram to serve as an example:

> Confucius called Ch'ien the greatest strength in the universe.
> Great strength engenders great and continuous motion.
> The creative principle is thus viewed as the most dynamic
> power in the universe, creating and transforming all things.
> It influences and governs the vast and distant masses of
> the nebulae no less precisely than it does the microcosmic

laws of the atom. Most mysteriously, it works within man as his creative energy, making him a potential sage capable of serving as an effective agent of the Creator and a moral leader of his fellow men.

The explanation generally serves as an introduction to the meaning of the hexagram and sums up the symbolism of the lines and how they interact with one another. In the case of the Ch'ien Hexagram, we have six solid lines, or six yang lines, and this, according to the commentaries, symbolises incredible strength as well as endless motion when put together. Because the trigram that contains three solid yang lines is known as the Ch'ien Trigram, what we actually have in the Ch'ien Hexagram is two Ch'ien Trigrams one above the other, and this symbolises the strength and meaning of this particular figure. After the general explanation of the hexagram in question, the I Ching then contains a Judgement, said to have been written by King Wen himself. These can be several paragraphs or just a few words long. All offer a greater understanding of the meaning of the hexagram.

After the Judgements of King Wen, we also find a more detailed explanation of these comments, thought to have been written by Confucius, the famous Chinese philosopher, and based on the writings of the Duke of Zhou, the grandson of King Wen. These comments have been collated from the 'Shih I', the 'Ten Wings' or 'Ten Appendices', the first five books of which are now printed with the I Ching itself. We do not know for sure whether Confucius wrote the Ten Wings, but over the centuries this belief has grown up amongst scholars.

These comments of Confucius are read if the person consulting the I Ching has any of the moving lines in their hexagram. For example, returning to the first hexagram, Ch'ien, if the person seeking guidance from the I Ching has an old yang line in line five, then they should read the extra explanation which reads as follows:

> Line 5 suggests: 'The dragon is flying in the sky. It is advantageous to see the great man.' What does this signify? The Master said: 'Notes of the same key echo one another. Creatures of the same nature seek one another. Water flows towards what is wet. Fires turn towards what is dry. Clouds accompany the dragon. Winds accompany the tiger. When a sage appears, all creatures look up to him. What is rooted in

heaven draws near to what is above. What is rooted in earth draws near to what is below. Thus, each thing goes with its kind.'

These added commentaries help unravel some of the deeper layers of the I Ching and reveal the meaning of the hexagrams and the symbolism behind them to the everyday person, not just to those steeped in the philosophies of the Book of Changes. In this way, it is possible for anyone to consult the I Ching and receive wisdom which will help them make some sense of their current predicament and aid them in answering the question they have asked for assistance with.

When we consult the I Ching, we see how apt the name Book of Changes is. Much of the wisdom imparted throughout the I Ching reveals that change is at the heart of the world and that how we deal with change in our own lives is the key to navigating events and circumstances in our day-to-day lives. The I Ching tells us that change is not something to be resisted or to rail against; rather, change is an unstoppable force, and whether we choose to embrace it or fight it, the truth is that the only real constant in life is that nothing ever stays the same for long, good or bad. Whether it is truly oracular in nature or simply a guide to avoiding the perils of life, the I Ching contains much wisdom on how best to deal with change, and that is probably the key to its longevity – because we can all benefit from such guidance at some point in our lives.

SEE ALSO: Divination

KABBALAH

Kabbalah is a complex Jewish spiritual tradition that claims to provide a way of achieving knowledge of the divine and the secrets of Creation and the universe through studying to discover the hidden meanings of Jewish texts and teachings. The term 'Kabbalah' is Hebrew for 'to receive', with convention stating that the divine sacred tradition, part of which was written down and part transmitted orally, was 'received' by Moses on Mount Sinai.

It is not certain when the oral tradition was first written down, but the earliest collection of works, known as the Book of Creation, is purported to date to sometime between the second and sixth centuries AD. However, what is known is that in the twelfth and thirteenth centuries groups of Jewish esoterics from Spain, France and Italy thought of themselves as the possessors of secret knowledge and tradition and of the secrets of language. They stated that the secrets related to the workings of the divine realm and were given by God to Moses and then passed down orally, underlining the idea that the medieval esoteric Kabbalah was not new but had an ancient and divine tradition. However, historians take a different view of the origins of the Kabbalah, considering it to be a new phenomenon that came about in the twelfth century, independently of any tradition, growing up from ideas developed by a number of individuals and schools.

It is thought that the Zohar ('the Book of Splendour'), Kabbalah's most famous and pivotal book, was written by Moses de Leon and first appeared in 1305. He claimed that he had copied it from an ancient manuscript by the second-century rabbi Simeon bar Yohai. On his death, however, his destitute wife was offered large sums to sell the ancient work, but she had to reject all offers saying that it did not exist, as the Zohar had been all her husband's effort.

The Zohar is a collection of treatises, the main part being a commentary on Judaic sacred texts and law, as well as discussions of the commandments (not just the Ten Commandments but the *mitzvot*, the 613 commandments that detail what a Jew can and cannot do) and revelations, all of which cover every possible theme. Joseph Dan, author of *Kabbalah: A Very Short Introduction*, considers the Zohar to be 'among the most daring and radical works of religious literature and mysticism' because of its 'radical descriptions of the divine powers, the unhesitating use of detailed erotic language, and the visionary character of many sections'.

There are many other texts and treatises that make up the teachings of Kabbalah. These include discourses on the structures of heaven and hell, how and why Creation came about, magical formulae and procedures (found in *The Sword of Moses* and *The Book of Secrets*), the names of angels, the realm of God, the emergence of the *sefirot*, or spheres, from the divine realm, the divine system that fashioned and governs the world, ways to ascend to the divine realm and, as Joseph Dan puts it, to 'face God in His glory', as well as how these ideas are applied to Jewish tradition, ritual and the commandments.

According to Kabbalah, Creation occurred when 'God wished to see God' and made a hole in the *ein sof*, the perfect, infinite and supreme being, which André Nataf describes in *The Wordsworth Dictionary of the Occult* as 'the Absolute All'. It was through this that existence appeared. Out of the hole in the ein sof, a ray of light shone from ten different levels, or sefirot, the ten attributes that make up the divine realm, also described as the ten faces of God or the tools of God. Joseph Dan makes the point that there is no one definitive description of Kabbalah, as it has been used in the past in many ways for many purposes. As such, medieval Kabbalah is slightly different to Kabbalah of other eras, and this is true with respect to the divine realm, which is depicted and explained in a number of ways. For example, there is the anthropological view: the sefirot arranged to form a human body, with the tenth being the female divine power.

Another, better-known depiction is of the divine realm as the Tree of Life. In this, the sefirot represent the ten states of being:

the fount of Creation, wisdom, intelligence, grace, power, beauty, permanence, reverberation, foundation and royalty or the earth. These ten have twenty-two interconnecting paths with each sefirot from the highest to the lowest interrelating with the others, whilst still maintaining its uniqueness. Hence the lowest realm, earth, is essential for the attainment of progress, with the spirit having to descend into the material body in order to achieve this. The Tree of Life also encompasses four worlds: the material, formation, creative and the abode of the uncreated divinity; it is divided into three pillars – the right, left and middle – with the ideal being to tread the Middle Way, which leads to the unity of the left and right paths and hence eternal balance. The sefirot themselves are governed by three hidden splendours of will, mercy and severity.

Another depiction of the divine realm is one that corresponds to the stages of divine emanation. The first emanation is ein sof; the second is *keter*, the shining point that was created; third is *binah*, the fountain from which divine existence pours forth; fourth is *hesed*, the right-hand path of love and mercy; fifth is *din*, the left-hand path of divine law and justice; sixth is *tiferet*, which unites the left and right; seventh and eighth are *nezad* and *hod*, the lowest forms of *hesed* and *din*; ninth is *yesod*, the means by which divine power is released into the lower realms; and tenth is *shekhinah*, the divine feminine power that brings revelation and, according to Joseph Dan, 'transfers the divine flow to creation'.

These systems are often interrelated and superimposed on each other, and in all these cases the sefirot are thought by Kabbalists to represent the secret names of God, as well as incorporating all the traditional Judaic terms and biblical characters: for example, King David is associated with shekhinah.

Shekhinah is a very important concept that translates as 'divine residence' in Hebrew and is one of the terms used for God without naming Him. In Kabbalah, it is the feminine divine power that prophets saw in their visions, and it is where the good and the just ascend to on death. It is the tenth and lowest emanation, and so closest to humans and our world. As such, shekhinah understands and appreciates our earthly trials and tribulations, but due to her closeness to the material world is also susceptible to evil forces that seek to tempt her away from her husband – the male divine. When this happens, great discord and disharmony is felt in the divine realm, and to alleviate this many Kabbalist rituals are concerned with the reuniting of shekhinah with her husband to ensure the return of perfect harmony.

It is stated in the Zohar that all divine commandments involve an integral and essential interaction between man and God, so that the commandments are the way in which man can directly influence events in the divine world, and so, as Dan states, can 'ultimately shape his own fate'. This interaction, known as the divine flow, brings spiritual power from the highest realms of ein sof down to the lowest level, and it is this divine flow that sustains everything. However, divine flow is not always equally distributed, as sometimes more is dispersed to one side or another, or else the flow is low, for example, in which case evil will prevail. The quality of the divine flow has a corresponding effect on our material world, and conversely, what we do on earth has a direct influence and consequences in the divine realm: good acts, observance of the commandments and rituals, and prayers spoken with real passion increase the divine flow, whilst the reverse decreases it. This enables humankind to play a proactive part in the divine realm and the processes within it; Joseph Dan states that the commandments are 'conceived as instruments that wield enormous spiritual power'. As is written in the Zohar, 'The soul of the just man transforms the dry place; love and passion are awakened above, and all is Unity.'

Other aspects of Kabbalism include the notion of the special nature of language. Kabbalists go one step beyond the concept of the universe being created by divine speech to the view that the laws of creation are the laws of language. Kabbalah finds hidden meaning in numbers and words, with the sacred texts revealing 'a fabric of sacred names which shines through countless combinations' (Isaiah Tishby, quoted in *The Wordsworth Dictionary of the Occult*). The Zohar reveals that it is therefore necessary to discover what hides beneath the words of a sacred text. It uses the analogy of 'ignorant people [who] consider only the clothes that are the story; they see nothing more than that and do not realise what the clothes conceal' and goes on to elaborate that those who know a bit more see the body beneath the clothes, while the wise see the soul.

Kabbalah maintains that numbers as well as words have hidden, arcane meanings, asserting that through numbers it is possible to find the 'essence' of a word. The Kabbalistic relationship between numbers, words and meaning is very intricate and complex, but on a basic level each letter in Hebrew represents a number and therefore each word has a numerical value by which the hidden meaning of the word can be discovered. Words that have similar numerical value are considered to be connected to each other. Thus, by substituting a word of the same numerical value for another, alternative meanings of Hebrew religious texts can be arrived at. This type of numerology is called gematria, and it is very complex: there are around 70 different ways of employing it. In addition to this, the idea of notarikon is also used in Kabbalah, whereby the first, middle and last letters of a word are used to form another, revealing a new meaning.

In Kabbalah, the Hebrew language is intimately connected with creation, for which God is essential. The concept of the creative word has been taken one step further by Kabbalists: folklore has it that by the use of the name of God and the Hebrew alphabet and words, an adept can create life in the form of a golem, a man-made almost-human being, devoid of a soul, speech, emotion and free thought, yet possessing immense strength. The making of a golem is understandably complicated and time-consuming; it is said to take nearly two days to complete the meditation and recitation of the letter combinations and the names of God required to complete the task of creating a more complex golem. However, a simpler version of the ritual, as espoused by the sixteenth-century Rabbi Leow, requires virgin soil and pure water to be mixed together to form a human shape. Over this at least three ritually pure participants must recite the necessary words and names that will slowly produce a change in the soil, which will gradually take on a more human appearance. When the golem is fully formed, the creature is animated either by writing the word 'Adam' or 'emet' (truth) on its forehead or forearm, writing the name of God on a piece of parchment and placing it in the golem's mouth or writing the name of God on an amulet for the golem to wear.

A golem may be created as a servant, but traditionally the primary purpose of making a golem was for the protection of Jews. It is for this reason that Rabbi Leow supposedly made a golem named Yosele during the time of a pogrom against the Jews in Prague. When Yosele was deactivated, the clay figure was hidden in the attic of the Old New Synagogue in the city, although during the Second World War it was reported that the golem protected the synagogue from German troops, who were going to destroy the building but fled in panic when they heard its footsteps and saw the shadow of a giant hand.

A golem, being created by a human, can never come near the

perfection of God's creations, and is generally considered little more than an automaton. It is, however, fearless and continues to grow in height and strength. When the golem becomes too difficult to control due to its size and strength, or when the reason for its creation no longer exists, it can be deactivated either by removing the amulet or the parchment from its mouth, or the word on its forehead or forearm can be altered from 'Adam' to '*dam*', meaning 'blood', or '*emet*' to '*met*', meaning 'death'.

Interest in Kabbalah has increased enormously since the 1970s, due mainly to its popularity among new-age groups, which may be in part the result of its associations with mythology, alchemy and magic. Within this time, the Kabbalah Centre established by Philip S. Berg has become popular worldwide among men and women of all groups, races and religions. Its profile has increased since celebrities, the most famous being the singer Madonna, have openly endorsed Kabbalah.

Thanks to the Kabbalah Centre and its well-known adherents, the teachings of Kabbalah have attained a level of recognition and prominence unheard of at any other time in its history. However, this modern version of Kabbalah is considered by many to be a distorted form of the classical, pure Kabbalah. According to the Zohar, Kabbalah is a 'quest for the secrets of the faith' and, as Will Bradbury points out in *Into the Unknown*, classical Kabbalah stresses the need to keep its teachings and knowledge secret because what is hidden can only be attained through 'mystical approaches and ritualistic study'. This is one of the main concerns of the Kabbalah Centre's detractors. Traditionally, only a few learned Jewish scholars had access to the complex system of Kabbalah as this elite had a thorough grounding in and understanding of the Torah, the Talmud and Jewish ritual and tradition, developed over a long period of study. However, the Kabbalah Centre has opened its doors to everyone, with no requirement that students be Jewish or have any knowledge of Judaism. The view of many is that this new form is effectively a 'dumbing down' of Kabbalah for the masses. The statements made by the Kabbalah Centre have done little to dispel this idea, claiming as it does to be able to cure illnesses such as cancer by the use of the Zohar and the centre's special Kabbalah water. It also states that the only way to get the full benefit of the Zohar is to read it in Aramaic and that even if the reader cannot decipher the words, simply running a finger over the text and scanning the words will allow them magically to absorb their meaning. Meditation on a Hebrew letter is supposed to promote

The zodiac from the Egyptian temple of Denderah, which is now
held at the Louvre in Paris. (Photographs © Mark Oxbrow)

Above: Satanic altar with pentagram of Baphomet, black candles, chalice, monkey skull and peacock feathers. (Photograph © Jenny Greenteeth)
Below: Wiccan altar with pentagram, Brigid cross, beeswax and white candles, chalice, water, salt, incense, bread, wine, fruit and flowers. (Photograph © Jenny Greenteeth

Above: Dowsing inside a crop circle. (Photograph © Andy Gough)
Below: Every year, thousands of people celebrate the ancient Druid festival of Beltane high above the city of Edinburgh on Calton Hill. (Photograph © Mark Foster)

Modern-day Druids at Stonehenge. (Photograph © Andy Gough)

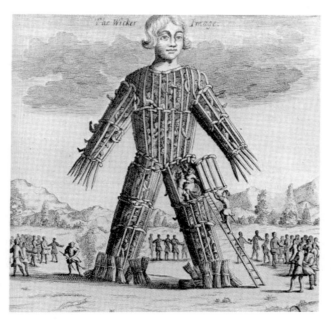

Julius Caesar wrote of the Druids in his *Commentaries on the Gallic War*: 'Others have figures of vast size, the limbs of which formed of osiers they fill with living men, which being set on fire, the men perish enveloped in the flames.'(Image courtesy of Jenny Greenteeth)

The Hanged Man card from the Tarot deck. The symbolism is often linked with that of Christ and of the Norse Odin, who is said to have hung from a tree for nine days and gained enlightenment. (© Alexander Briel Perez)

An engraving of the magician John Dee, together with a
magical glyph of his devising, the Monas Heiroglyphica.

The church in Mortlake, London, beneath which John Dee is buried. There is a stone in the graveyard (bottom right) that is claimed to have come from Dee's house, which has since been demolished. (Photographs © Andy Gough)

A statue from the church at Rennes-le-Château, France, thought to represent Asmodeus, one of the demons listed in grimoires which instruct on the practice of goetia. (Photograph © Andy Gough)

health, wealth and happiness. Unlike classical Kabbalah, modern Kabbalism has a strong belief in astrology and in the protective effect of the iconic red string, which is worn on the left wrist and said to protect the wearer against the evil eye.

SEE ALSO: Astrology; Divination; Evil Eye; Numerology

LÉVI, ELIPHAS

Arguably the most famous of all modern magicians and certainly one of the most infuential, Eliphas Lévi was born in Paris on 8 February 1810. The son of a shoemaker, he was christened Alphonse Louis Constant but changed his name to the Judaised form Eliphas Lévi Zahed in 1845. Referred to by some as 'the Last Magi', he had a fascinating and controversial life driven by many passions. The one that outshone all the others and for which he is famous was his lifelong fascination with esoteric beliefs and the occult.

As a young man, in 1832, he was sent to the seminary of St Nicholas du Chardonnet, before moving on to the higher seminary of St Sulpice at Issy. It was here that his interest in magic was first awakened, by the Abbot of St Sulpice. This was not the only thing that was awakened! After becoming a deacon, he fell for a girl named Adèle Allenbach, who was in his class for catechism. According to André Nataf, in his *Dictionary of the Occult*, Constant saw her as 'the embodiment of the Virgin' and said that: 'God had rewarded his sincere zeal by sending him what the uncharitable and sanctimonious called "temptation" but he himself called "initiation to life".' Although the relationship did not develop, it was to change his life.

He resigned from the seminary in 1836, before his ordination, which sadly resulted in his widowed mother committing suicide. During the depression he suffered following this event, he met Flora Tristan, a leading figure in the French feminist movement (and later the grandmother of the painter Paul Gauguin). Their relationship was a stormy one and didn't last long, but it was through Flora that he was first introduced to the literary circle of Paris.

In 1839, he returned to his religious vocation and entered the Abbey of Solesmes, where he remained for only a year before arguing with his superiors and leaving the priesthood, this time for good. During this short time at Solesmes, he studied the writings of the ancient Christian Fathers, the Gnostics and numerous Christian mystics such as Madame de Guyon (1648–1717), who was viewed by the church as a heretic and imprisoned for her radical beliefs.

By 1840, Constant was back in Paris and following a writing career. Not all his works were on magic, but most of them were controversial in one way or another. In 1841, he found himself imprisoned for eight months for writing a publication called *La Bible de la Liberté*, which was seen as a subversive work. Incarcerated in Sainte-Pélagie prison in Paris (where the Marquis de Sade was imprisoned after the Revolution), he discovered and studied the works of the eighteenth-century Christian mystic, Emanuel Swedenborg, which were in the library there.

In 1846, Lévi fell in love with and married the 18-year-old Noémie Cadiot. Two years later, however, he was back in prison during the 1848 revolution for publishing a pamphlet entitled *La Voix de la Famine*, once again deemed subversive. The marriage produced one child, a girl who died in infancy, and seven years after they married, Noémie decided to leave him. In 1854, Lévi left Paris and moved to London for the next few years. Whilst there, he met a number of people who had an active interest in magic and the occult. The most notable of these was the English writer and Rosicrucian Sir Edward Bulwer-Lytton, who had undertaken extensive study of many magical works, including the writings of the alchemist Heinrich Cornelius Agrippa. It was this friendship that inspired Lévi to write and publish his magical studies.

During this time in London, Lévi performed what was to be his most famous magical act – the raising of the dead! He claimed that he successfully summoned up the spirit of Apollonius of Tyana after weeks of preparation that included meditation and a strict vegetarian diet. Apollonius, who lived in the first century AD, is regarded as having been one of the greatest magicians of all time and was once the guardian of the Emerald Tablet of Hermes Trismegistus. Lévi's account of the encounter was published in his 1856 book *Dogme et Rituel de la Haute Magie (The Dogma and Ritual of High Magic).* The ceremony was to have been performed by Lévi and a mysterious female who claimed to be an adept, but at the last moment she apparently became faint-hearted, and he was left to evoke the spirit himself.

Of the event, he wrote:

> All was ready by the 24th of July; our purpose was to evoke the phantom of the Divine Apollonius and interrogate him as to two secrets . . . I was clothed in a white robe . . . I began at first in a low voice; then louder by degrees, the invocations of the Ritual . . . a whitish form there developed itself . . . I called three times upon Apollonius, at the same time closing my eyes; and, when I re-opened them, a man was before me . . . I twice repeated, in the course of a few days, the same experiment. The result of these two other evocations was to reveal to me two Cabalistic secrets, which might, if they were known by everyone, change in a short time the foundations and laws of the whole of society.

The Dogma and Ritual of High Magic is perhaps the work that is most often credited with having influenced the magical revival in the late nineteenth and early twentieth centuries. This work was followed in 1860 with a *History of Magic*, again an extremely influential work. Both of these books were translated into English by the Freemason and mystic A.E. Waite and remain in print over 100 years after Eliphas Lévi's death.

Not so widely known is the fact that Lévi was also a Freemason. He was initiated into Lodge Rose du Parfait Silence under the Grand Orient of France but does not appear to have pursued this interest. No evidence that he was particularly active as a Mason exists, and he is not mentioned in the records of the fraternity after 21 August 1861.

The magical works of Waite, along with those of a number of other members of the Hermetic Order of the Golden Dawn – most notably Aleister Crowley, the 'Great Beast' – were greatly influenced by the French magician. Crowley was born in the same year that Eliphas Lévi died, and he would declare that he was in fact the reincarnation of the magician. Other esotericists to have been influenced by Lévi include Albert Pike, the writer of *Morals and Dogma of the Ancient and Accepted Rite of Freemasonry*, and Madame Blavatsky, founder of the Theosophical Society and writer of *The Secret Doctrine*.

Lévi died in 1875 at the age of 65; he is said to have returned once again to the Roman Catholic faith and received the last rites before passing on to the next life.

SEE ALSO: Alchemy; Crowley, Aleister; Gnosticism; Hermeticism; Magic; Rosicrucianism

MAGIC

The use of magic is both ancient and universal, taking the form of rituals and spells to cure illness, for love, protection, fertility, revelation, curses, vengeance, attraction, domination and sorcery – in fact all concerns that resonate with human beings.

The antiquity of magic is hard to pinpoint, but some researchers believe that the Palaeolithic cave paintings of animals found in Europe and dating from around 25,000 years ago are the earliest attempts by humans to influence their environment by utilising magical forces, creating the drawings in order to be successful in hunting the animals depicted. Sir James Frazer, who made a study of beliefs and superstitions worldwide and presented the results in his seminal 1922 work *The Golden Bough*, asserted that magic is far older than religion, although his view was based not on historical research but on his belief that religion evolved from the 'inherent falsehood and barrenness' of magic, which predated the 'purer and truer principle' of religion.

Frazer declared that magic belonged to the uneducated masses and described it as 'the bastard sister of science'. Despite his view of the 'fallacy' of magic, his studies show that it was universally believed in and practised, as it still is in many parts of the world. Regardless of differences in society, culture and environment, and whilst religious beliefs vary considerably, 'the system of sympathetic magic remains everywhere and at all times substantially alike in its principles and practice'.

MAGIC

It is unfortunate that the term 'magic' is often used negatively to describe a practice seen as primitive, false and less meaningful than religion. The term derives from the Greek *mageia*, which stemmed from the Persian Zoroastrian astrological priests of the fifth century AD, known as 'magi' and famed for their understanding of magic and the occult. Because of the Ancient Greek fear of all things foreign, they saw the 'exotic' magical arts of the Zoroastrians as illegal and fraudulent, a view that has coloured our modern conception of magic, hence the Western prejudice against it as worthless mumbo-jumbo. The study of magic in the ancient world has therefore suffered in the past from the tendency to reflect the 'sorcery' aspect rather than the positive areas of everyday magic. Scholars have generally done little to hide their disdain for magic; in *Egyptian Magic* (1899), the Egyptologist E.A. Wallis Budge stated that magic consisted of 'beliefs and superstitions of the most degraded character'. However, in the past 40 years scholars have moved away from this negative view and towards a realisation of magic's validity and relevance to the people who believed in its power and actively used and manipulated its properties.

In his book *Arcana Mundi*, the historian Georg Luck states that magic was 'very much a part of life in the ancient world', Greece and Rome included, and was a 'permanent and universal' feature. Although banned or otherwise controlled by many Greek city states, magic was not ubiquitously legislated against in Greece. However, in Rome, as in Greece, the marginalisation of magic was mainly due to xenophobia and fear that foreign magic would be misused, leading to a decree in AD 199 of Q. Aemilius Saturninus, the Prefect of Egypt, prohibiting oracles, which were seen, according to Egyptologist Robert Ritner, as 'non religious "charlatanry"'. However, this had not always been the case, for in pharaonic Egypt magic permeated every aspect of society from the highest to the lowest, from birth to death and beyond. Magic was integral and inherent to the culture, and completely accepted in all its many forms; indeed it was almost indistinguishable from religion, with prayers to gods used alongside magical incantations and rituals.

In Mesopotamia (from 3000 BC), magic was not despised by any section of society but used for a variety of purposes, for example as a protection against slander, to escape from a ghost, protection against demons, for consulting the dead and in medicine. It pervaded all levels, from the ruler through to the lowliest slave, and was approved of and openly practised by all. However, unlike Ancient Egyptian magic, that of Mesopotamia was principally used as a protection against the multitude of demons that were thought to infiltrate the world of the living, bringing harm, disease and other assorted problems.

André Nataf states in his *Dictionary of the Occult* that there are four basic types of magical practice: consecration (the empowering of objects and gods), execration (the removal of evil from objects and people), invocation (the ritual chanting and saying of spells in order to obtain help from spirits and other entities) and evocation (the ordering of an entity to show itself). Nataf emphasises that in magic the spoken word plays an integral role in rituals and spells, with the correct words and form of speech being essential to ensure their potency. All things and objects contain their own life force and an utterance is thought to have the power to draw out the life force of the object invoked, which therefore makes the words themselves a real and effective force. Whilst words and ritual are both intrinsic factors in spells, it is the words themselves that are considered to be the ultimate power behind their efficacy.

Accordingly, once uttered, a spell is judged to be active and powerful. In his 1960s study of magic in Papua New Guinea, *Coral Gardens and their Magic*, Bronislaw Malinowski noted that the Trobriands of that region often focused their voices towards the required direction by the use of a hand clasped around the mouth, a posture also found in Ancient Egyptian tomb scenes that show magic in practice. It is thought that this action was intended to ensure that the words reached their correct target.

In the early 1900s, Sir James Frazer pioneered the theory of sympathetic magic, which he broke down into two parts: the law of similarity (homoeopathic magic) and the law of contact (contagious magic). Homoeopathic magic is based on the concept that what is done to an object relating to the target will be replicated in the target itself: for example, a spell or curse could be applied to a doll that represents a specific person. Contagious magic, however, involves the idea that a person can be affected by something that once belonged to them or with which they once had physical contact, even long after the contact has been disconnected: for example, nail clippings could be used in a spell aimed at their owner.

So how then can we define magic? A universal definition is hard to achieve because it is subject to so many different viewpoints and perceptions; after all, one person's magic may be another's religious experience. Dictionaries tend to avoid actually defining magic, concentrating instead on describing the effects its practitioners aim to achieve. Stuart Gordon has gone further, however, and in *The Paranormal: An Illustrated Encyclopaedia* he defines magic as 'the art of influencing the external world . . . by will and imagination combined'. Hence, as defined by Gordon, magic is the creation of mental images and the projection of these images into reality to produce a desired effect.

Magic could thus be said to be the utilisation and control of both natural and supernatural forces by means of words, incantations, rituals and spells in order to attain a result considered unattainable by natural means. Frazer thought that magic often worked by forcing higher powers to help in order to achieve its goals, unlike religion, which worked with deities and appeased these powers. Interestingly, the very terms used are often biased: magic is aggressive, demanding, cajoles or seeks submission, whereas religion is dignified, addresses gods, seeks their assistance and in return rites are performed and prayers said in adoration and gratitude.

In trying to distinguish magic from religion, Malinowski concluded that unlike religion, magic had a clear aim: people using magic were trying to exert some form of control over situations and tasks in which a high degree of luck or fate was involved and thus the outcome was not assured by ordinary means, as magic 'flourishes in . . . all dangerous enterprises, above all, in disease and in the shadow of death'. Therefore, where there is an element of chance, where the consequences are uncertain or all else has failed, magic would be used. By making use of this force, the individual is able to gain an element of control over a situation in which they might otherwise feel powerless. Magic is an area of human activity that helps the individual to cope and respond, so that no matter how (in)effective a ritual or spell might be, something positive is seen to be done.

Black magic, however, is a different matter altogether, because it involves the evocation of demons and their legions in order that the sorcerer can command them to do his or her bidding. This practice is far removed from the everyday magical practices of the majority, but, unfortunately, because of black magic's notoriety, it is the form of magic that is foremost in people's imaginations.

Since it is generally not understood how magic is practised and what it means to an individual or a society as a whole, it is often dismissed out of hand and its relevance is not considered. There are in fact many ways in which magic can be useful to its practitioner – socially, psychologically, spiritually – and its lasting testament is the fact that magical practices have survived for so long. Magic remains important to many people because it appears to work, even if not immediately, and because if it does fail, it is thought to be the result of errors in the ritual or spell, or of hostile forces, and not because the individual is unworthy, nor indeed because the magic itself is ineffective. Today, however, in Western society, with our reliance on science and desire for a logical explanation for everything, magic has fallen from favour, enjoyed by the majority for its entertainment value and no longer given credence as a belief system.

SEE ALSO: Lévi, Eliphas

MAGICAL WORDS

Magical words are often used in rituals, to focus the practitioner's mind, for example, or to summon forces to aid with the magical intent of the ceremony. Words of power originated in the earliest communities, and we find evidence of their existence in Ancient Egypt in the funerary texts, which include spells and words of power to be said over the body of the dead pharaoh as he was interred in his tomb and his soul was sent on its tortuous journey to the afterlife. To navigate the many pathways of the underworld, the pharaoh's soul had to pass many gates and guardians on the way to the final meeting with Osiris and the weighing-of-the-heart ceremony, where the deceased's earthly deeds were judged. Magical words were needed to pass certain gates and, to assist the dead pharaoh, these were spoken in the tomb by the king's priests in an elaborate ritual.

In the Papyrus of Ani, a version of the Egyptian Book of Coming Forth by Day (sometimes known as the Book of the Dead), we find an example of these magical words and phrases:

> Behold, these things have been told to me concerning the one to whom I shall speak when he shall be weighed in our midst.
>
> Then shall say the Majesty of Anubis concerning this: Do you know the name of this gateway, as many say to me?
>
> Then the Osiris, the Scribe Ani, the vindicated, shall say: In peace and in vindication: 'You Dispel Light' is the name of this gate.

Magical words have been used ever since in many cultures. In the New Testament, we witness Jesus using magical phrases and words to heal. For example, in the Gospel of Mark, we read: 'And he took the damsel by the hand, and said unto her, Talitha cumi; which is, being interpreted, Damsel, I say unto thee, arise.'

When alchemy and magic spread throughout Europe and the Middle East, magical words were used to shroud their practices and rituals in secrecy, as well as to confer unique powers on the speaker. We have all heard of the phrase 'open sesame', made famous in the Arabic magnum opus *The Thousand and One Nights*, in which Ali Baba stumbles upon a cave that opens with the phrase and is shut when 'close sesame' is spoken. This is just one example of the belief in magic words throughout the Middle Ages, as magicians and alchemists sought to answer some of the questions that science could not, and superstition and belief in the supernatural was rife amongst the general populace.

Aleister Crowley spent years searching for magical words, and he is attributed with documenting the form 'abrahadabra', a variant of the ancient magic word 'abracadabra'. In its oldest form, abracadabra was used in Roman times, inscribed onto amulets as a cure or to ward off sickness. There have been many attempts by scholars to trace the word's origins, and the following Hebrew-Aramaic phrases have been suggested as possibilities: *avarah k'davarah*, which means 'I will create as I speak', which certainly makes sense as the derivation for a word of power; *abhadda kedkabhra*, 'disappear like a word'; and *abreq ad habra*, 'hurl your death-bolt even unto death'.

To Crowley, his new form, abrahadabra, signified a new age brought about by revelations that were made to him when he received the Law of Thelema, the basis of his *Book of the Law*. Of abrahadabra, Crowley said that it was his knowledge of gematria that caused him to make the change to the original word abracadabra. Gematria is the system of numerology used in the Hebrew language, whereby each letter has a specific numerical value, as does each word when the values of its component letters are added up. Changing the 'c' of abracadabra to 'h' gave the new word a value of 418, which equates it, with, amongst other things, the demiurge, the creator of the universe, known to the Greeks as Iao and to the Gnostics as Yao.

Expounding further the word's meaning, Crowley wrote in *The Book of the Law*:

> This book shall be translated into all tongues: but always
> with the original in the writing of the Beast; for in the chance
> shape of the letters and their position to one another: in
> these are mysteries that no Beast shall divine. Let him not
> seek to try: but one cometh after him, whence I say not,
> who shall discover the Key of it all. Then this line drawn is a
> key: then this circle squared in its failure is a key also. And
> Abrahadabra. It shall be his child & that strangely. Let him
> not seek after this; for thereby alone can he fall from it.

Some phrases have stepped outside the secretive world of the private magical ritual and gained a usage outside of true magic. Many of these were picked up by conjurers and tricksters, magicians who were interested less in the discipline's esoteric aims and more in fooling people for amusement or profit. These phrases were adopted for many reasons: for example, to imply that the conjurer knew mysterious words of power and could summon magical forces and powers, but also in large part to distract the audience and so aid the trick being performed in front of them.

One of the most common phrases that has come into popular usage is 'hocus pocus'. The true origins of this phrase are not clear, but several theories have been put forward. The most likely is that it is a corruption of the Latin phrase '*Hoc est corpus meum*', which means 'this is my body' and refers specifically to the words of Jesus at the Last Supper. It has been suggested that this phrase may have been corrupted into 'hocus pocus', signifying the Roman Catholic's ritual of the Eucharist, where the focus is on the transubstantiation of the bread and wine of the Last Supper into the flesh and blood of Jesus – itself a magical transformation.

Thomas Ady, an English doctor of the seventeenth century who wrote three books concerning witchcraft, airing his belief that the Church's witch-hunt was misguided, demonstrates the use of the word in his *Candle in the Dark* (printed in 1656), when he discusses the tricks that jugglers employed ('juggler' at the time was a general term for conjurers; the word originally meant 'magician'):

> First, In slight of hand, or cleanly conveyance. Secondly, In
> confederacy; and Thirdly, In the abuse of Natural Magick.
> The first is profitably seen in our common Juglers, that go up
> and down to play their Tricks in Fayrs and Markets, I will

speak of one man more excelling in that craft than others, that went about in King James his time, and long since, who called himself, The Kings Majesties most excellent Hocus Pocus, and so was he called, because that at the playing of every Trick, he used to say, *Hocus pocus, tontus talontus, vade celeriter jubeo*, a dark composure of words, to blinde the eyes of the beholders, to make his Trick pass the more currantly without discovery, because when the eye and the ear of the beholder are both earnestly busied, the Trick is not so easily discovered, nor the Imposture discerned.

One of the most mysterious magical words is 'abraxas'. This word has been found engraved on Graeco-Roman stones that we call simply abraxas stones. It is believed that these were used as sacred amulets of power and warding. The meaning of the word has never been discovered, but it is thought to suggest the power of infinity and the concept that there is a greater force in the world than we can ever fully comprehend.

In Ancient Greek numerology, the letters that make up the word abraxas amount to 365, the number of days in the year. Furthermore, there is evidence that the Alexandrian Gnostic sect of the second century known as the Basilideans believed that abraxas was a pantheon of 365 gods who were the constituent parts of a supreme god. E.A. Wallis Budge, the Victorian Egyptologist, had this to say on the subject:

> Abraxas represented the 365 Aeons or emanations from the First Cause, and as a Pantheus, i.e. All-God, he appears on the amulets with the head of a cock (Phoebus) or of a lion (Ra or Mithras), the body of a man, and his legs are serpents which terminate in scorpions, types of the Agathodaimon. In his right hand he grasps a club, or a flail, and in his left is a round or oval shield.

The origin of the word is controversial, with some scholars maintaining that it belongs to no one particular dialect. Whatever its source, it seems to sum up all that is magical and mysterious about such words of power, words designed to instil in the listener a feeling of the supernatural, a sense that somehow voicing the words is enough to penetrate that thin veil that separates this world from the mystery and romance of the other world. We might at this stage cast our minds back to the Bible and remember the line: 'In the beginning was the Word, and the Word was with God, and the Word was God.'

SEE ALSO: Alchemy; Crowley, Aleister; Gnosticism; Numerology

MARTINISM

The term 'Martinism' can refer to a number of esoteric groups and systems of thought, so Martinism means different things to different people. Its roots are most certainly to be found in the theurgic (that is, divine magical) doctrine and practices of Martinez Pasqually (1710–74). It also refers, however, to the theosophical system developed by his pupil Louis-Claude de Saint-Martin (1743–1803). Equally, it can also be used to describe the Freemasonic Rectified Scottish Rite created by another of Pasqually's pupils, Jean-Baptiste Willermoz (1730–1824). The secret teachings of this rite were hailed as the 'jewel in the crown' of Freemasonry by the English occultist Arthur Edward Waite.

In its modern form, Martinism is practised today mainly by the many offshoots of the Martinist Order established by the French occultist Papus (1865–1916). He founded the order in 1887 to preserve the teachings of Pasqually and his disciple Saint-Martin, as he felt that these were far too important within the Western esoteric tradition to be lost. What he created was a three-degree system based on the Freemasonic model. The first two levels were preparatory; only when one reached the third degree were the teachings proper revealed.

Little is known of the private life of Martinez Pasqually, but we do know that he was the founder of a Masonic-theurgic order, l'Ordre des Chevaliers Maçon Elus Cohens de l'Univers' (the Order of Knights Mason Elect Priests of the Universe) generally shortened to just Elus Cohen. The Elus Cohen believed they were direct descendants of Aaron, the brother of Moses, and were continuing his priestly work.

Pasqually operated his system within French lodges, based on the authority granted in a Masonic charter issued to his father by Charles Edward Stewart, the exiled Scottish king. Dated 20 May 1738, this charter and the powers it conferred allowed his father, as Deputy Grand Master, 'to erect temples to the glory of God and the Grand Architect'. All rights and privileges transferred to Pasqually, as hereditary successor, when his father died in 1758. This marked the active beginning of the Elus Cohen and Pasqually's spiritual mission.

The doctrine of the Elus Cohen describes the occult history of humanity, its divine origins, the meaning of 'The Fall' and, most importantly, the means by which humans can discover their true nature by reintegrating with God. Pasqually did not profess to have created this doctrine but claimed that, as an initiate himself, these teachings had been conferred upon him. From whom he received the teachings we have no record. What he did leave behind, however, was an unfinished work entitled *Treatise on the Reintegration of Beings into their original virtues, powers and qualities*, which outlines the doctrine of the Elus Cohen.

It was whilst Louis-Claude de Saint-Martin, a soldier, was stationed in Bordeaux that he met Pasqually. In 1768, when he was 25 years old, he was initiated into the Rite of the Elus Cohen. He later wrote: 'It is to Martinez Pasqually that I owe my introduction to the higher truths.' By 1770, Saint-Martin had resigned from the army to pursue his religious and philosophical interests. Always a very spiritual man, Saint-Martin dedicated himself to seeking out the hidden truths in life. He became personal secretary to Pasqually and over the coming years progressed through the grades of the Elus Cohen until eventually he reached the sublime grade of the order, known as the Réau+Croix.

The priests performing this ceremony called on God's will to put initiates in touch with the worlds beyond, in order to draw celestial powers to earth. One such power was referred to by Saint-Martin as 'the Repairer', thought by some to have been Jesus Christ himself.

The importance and solemnity of the work was such that before taking the Réau+Croix grade, members engaged in lengthy meditation and physical purification. An exact diet similar to that eaten by the ancient Levites was followed, as was abstinence from sex, alcohol and other stimulants for a number of days leading up to the ceremony.

Pasqually died in 1774, whilst abroad at Port-au-Prince in Haiti. In the same year, Saint-Martin experienced the turning point in his life within the Elus Cohen. He had an encounter with an 'Unknown

Agent', a being from the higher spiritual planes. This being manifested itself within the lodge at Lyons during a ceremony. The outside world will never know the full details, as such manifestations were too sacred to the initiates to be discussed in any way with the profane.

Saint-Martin's own spiritual mission continued to develop in a different direction after the death of his mentor. His first book came out in 1775, and was called *Of Errors and of Truth*, which he published under the pseudonym of 'the Unknown Philosopher'. All his writings would appear under this nom de plume until after his death.

As time went on, Saint-Martin grew uneasy with the powerful magical work of the Elus Cohen and chose another way to follow the spiritual path. In 1790, he left the order behind to focus on a path that he termed 'the Way of the Heart'. This was an inner way, a way of prayer rather than ceremonial magic. Instead of following doctrine, he promoted the art of self-knowledge. 'Books are the window to the truth but they are not the door; they point things out to men but they do not impart them,' he wrote. His later teachings can be summed up in the phrase: 'Look within for that which is of Truth.'

Saint-Martin acquired followers in many countries and with those he felt were worthy of initiation, he personally shared his truths. These secret initiates were referred to as 'Supérieurs Inconnus' (Unknown Superiors), or S.I. for short. Each S.I. in turn could pass on this initiation to other worthy candidates. Saint-Martin conferred initiations up until his death in 1803, but he never returned to Freemasonry or the Elus Cohen, and he himself never established an order for his teachings.

Another of Pasqually's pupils, however, did create an organisation to preserve his masters' wisdom. Jean-Baptiste Willermoz incorporated the higher teachings of the Elus Cohen into a Masonic system known as the Rectified Scottish Rite. The origins of this rite go back to the system of Strict Observance, founded in 1756 by Baron von Hund. Like Pasqually's father, Baron von Hund had Masonic authority bestowed upon him by Charles Edward Stewart, in 1754. This resulted in him becoming the head of the Rite of Strict Observance, an elite order of Knights Templar.

At the lodge in Lyons in 1778, Willermoz brought about significant changes to the rite in France. He replaced the Strict Observance Templars with the Chevaliers Bienfaisants de la Cité Sainte (the Beneficent Knights of the Holy City), shortened to CBCS. The secret grades of the CBCS were to incorporate the essential teachings of the Elus Cohen. As a Freemason belonging to many 'high grades', Willermoz considered the Strict Observance to be only a preparatory school, from where the Elect could be introduced into the higher truths within the inner circle of Martinism (as we now call it).

However, Martinism as most understand it today has Papus (his real name was Dr Gérard Encausse) to thank for its preservation. After Saint-Martin's death, the S.I. initiation continued to be transmitted from person to person, as each initiate had to choose at least one successor to receive the teachings before he died. Papus, an avid occultist, received the initiation himself in 1880. Soon afterwards he discovered by chance that his friend Augustine Chaboseau was also an S.I. Viewing this occurrence as a signal, he decided to create an order as a home for all those who shared this 'mysterious gift', as a way of preserving the tradition. In 1887, the Ordre Martiniste was created. Papus defined the aims and purpose of his Order in the following way:

> the Order, as a whole, is especially a school of moral knighthood, endeavouring to develop the spirituality of its members by the study of the invisible world and its laws, by the exercise of devotion and the intellectual assistance and by the creation in each spirit of an all the more solid faith as it is based on observation and science.

Although today there are dozens of offshoots from the original order created by Papus, they all have one thing in common: the theosophical teachings of Martinez Pasqually and his pupil Louis-Claude de Saint-Martin.

MEDITATION

Meditation is a part of many disciplines and is integral to several of the world's religions. Generally, the term describes the art of controlling the thoughts and involves quietening and calming the thought processes and directing their flow. Usually, the person meditating turns their thoughts inward and away from the outside world, looking towards the inner, more personal world. Sometimes the aim is to stop all thoughts entirely and focus on that stillness, but often there is a specific purpose to a meditation and the aim is to concentrate the thoughts on a definite goal.

People meditate for many different reasons, some to achieve unity with a higher being, such as God, or with the universe itself, some simply to find peace and tranquillity within their minds, and others to work through life experiences and memories.

Many religions and traditions make use of meditation, including Buddhism, Taoism, yoga, Sikhism, Judaism and Kabbalah, Hinduism, Sufism and even Christianity.

While meditation alone is often enough, certain disciplines have additional requirements, such as meditation postures and breathing techniques. In Buddhism and many other traditions, it is considered important to sit upright with the spine straight, so that the life force – known also as prana or chi – of the body can flow upwards through the chakras; this posture also aids the breathing of the person meditating. Silence is nearly always a prerequisite, although chanting is also used in some instances, to force the mind into certain states and to alter the normal thought patterns.

Breathing is often very important, and in Buddhism breath work is considered vital. Concentrating on one's breathing can often bring about a change in consciousness and help the mind turn inwards on the rhythms of the body rather than focusing on exterior distractions. Beginners often count as they exhale and count as they inhale, building up regular, slow breathing patterns. Variations in the count are developed in some traditions and can lead to radical changes in thought processes.

Buddha himself taught that breathing is a vital element for reaching true enlightenment. The Buddhist scripture known as Samyutta Nikaya contains the story of how Ananda, Buddha's devoted disciple, asked Buddha to describe one quality that would allow him to bring about full realisation. Buddha replied that it was breathing, telling Ananda:

> There is the case where a monk, having gone to the wilderness, to the shade of a tree, or to an empty building, sits down folding his legs crosswise, holding his body erect, and setting mindfulness to the fore. Always mindful, he breathes in; mindful he breathes out.
>
> Breathing in long, he discerns that he is breathing in long; or breathing out long, he discerns that he is breathing out long.
>
> Or breathing in short, he discerns that he is breathing in short; or breathing out short, he discerns that he is breathing out short.
>
> He trains himself to breathe in sensitive to the entire body, and to breathe out sensitive to the entire body.
>
> He trains himself to breathe in calming the bodily processes, and to breathe out calming the bodily processes.

When attempting meditation for the first time, many people feel baffled and lost, but, quite simply, all it involves is quietening the mind and focusing on the self and the now. For even this simple act is meditation – nothing more is needed. Of course, there are more complex forms of meditation, with structured elements and tangible results, but at its heart, the essence of meditation is simply taking the time and the effort to look inward.

Many schools of Eastern thought, such as Taoism, teach that in truth the past and the future do not exist, that only the present moment is reality. While this is a complex concept that we cannot hope to discuss in a few sentences, the truth of it can probably be seen by everyone. We know that the past has happened and that the future will be upon us, but all that really exists is the here and now. It is this concept that meditation is designed to help us focus on. So much of our lives is concerned with what happened in the past and what will happen to us in the future, and we worry endlessly, trying to make preparations for tomorrow. While that is not to be neglected, meditating on the now helps us realise that if we spend all of our time concerning ourselves with the future or what happened long ago, all we are doing is destroying the now, negating the present moment. Meditation allows us to retrieve the now, to bring it clearly into focus and to brush away everything else, even if only for a short time. If we can achieve that through meditation alone, then we have already benefited from the many gifts it can offer.

SEE ALSO: Taoism

NECROMANCY

The meaning of this old word is 'divination by communication with the dead'. Necromancy is essentially the summoning of spirits to aid the practitioner, generally for the purposes of gaining knowledge and wisdom.

Necromancy clearly works on the assumption that there is a soul that lives on after a person has died and that this soul or spirit can then be summoned back to earth to communicate with the living. The words 'necromancy' and 'necromancer' have dark connotations and are thought of as being part of the 'black arts'. The etymology of the word also suggests this, the old Middle English version being '*nygromauncy*', which was influenced by the Latin word '*niger*' meaning 'black'.

Early necromancy is thought to have been similar in principle to shamanism, where village elders would communicate with the dead ancestors of the tribe in an attempt to answer certain questions or to heal an individual.

There is reference to the art of necromancy in Ancient Greek texts, where we see that the practice of it involved a trip into Hades, the underworld, so that the dead need not be summoned to the living world. The most famous account of such a journey is found in Homer's *Odyssey*, in which Odysseus ventures into Hades in an attempt to raise the spirit of Tiresias.

Necromancy was also used in Ancient Rome, as well as later in Israel and the Middle East. In Australia, the Aborigines made use of necromancers who were known amongst the tribes as Birraark, and they would summon ghosts that they called *mrarts*. The discipline was also practised in Japan, where one process involved thrusting 100 rushlights into a lit paper lantern.

In medieval times, there seems to have been a fascination with necromancy throughout Europe, but possibly no more so than in earlier times; it may simply be the fact that we have more surviving texts from the Middle Ages that colours our view that there was an explosion of necromancy during this time. It is easy to confuse necromancy with the summoning of demons and devils, which was done with the aid of a grimoire, or book of magical instruction, but it must not be forgotten that necromancy deals specifically with attempting to raise spirits of the dead, not demons.

There was a separate form of necromancy – the purest form, it could be said – that involved actually returning the corpse to life (the Latin *necromantia* means literally 'divination from an exhumed corpse'). However, for obvious reasons (digging up a foul, stinking cadaver is not an endeavour to undertake lightly unless absolutely necessary), this form of necromancy was rarely practised, and generally attempts were made to revive only the spirit of the deceased, not the body as well.

Despite it not being necessary to raise the corpse to practise necromancy, rituals of the Middle Ages were often very elaborate and sometimes macabre affairs. Lewis Spence, in his 1920 book *An Encyclopaedia of Occultism*, detailed the lengths to which necromancers went, relating the intricate process they embarked upon before carrying out the summoning. He tells us that a remote location must first be chosen, either that or an underground vault, and then a magic circle must be constructed for the protection of the necromancer:

> A piece of ground is usually chosen, nine feet square, at the full extent of which parallel lines are drawn within the other, having sundry crosses and triangles described between them . . . The vacancies formed by the various lines and angles of the figure are filled up with the holy names of God, having crosses and triangles described between them. The reason assigned by magicians and others for this institution and use of circles, is, that so much ground being blessed and consecrated by such holy words and ceremonies as they make use of forming it, hath a secret force to expel all evil spirits from the bounds

thereof, and, being sprinkled with pure, sanctified water, the ground is purified from all uncleanliness.

Spence also detailed the attire of the necromancer and the words and rituals he went through to bring about the summoning of the dead spirit, together with all the other minutiae that were necessary if he was to be successful in his aims, including shutting himself away for 21 days before the summoning, during which time simple meals and purity of body and thought must be maintained. All in all, it demonstrates just what a complex process it was to summon a spirit of the dead. The job was certainly not for the faint of heart, or indeed the impatient. If the necromancer was lucky and all the preparations had been made correctly, the spirit arrived, and Spence details some such successful incidents:

> Exactly at midnight the spirit came. Sometimes the door opened slowly, and there glided in noiselessly a lady sheeted in white, with a face of woe and told her story to the man on his asking her in the name of God what she wanted. What she wanted was done in the morning, and the spirit rested ever after. Sometimes the spirit rose from the floor, and sometimes came forth from the wall. There was one who burst into the room with a strong bound, danced wildly round the circle, and flourished a long whip round the man's head, but never dared to step into the circle. During a pause in his frantic dance he was asked, in God's name, what he wanted. He ceased his dance and told his wishes. His wishes were carried out, and the spirit was in peace.

Christian and Judaic texts specify quite clearly that necromancy is forbidden and that those who attempt it will be shunned by God. Leviticus, the third book of the Old Testament, mentions that it is a crime and says:

> If a person turns to the mediums and oracles so as to prostitute himself to their ways, I will direct My anger against him, and cut him off spiritually from his people.
>
> You must sanctify yourselves and be holy, for I am God your Lord.

It was considered a great crime because it was believed at the time that the scriptures were being composed that a demon could appear to the necromancer, pretending to be a dead person's spirit, and so work its dark will through the summoner, even to the extent of taking possession of the necromancer.

Today, society is not so strict when it comes to the subject of speaking to dead spirits, although the word 'necromancy' is still rather taboo. This is probably because necromancy surely exists in a form known today as spiritualism. While the word 'spiritualism' doesn't conjure up the dark images that necromancy invokes, the two are very similar, if not one and the same. The spiritualist attempts to contact spirits of the dead, and even if the methods are different, the act and the alleged results are very close. Many people, such as members of the Spiritual Church, use spiritualism to heal, contacting the spirits of the dead for benign reasons, so perhaps through such channels the concept of communication with the dead has come to seem more wholesome and no longer entails the negative connotations that have been associated with necromancy over the centuries. Whether it actually works or not is still open to debate, but the art of necromancy is alive and well in the world today.

SEE ALSO: Divination; Grimoires; Shamanism

NOSTRADAMUS

Nostradamus is perhaps the world's most famous prophet. His book *Les Prophéties* is in print to this day, and his predictions are frequently debated and quoted in modern times.

He was born in the south of France in 1503, and his full name was Michel de Nostredame. He grew up to be conversant in a wide range of subjects, especially philosophy, grammar, classical literature, medicine (both conventional and herbal) and astrology.

The famous predictions were not written down until he was 46. Before this, he concentrated on medicine and entered the University of Montpellier in 1529, after which he would specialise in fighting the bubonic plague, which was rife throughout Europe at the time. Nostradamus had some success in developing a treatment for the plague that contained rose petals and rose hips, now known to contain high levels of vitamin C, and he became well known for his cures and treatment of the plague.

Unfortunately, in 1537 his own wife and children succumbed to the illness, and after their deaths Nostradamus began travelling Europe. It was after visiting Italy that Nostradamus began to move more towards his interest in all things occult. In 1550, remarried and now living back in France, at Salon in Provence, he changed his name to Nostradamus, the Latinised version of his surname, Nostredame, and published an almanac for the year, containing predictions regarding the future. It was so successful that he would write one every year until his death in 1566, and these works contain over 6,000 prophecies altogether. Sometimes he would publish two or three almanacs in a single year under different titles: *Almanachs*, which contained detailed predictions, and *Prognostications* or *Presages*, both of which contained more general forecasts.

The success of these almanacs resulted in Nostradamus being asked to submit horoscopes for notable members of society, and this proved quite a lucrative career. It even led to him being installed as an adviser to King Henri II of France after the king's consort, Catherine de' Medici, read one of Nostradamus's almanacs and asked him to travel to the court to explain his predictions relating to the royal family.

Inspired by the success of the almanacs, Nostradamus began to work on a larger project that was to contain 1,000 predictions, this time written in rhyming quatrains (stanzas of four lines). The result of this endeavour was *Les Prophéties*, the first part of which was published in 1555. This book was never as popular as his yearly almanacs, yet, ironically, it is the work that has ensured Nostradamus's lasting fame.

The methods of Nostradamus have been debated for centuries, and in *Les Prophéties* we get a glimpse of his technique for divining the future and setting it in verse:

> Sitting by night in my secret study,
> Alone, resting upon the stool of brass,
> A slight flame, going out of the solitude,
> Makes me pronounce what is not to be believed vain.

> The wand in hand, set in the middle of the branches,
> From the wave I wet both the hem and the foot,
> In fear I write, trembling in the sleeves,
> Divine splendour: the Divine seated nearby.

It is thought that Nostradamus also used a scrying bowl in his study, and it is possible that he took mind-altering herbs when seeking his visions of the future.

Nostradamus's predictions have come to prominence again in recent times, as they do every few years, because it was suggested that his quatrains had predicted the 9/11 attack on the Twin Towers in New York. One of the verses cited was this one:

> Latitude forty-five, the sky shall burn:

To great 'New City' shall the fire draw nigh.
With vehemence the flames shall spread and churn
When with the North conclusions they shall try.

Much was made of the supposition that 'latitude forty-five' indicated New York, but it does not precisely match, and is actually several hundred miles off. The New City, rather than being New York – and incidentally Nostradamus makes no reference at all to America in any of his quatrains – seems to represent Naples in Italy, whose name comes from the Greek *neapolis*, which literally means 'new city'. According to Peter Lemesurier, author of *Nostradamus: The Illustrated Prophecies*:

> If, though, Nostradamus was really thinking of 40 degrees 50'
> North, rather than 45 degrees 00' North, then he is clearly
> talking about Naples (Greek 'Neapolis' = New City), with the
> 'fire from the sky' the volcano of nearby Mount Vesuvius.

Other attempts by amateur translators of Nostradamus's quatrains to try to make the predictions fit the circumstances of 9/11 include either deliberate misinterpretations of the material or entirely fictional lines, inserted at will. However, as with many of these cases in which Nostradamus is quoted as having predicted an event that has just happened, critical mass is reached, a large section of the population hears that Nostradamus predicted the event and only a small percentage of these will ever check the original source material – and so the myth continues until soon it is spoken of as fact.

Critics suggest that Nostradamus deliberately phrased his quatrains so that there would be a certain amount of ambiguity, in order to allow various interpretations of his predictions. There is no doubt that Nostradamus deliberately obscured some facts by such methods as removing letters from names, though he himself claimed that the reason for this was simply to avoid being arrested and punished as a magician. Furthermore, maybe for the same reason or perhaps to conceal the real truth hidden in the quatrains, Nostradamus didn't use only French to compose the verses, but also added Provençal, Italian, Ancient Greek and Latin.

In his defence, Nostradamus never went so far as to claim that he was a prophet; he always maintained that he used his skills in astrology and research to the best of his abilities but that he was not prescient. He wrote this on the subject:

> . . . although I have inserted the name of prophet, I do not desire to assume a title of so high sublimity at the present moment . . .
>
> . . . Still, by the means of some eternal power, by an epileptic Herculean agitation, the causes by the celestial movement become known. I do not say, my son, in order that you may fully understand me, that the knowledge of this matter cannot yet impress itself upon thy feeble brain, that very remote future causes may not come within the cognizance of a reasonable being; if they are, notwithstanding, purely the creation of the intellectual soul of things present, future things are not by any means too hidden or concealed.

Some researchers have claimed that Nostradamus inherited the gift of prophecy from the Israelite tribe of Issachar, son of Jacob, and it is known that his paternal grandfather converted from Judaism to Catholicism some 50 years before his birth. However, Nostradamus himself believed that he had received his gifts from his mother's side.

Nostradamus finally succumbed to dropsy after suffering from gout for many years. He died in 1566, aged 62, but not before he supposedly predicted his own death. One of his last writings was this verse, found in his unfinished last almanac:

> On his return from the Embassy, the King's gift put in place,
> He will do nothing more. He will be gone to God.
> Close relatives, friends, brothers by blood (will find him)
> Completely dead near the bed and the bench.

This was exactly what happened on the day of his death, but it has been suggested since that the verse was edited by his secretary, Jean de Chavigny, so that it would fit events and keep alive the great foresight of Nostradamus, but it makes for a fitting epitaph nonetheless.

Nostradamus's last wish was to be buried upright and for his coffin to be sealed inside the walls of the Church of the Cordeliers in Salon, where he had lived the last days of his life. A stone in the church reads:

Here rest the bones of the illustrious Michaelis Nostradamus, alone of all mortals judged worthy to record with his almost divine pen, under the influence of the stars, the future events of the whole world. He lived 62 years, 6 months and 17 days. He died at Salon in the year 1566. Let not posterity disturb his rest. Anne Pons Gemelle wishes her husband true happiness.

We will end with Nostradamus's own words, written to his newly born son in the form of a preface to his book *Les Prophéties*:

Thy late arrival, César Nostradamus my son, has made me bestow much time, through nightly vigils, to leave you in writing a memorial to refer to, after the corporal extinction of your progenitor, that might serve for the common profit of mankind, out of what the Divine Being has permitted me to learn from the revolution of the stars . . . Considering that events of human proposal are uncertain, whilst all is governed and directed by the incalculable power of Heaven, guiding us, not by Bacchic fury, nor yet by Lymphatic motion, but by astronomical assertion.

SEE ALSO: Astrology

NUMEROLOGY

The Ancient Greek philosopher and mathematician Pythagoras flourished c. 530 BC, and it was his assertion that all things can be expressed in numerical terms, because they are ultimately reducible to numbers. There are those who believe that numbers have an arcane, mystical relationship with animate and inanimate objects and with words. Numerology is the science of the exploration of this relationship in order to discover hidden meanings, forecast the future or interpret the character of a person. In its modern form, a series of figures which correspond to an individual's name and date of birth are calculated, and practitioners claim to be able to divine the fortune, prospects and character of the subject from the results.

St Augustine of Hippo (born AD 354) believed that numbers formed a special language through which God could speak to man to show him what was truth. Other Christians of his day, however, having considered what formed true belief and what ought to be condemned as unorthodox, frowned upon numerology, along with other supposed dark arts such as astrology. This did not, however, stamp out such practices.

In many cultures, number symbolism is used to give structure to and allow understanding of that other world which is inhabited by gods, spirits and demons. Duality appears, for instance, in the nature of Christ as God and man, or the pairing of God and the Devil as two opposing forces. The Christian Holy Trinity, of course, involves the number three, and Egyptian Triads comprised three gods, usually as father, mother and child, linked together during the New Kingdom period, when formerly unrelated deities were joined in neat packages.

Aspects of numerology are significant in the Islamic faith too. Many Muslim legends, stories and traditions are based on the mystical value of numbers. One way in which this manifests itself is in the fact that there is often an emphasis on repeating certain religious rites three or seven times. It is taught that the Prophet himself found the repetition of religious formulae more efficacious than performing them only once. In both the Koran and the Bible the number 40 has a certain power – 40 days of fasting, preparation or repentance, for instance. The Prophet is said to have attributed particular qualities to numbers (and days of the week), so that certain numbers are of great significance in Islam. (For example, seven: it is the number of the heavens and the number of heinous sins leading directly to hell, and when undertaking the Hajj, the pilgrimage to Mecca, pious Muslims process seven times around the sacred Black Stone and ritually throw seven stones at the Devil.) Letters of the alphabet each have numerical values peculiar to themselves, for instance the first is valued as one, which symbolises the special quality of Allah. Many centuries previously, the Assyrians and Babylonians also regarded the number one as very special, since when moving from zero to one you progress from non-existence to existence. The second letter begins the Koran, and signifies the Creative Power through which everything was made.

The number four is thought of in Christianity, Islam and Judaism as symbolising perfection. It relates to the cardinal points of the compass. The Zoroastrians knew of only seven planets and, recognising this as a special number, incorporated it into their religious beliefs regarding celestial beings. Assyrians and Babylonians assigned their great goddess Ishtar (the planet Venus) the number 15, while the moon god, Sin, and earth's satellite itself were associated with 30.

In the biblical Book of Revelation, the Antichrist is assigned the 'number of the beast', 666. The author of Revelation also has a fascination for the number seven: seven seals opened, seven trumpets, seven bowls poured out.

The number nine has a special significance in many cultures because if it is multiplied by any whole number except zero, when the digits of the answer are added until a single digit remains, this number will always be nine. For example: $2 \times 9 = 18$ and $1 + 8 = 9$; $6 \times 9 = 54$ and $5 + 4 = 9$; $121 \times 9 = 1,089$ and $1 + 0 + 8 + 9 = 18$ and $1 + 8 = 9$.

While numerology was thought of in earlier times as a branch of mathematics, today it is no longer seen in this light. Just as twenty-first-century astrology is not usually accepted as being the concern of astronomers any longer, numerology is viewed today as being simply part of the occult.

One of the most famous numerologists of modern times was Ivan Panin, a Russian born in 1855 who claimed that mathematical patterns could be found in the Hebrew text of the Psalms. He devoted more than 50 years to these supposed numerical structures, lecturing on what he alleged he had discovered and publishing some of his findings. It is now generally accepted that he fudged at least some of the evidence, accepting only what suited his theories and rejecting the rest. Those who have researched the matter say that similar numerical patterns occur in most, if not all, texts. Perhaps they can even be found in this work.

That man of mystery, self-professed psychic Uri Geller, is on record as claiming that numerology can help those with the knowledge of these things to a profounder understanding of occurrences such as the infamous 9/11 attack.

Just as astrologers make a living from clients who will pay them to forecast their futures and advise on their actions by taking account of the position of the heavenly bodies at a given time, so numerologists offer similar services. For example, using a chart, they can ascribe numbers to the letters of a client's name, and the birth date may also be taken into account. Analysis of this information is supposed to lead to a better understanding of the subject's situation. Some who practise this skill considered it possible that if a life is not going well, a change of name may be a solution. A couple whose numerical make-up is incompatible might be persuaded to each find a more suitable partner, although numerology alone would not be a good basis for ending a relationship. It has been said that while numerology is a fairly easily accessible spiritual study, it is the least understood. Palmistry, astrology and the reading of Tarot cards are more common and more accepted, it seems.

We should ask ourselves whether numerology's claim to be able to allot you a number, based solely on a name and date, which reveals your characteristics and personality makes any sense. If the answer is in the affirmative, then how does it compare with fortune telling using cards, tea leaves, a horoscope or other such methods? Since it is difficult to know oneself, it may be better to ask others to what extent their personal observations of you are a match for your numerology reading. It is all too easy just to pick and choose those traits which you believe or hope you have and to reject the others out of hand.

SEE ALSO: Astrology; Pythagoras; Tarot

ORDO TEMPLI ORIENTIS

The Ordo Templi Orientis, or O.T.O., is a magical order that was founded in Germany probably around 1896 (although some sources state 1906). It has attracted the label 'satanic' because sex magic is performed within the higher degrees of the order. Members argue strongly, however, that they are not satanists and in actual fact the rites that they perform are some of the most holy to be found anywhere. As the tantric system in the East uses sex as part of its practices in pursuit of spiritual enlightenment, so O.T.O. members argue that their use of sex acts within their sacred rites are employed to achieve an end.

Magical practitioners of the high rites of the O.T.O. system apparently assume the identities of gods and goddesses, and through their union, they believe, they achieve higher states of consciousness, knowledge and understanding of this world and the worlds beyond. Some claim that here in the West practices such as these hark back to the *heiros gamos*, the sacred marriage, part of the rites practised within the Eleusinian mystery schools of the ancient world.

These explanations aside, the negative image that the order suffers from in the popular consciousness also has very much to do with its most infamous leader: Aleister Crowley. Crowley once stated that he wanted to be the Saint of Satan, the Devil's chief emissary on earth, and he identified himself as 'the Great Beast' whose number is 666 in the Book of Revelation. When he took over the leadership of the O.T.O., he set about incorporating into it the teachings of his own Church of Thelema, a faith that Crowley hoped would one day become the natural successor to Christianity. The O.T.O. accepted the Law of Thelema, the doctrine of which is contained in his *Book of the Law* and which is summarised in the motto 'Do what thou wilt shall be the whole of the Law'.

The O.T.O. as it exists today claims descent from Carl Kellner, who founded the order in 1896. Kellner, who was interested in Freemasonry and Eastern esotericism, started a group that practised sex magic, incorporating tantric exercises. In his house, he had a room without windows where these ceremonies were performed. He acted as priest while his wife performed the role of the great goddess. As part of the ceremony, they apparently created an 'elixir', produced by mixing together male and female sexual fluids.

In 1903, an ardent occultist, Theodor Reuss, became a member of Kellner's group. When Kellner died in 1905, Reuss took control of the society, and it is said that it was he who then restructured the group along Freemasonic lines. This pseudo-Templar Freemasonic system included seven degrees, each of which was supposed to open one of the seven chakras. The system apparently borrowed much from the esoteric Memphis Misraim Masonic rite, but obviously the sexual aspects that Kellner had practised were added.

In 1910, Theodor Reuss and Aleister Crowley met. Soon afterwards, Crowley was admitted into the O.T.O., becoming an active member. Within two short years, he became the head of the British section of the order. In 1913, whilst he was in Moscow, he wrote a Gnostic Mass, which was similar to the Christian ceremony in so far as it involved eating cakes and drinking wine but which was based on Crowley's own writings and made no reference to Christ. On his production of this, it was introduced into the practices of the order. When Reuss died in 1923, Crowley moved in to assume overall control of the whole organisation and introduced his Thelematic system, which has remained in use within the order to this day.

According to a contemporary O.T.O. source, initiation into the order is designed 'to instruct the individual by allegory and symbol in the profound mysteries of nature, and thereby to assist each to discover his or her own true identity'. The order has developed into a system of thirteen numbered and twelve un-numbered degrees. These are further divided into three grades or triads. The degrees have various titles, including Magician, Prince of the Royal Secret and Bishop of Ecclesia Gnostica Catholica.

The Ecclesia Gnostica Catholica is the ecclesiastical arm of the

O.T.O. and was born out of the Gnostic Catholic Church, which was founded in France in 1907 by the occultists Jean Bricaud, Gérard Encausse (also known as Papus) and Louis-Sophrone Fugairon. During his lifetime, Reuss borrowed from many systems and was active in numerous occult groups across Europe as he continued to develop the O.T.O. He had a network of contacts in Martinism, Rosicrucianism and fringe Freemasonry. He received consecration into the Gnostic Catholic Church from its founders in gratitude for the Memphis Misraim Masonic charter that he had issued to them. As with many of his other affiliations, he assimilated the practices and rites of the Gnostic Catholic Church into his O.T.O. Crowley changed the name from Gnostic Catholic Church to Ecclesia Gnostica Catholica. The most significant change came about when his Gnostic Mass was introduced. This marked the removal of the last remotely Christian elements from the Church and its transformation into a vehicle for the Law of Thelema. This move separated it from the Church of Bricaud, Papus and Fugairon, which was essentially a Christian Gnostic Church.

Although Kellner and Reuss are major figures in the history and development of the O.T.O., it is Crowley who is the most noted. Today, the followers of the order that carries out the magical practices that he influenced number more than ever before. After more than a century in existence, it is particularly strong in the United States, and it is thought that there are between 2,000 and 3,000 members worldwide.

SEE ALSO: Crowley, Aleister; Gnosticism; Rosicrucianism

OUIJA BOARD

It is remarkable to think that the Ouija board, often portrayed as a dangerous method of raising spirits from the dead, has in the past been, and continues to be, used as an after-dinner parlour game and even a children's board game.

The board which is sold today was patented in 1891, with the inventor listed as Elijah Bond and with Charles Kennard as one of the assignees. Kennard began selling the boards commercially through the Kennard Novelty Company, but he was eventually supplanted by William Fuld, who achieved great success with the 'talking boards'. Fuld fell to his death in 1927 from the roof of his factory in Baltimore, either by accident while erecting a flagpole or by suicide, depending upon how lurid a tale one prefers. This certainly did not harm the company, which was continued by his descendants until it was sold to Parker Brothers in 1966. Parker Brothers, who made other popular games such as Monopoly, moved production of the boards to their factory in Salem, Massachusetts. This connection with the location of the famous Salem witch trials is a delightful twist in the story.

Two main versions of the origin of the word 'Ouija' exist. One, offered by Fuld, is that it is an amalgamation of the French word 'oui' and the German word 'ja', both meaning 'yes'. The other suggestion is that Charles Kennard named the board after what he incorrectly believed was the Egyptian word for luck. The name 'Ouija' is patented by Hasbro, the game manufacturers who now own Parker Brothers. Any other boards should be referred to generically as talking boards, although this convention is little used, in the same way that the dominance of one manufacturer in the market results in vacuum cleaners being generally referred to as Hoovers. Several other companies have produced their own versions of the talking board, decorated in many cases with imagery from the Tarot cards or other occult designs.

The board consists of the letters of the alphabet, numbers one to nine and the words 'yes' and 'no', usually accompanied by one or two other simple words such as 'goodnight' or 'goodbye'. Participants sit around the board, and each lightly places a finger on a moving plate called the planchette. In the nineteenth century, before the invention of the Ouija board, the planchette was used alone with a pen inserted through it, and a spiritualist would receive messages spelt out by the device. The huge popularity of the Ouija board resulted in part from the fact that it did not require a spiritualist with special powers to operate it and could therefore be used directly by anyone with either a curiosity to discover secrets from the spirit world or a desire to entertain themselves and their friends.

As a means of divination, it is customary to ask the board a question, which, by the movement of the planchette, is answered 'yes' or 'no' or the reply is spelt out. To what extent the device moves spontaneously, under spirit guidance, or by the conscious or unconscious design of the operators is very difficult to tell. Most proponents of the boards advise that anyone unwilling to risk receiving an answer he does not want refrains from taking part in sessions. The slogan used by Parker Brothers to market the Ouija board was 'It's only a game − isn't it?', which, however, seems to contrast with a glow-in-the-dark version of the board that is currently on sale as a game suitable for children aged 8 to 12 years.

In popular culture, the use of the Ouija board generally appears as a sinister practice, resulting in terror and torment for the practitioners. For example, in the 1973 movie *The Exorcist*, the central child character, Regan, becomes possessed by a demon called Captain Howdy after using a Ouija board in the presence of her mother. In another context, however, the Pulitzer Prize-winning American poet James Merrill used a Ouija board to conduct several conversations with the spirits of both fictional characters and real people, including the poet W.H. Auden. He incorporated these conversations into his epic poem *The Changing Light at Sandover*, a work that considerably enhanced his reputation and received the National Book Critics Circle Award in 1983.

OUIJA BOARD

A political scandal haunted the Italian former European Commission president and current prime minister Romano Prodi after he gave information to a judicial hearing that he had participated in a seance in 1978. At the seance, Prodi claimed, he and a group of friends received information through a Ouija board regarding the location of a kidnapped former prime minister, Aldo Moro. The spirit of a recently deceased Christian Democrat politician, Giorgio La Pira, spelled out to the assembled participants several words, including 'Gradoli' — which turned out to refer to the Via Gradoli in Rome, where terrorists were holding Moro. Sadly, although the information was passed to the police, they were unable to make the link to the terrorist hiding place, searching instead a small village by that name, and Moro's murdered body was discovered weeks later in Rome. That a senior politician, in a country where the Roman Catholic Church strongly disapproves of such activities, would admit to taking part in a session with a Ouija board to summon up spirits seems incredible. Some of Prodi's opponents have suggested that the story was made up to protect the identity of a source who leaked to him the name Gradoli.

Whether we see the Ouija board as a harmless toy, a source of information from the spirit world or a dangerous portal to the underworld, it has without doubt become an iconic piece of occult paraphernalia.

SEE ALSO: Divination

OUROBOROS

The ouroboros is the figure of a serpent in the form of a perfect circle, devouring its own tail. Some depictions, especially in alchemical works, show a double ouroboros, which takes the form of a lemniscate, the traditional symbol for infinity, very much like the figure 8 turned on its side. The Latin word *'lemniscus'* means simply 'ribbon' and that is exactly what this infinite loop looks like. The word 'ouroboros' comes to us from Ancient Greek, although the symbol itself has been traced back as far as Ancient Egypt, and it means literally 'tail-swallower'. The symbol is a very powerful image; it suggests the cyclical nature of the universe, that through destruction comes creation, a literal representation of life through death. As the ouroboros devours itself, so it is nourished and so life continues.

The ouroboros has been much used in religious and mystical symbolism, and also in alchemy, in which context it often appeared as half black and half white, emphasising the opposing forces of nature — in a similar way to the concept of yin and yang — that make life and creation possible. Alchemists used the ouroboros as a purifying glyph when carrying out their transmutations and experiments.

There is an interesting account of how the famous chemist August Kekulé discovered the chemical structure of benzene while dreaming about the ouroboros. He is quoted in Royston M. Roberts' *Serendipity: Accidental Discoveries in Science*:

> I was sitting writing on my textbook, but the work did not progress; my thoughts were elsewhere. I turned my chair to

the fire and dozed. Again the atoms were gambolling before
my eyes . . . My mental eye, rendered more acute by repeated
visions of the kind, could now distinguish larger structures
of manifold conformation: long rows sometimes more closely
fitted together all twining and twisting in snake-like motion.
But look! What was that? One of the snakes had seized hold
of its own tail, and the form whirled mockingly before my
eyes. As if by a flash of lightning I awoke.

Gnostic Christians also adopted the ouroboros, and to them it
symbolised that the world that we know is small in comparison to
the universe that exists outside of it. It is even referred to in Ancient
Greece as existing on the edge of the 'sea which surrounds the world',
again a clue as to its meaning: the known universe is symbolised
by the space enclosed by the serpent, with the unknown universe
outside it. This idea of the world without and the world within can
also be taken as a metaphor for the world inside our heads; in other
words, the ouroboros tells us that our minds do not contain the whole
of reality, only a very small portion that we create for ourselves, while
all the time there is a greater reality outside of our being to connect
with.

Going back even further in time than the Gnostics, Plato tells us
in his *Timaeus* about a creature brought to life by the Creator that
sounds very similar to the serpent of the ouroboros:

> The shape he gave it was suitable to its nature . . . Therefore
> he turned it into a rounded spherical shape, with the
> extremes equidistant in all directions from the centre, a figure
> that has the greatest degree of completeness and uniformity,
> as he judged uniformity to be incalculably superior to its
> opposite. And he gave it a perfectly smooth external finish all
> round, for many reasons. For it had no need of eyes, as there
> remained nothing visible outside it, nor of hearing, as there
> remained nothing audible; there was no surrounding air
> which it needed to breathe in, nor was it in need of any organ
> by which to take food into itself or discharge it later after
> digestion. Nothing was taken from it or added to it, for there
> was nothing that could be; for it was designed to supply its
> own nourishment from its own decay and to comprise and
> cause all processes, as its creator thought that it was better

for it to be self-sufficient than dependent on anything else.
He did not think there was any purpose in providing it with
hands as it had no need to grasp anything or defend itself,
nor with feet or any other means of support . . . [he] made
it move with a uniform circular motion on the same spot
and because for its revolution it needed no feet he created it
without feet or legs.

This is an incredible description and sounds remarkably like the earth
itself, especially as the ancients regarded the earth to be self-sustaining.
The ouroboros signifies the endless cycles of the earth as well as hinting
that humankind too is subject to such cycles, as, in fact, is all life.
The ouroboros, then, symbolises the eternal return, the concept that
the universe is never-ending, that all life springs eternal. This idea has
been with us since Ancient Egyptian times, when it was believed that
the scarab beetle, in the form of the god Khepri, rolled the sun across
the sky each day only to enter the mouth of the sky goddess, Nut, and
pass through her body to emerge from her womb as the new day at
dawn. In fact, the concept of the goddess Nut herself can be seen as a
precursor of the ouroboros itself and many depictions of her show her
arched over the earth, echoing the shape of the ouroboros, although
she does not often form a closed circle exactly like it.

The ouroboros is a symbol found worldwide, and there are variants
on the theme in, for example, the Aztec culture of South America,
in Native American art, in China and Japan, in Norse legend and in
India. It is clear that it is a symbol that has been used in almost every
culture, and although it is not certain where it first originated, it
seems to speak to us a universal language of death and rebirth and to
sum up the physical world which we inhabit.

Carl Jung, the renowned psychiatrist, became fascinated by the
ouroboros, and he considered the symbol to be an archetype, a
template that could be used to explain certain processes that occurred
within the human psyche, which would explain why it is found in
many different cultures around the world. He states:

The uroboros is a dramatic symbol for the integration and
assimilation of the opposite, i.e. of the shadow. This 'feed-
back' process is at the same time a symbol of immortality,
since it is said of the uroboros that he slays himself and
brings himself to life, fertilises himself and gives birth to

himself. He symbolises the One, who proceeds from the clash of opposites, and he therefore constitutes the secret of the prima materia which . . . unquestionably stems from man's unconscious.

(The Collected Works of Carl Jung, Vol. 1)

To Jung, the ouroboros represents the true self before the ego has had a chance to alter and defile it.

Furthermore, the ouroboros holds the promise that whether we retain our true sense of self or not, the very matter we are made of will return to where it came from, the process of rebirth and renewal will continue eternally. Even when this world that we inhabit dissolves into the stars and becomes dust, the serpent will still continue to devour its tail; our world will be absorbed into the universe and will be reborn as something new.

SEE ALSO: Alchemy; Gnosticism

PENTAGRAM

The pentagram, a five-pointed star (often drawn in a single movement, without, for example, removing pen from paper), is an ancient and arcane symbol having numerous meanings. Its origins are obscure, although its use can be traced back to Ancient Sumer, where it was used to represent the word 'corner' or 'angle', as well as Ancient Egypt where it was a hieroglyph meaning 'praise', 'worship', 'rise'. However, these five-pointed Sumerian and Egyptian symbols did not have the same connotations that the pentagram has now attained. It is interesting to note that in Ancient Egypt all stars were depicted with five points, although the reason for this is uncertain. One possibility is the pentagram's relationship with the planet Venus: the ancient astronomers noticed that every eight years the planet's movements completed the drawing of a pentagram in the sky.

One of the earliest recorded geometric pentagrams was the work of Pythagoras (c. 580–c. 500 BC), who called the symbol 'health' because he saw it as mathematically perfect, incorporating as it does the golden ratio, the value of which is approximately 1.618. The Pythagorean school drew the pentagram meaning 'health' with the two points at the top – the 'inverted' pentagram that has acquired sinister connotations in modern times. When the Pythagoreans depicted the pentagram with one point uppermost, it became representative of humankind, the point upwards being the head and the other four being the outstretched arms and legs. This representation was seen as highly significant, as not only was five an important number in

174

itself to the Pythagoreans, but it was also the sum of the number two, the feminine aspect, and three, the masculine aspect, which, when combined, created the unity of man and woman. Five was therefore considered the perfect number for humankind.

By the medieval period, the pentagram represented a number of things including the five elements of earth, air, fire, water and quintessence, the divine idea (the essential matter or essence that was present in all things and of which the celestial bodies were thought to be made). This conception of the elements was a belief that had been borrowed from original Pythagorean thinking. In addition to this, the pentagram represented the five wounds of Christ (being the nail wounds to his hands and feet and the spear wound to his side). The fourteenth-century poem *Sir Gawain and the Green Knight* emphasises medieval thinking regarding the pentagram, which is emblazoned on Sir Gawain's shield, stating that, as well as representing the five wounds of Christ, the pentagram signifies the five senses, the five fingers, the five joys of Mary (the Annunciation, Nativity, Resurrection, Ascension and Assumption) and the five knightly virtues of generosity, courtesy, chastity, chivalry and piety.

In Christianity, the pentagram is also symbolic of the Star of Bethlehem, which is always depicted as a five-pointed star. In many cultures and for many centuries, stellar symbolism was familiar and all-encompassing, possessing as it did an innate association with the power of God, the source of life itself. As Freke and Gandy relate in their book *Jesus and the Goddess*, the symbolism of the stars represents one of 'the permanent archetypes of which the world is a mutable expression'. They go on to state that according to Gnostic belief the Star of Bethlehem is symbolic of Jesus's intrinsic nature, the fact that he was incarnated in order to light humankind's way back to heaven. Adrian Gilbert notes in his book *Magi* that the Star of Bethlehem must have an association with Egypt because the Egyptians always depicted stars as five-pointed. On the other hand, Raymond Buckland in *An Illustrated Guide to Magical and Spiritual Symbolism* notes that the pentagram is used to represent the Star of Bethlehem as a result of the pagan concept of the pentagram as a life force.

The use of the pentagram in a Christian context is less common today than it once was, partly because the star has increasingly become associated with black magic and satanism. Thanks to the books of Dennis Wheatley, such as *The Devil Rides Out* and *To the Devil a Daughter*, and the many films that have featured ceremonial magic, the pentagram is probably best known in connection with pagan and magical rites. The pentagram's primary use in magic is as a protection against demons and witches, an association that, as Udo Becker states in *The Continuum Encyclopedia of Symbols*, dates back at least to the medieval period. The function of the pentagram within ritual or low magic is both as a protection and as a means of commanding. It defends the sorcerer from the dark forces that have been conjured up and enables him to order the spirit to obey his will.

The protective aspect of the pentagram is, then, an essential component in the conjuration of spirits. For this purpose, Aleister Crowley recommended the pentagram of Solomon, which, he explains in his book *The Goetia*, is to be used in order 'to preserve thee from danger, and also to command the Spirits by'. To evoke spirits, the pentagram is placed within a circle; the circle and pentagram, as well as the names and symbols that appear within these, are drawn in black. The word 'Tetragammaton', an allusion to the sacred Hebrew name for God, is written in red letters around the outside of the pentagram; the inner pentagon of the pentagram is green, and the five triangular points are blue. Crowley states that the pentagram of Solomon is to be worn on the sorcerer's chest, on a pure white robe and covered by a square of pure linen. Once the entity has been conjured up, the sorcerer is to raise the linen cloth to reveal the pentagram to it, and by this action and by saying certain words, the spirit's obedience will be ensured. A pentagram is also to protect the magical circle of King Solomon, which Crowley explains the sorcerer must use to ensure the entity's compliance, saying, 'by the pentacle of Solomon have I called thee! Give unto me a true answer.'

Probably the most recognised, and contentious, form of the pentagram is the inverted version drawn so that two of its points are uppermost and thus easily identifiable with the horns of Satan, whose face covers the rest of the pentagram. This figure is usually known as the 'Goat of Mendes pentagram'. The inverted pentagram is also thought by some to represent the Devil's footprint. The first such connection between the pentagram and devil worship is generally believed to have been made in the late nineteenth century by Eliphas Lévi, the occult writer and practitioner. The frontispiece of Lévi's 1854 book *Dogma and Ritual of High Magic* features his drawing of a half-goat, half-man entity named Baphomet, which was shown with a pentagram on its forehead. However, despite this portrayal, Baphomet was not an evil being; rather he was associated with the Knights Templar, who supposedly worshipped him. According to Christopher Knight and Robert Lomas in *The Hiram Key*, the mysterious name Baphomet, when rendered into Hebrew and a Hebrew cipher employed, becomes the word 'Sophia', the Greek for wisdom.

Whilst it is certain that the Knights Templar never used the pentagram as one of their symbols, it is known that early Freemasonry incorporated the pentagram into its paraphernalia. Because many of the United States' founding fathers were Freemasons, the pentagram can be seen on the Great Seal of the United States. However, the pentagram is rarely used in Freemasonry today, perhaps as a result of its link to satanism.

In Wicca, an inverted pentagram is not an emblem of evil but a five-fold salute for the second-degree witch, and as Raymond Buckland explains, the symbol indicates the order in which particular points are to be kissed by way of salute: genitals, right breast, left hip, right hip, left breast, genitals. An upright pentagram in witchcraft is associated with life, and is depicted in the Pythagorean way, with a person extended within the star. The 'Star of Knowledge' is also associated with witchcraft and paganism, being a natural pentagram formed by the seeds of an apple when it is cut horizontally.

Henry Lincoln's book *The Holy Place* suggests that an immense pentagram can be found mapped out in the mountains of the Languedoc in France around the village of Rennes-le-Château in the foothills of the Pyrenees. From clues within parchments, on tombstones and in artwork, Henry Lincoln (and David Wood before him in his 1985 book *Genisis*) discovered a natural symmetrical pentagram with its points marked by mountain peaks, three of which are topped with castles. As well as the geological pentagram, which is 15 miles in circumference, there are a number of man-made pentagrams in the region, incorporating villages, towers and natural phenomena, underlining our fascination and on-going relationship with the pentagram.

SEE ALSO: Crowley, Aleister; Gnosticism; Goetia; Lévi, Eliphas; Pythagoras; Wicca

PHILOSOPHER'S STONE

The secrets of the alchemists are veiled behind numerous symbols and strange language. Alchemy, the spiritual aspect of which is often referred to as 'the Great Work', employs the terms 'earth', 'air', 'fire', 'water', 'sulphur', 'mercury' and 'salt'. These, however, are not simply the physical substances; rather, they are the four elements and three principles of alchemy, representing the forces and qualities that lie behind everything in creation. Earth represents things in nature that have cold and dry qualities; air, hot and wet; fire, hot and dry; and, finally, water, cold and wet. As well as working adeptly with these four elements, the alchemist also needs to apply the principles of sulphur and mercury to his experiments. One represents male and the other female, one fixed and the other volatile. In the sixteenth century, Paracelsus added to these a third principle, that of salt. The mastery of the four elements and the three principles would lead the adept ultimately to the prize: the philosopher's stone.

This elusive substance has been identified with Jesus Christ, the elixir of life and the Holy Grail. It represents the force behind all things, the unifying cause, the thing in creation from which all others derive. It was said that once this had been discovered by the alchemist, he would gain immortality. Medieval legends also have it that the stone allowed base metals to be turned into gold. Many believe this to be no more than an allegory for the transmutation of a base human into a purified and perfected being. Aristotle said that 'Nature strives towards Perfection', and this was certainly the goal of the alchemist in his quest for the philosopher's stone.

Down through the centuries, many have been drawn to the search for the philosopher's stone by stories of alchemists creating gold, but true alchemists seem to have looked on this as only a minor by-product of their real work. It is often said that modern chemistry evolved from alchemy, but in fact the alchemical workshops that were set up to produce gold belonged to the 'puffers', or pseudo-alchemists, as opposed to the adepts, who truly wanted to find out the secrets of creation.

The origins of alchemy are lost in antiquity, but the traditions all claim one legendary founder: Hermes Trismegistus. It is from this character that we derive the words hermetic and hermeticism, as applied in Western occultism. He is said to have been the creator of a magical emerald tablet upon which he had embossed the very secrets of creation. Tales of the existence of this object came to Europe via Moorish Spain from around the eighth century onwards. The influence of the Emerald Tablet on Western esotericism is immense and cannot be underestimated. Famous mystics who have translated its wisdom have included Apollonius of Tyana, Albertus Magnus, Roger Bacon, Michael Maier, Sir Isaac Newton, Helena Blavatsky and Fulcanelli. Its philosophical ideas have been applied by alchemists, Kabbalists, Rosicrucians, Freemasons and theosophists.

The tablet almost certainly influenced early legends of the Holy Grail. In the Middle Ages, the kings of Spain possessed an emerald table, as well as a green dish known as the *sacro catino*, which was said to have once belonged to the Queen of Sheba. It was made of emerald or green glass and according to legend was the cup used at the Last Supper. Muslim influences may be present here because the colour green is sacred in Islam, associated with the Prophet Muhammad. It is also the colour associated with Venus, whose holy day is a Friday, which is also the Muslim Sabbath.

In his *Parzival*, Wolfram von Eschenbach, one of the most famous Grail romancers, describes the Holy Grail not as a cup but as a green stone with alchemical powers. This association between the philosopher's stone and the Grail legend gave rise to the tradition that drinking from the Holy Chalice offered the recipient life eternal in the same way that the philosopher's stone did.

The traditions concerning these two elusive, life-giving objects came to Europe during the same period, and one might speculate that the philosopher's stone and the Holy Grail were in fact one and the same.

The Emerald Tablet has been lost to us for centuries. It was publicly displayed within the great library at Alexandria during and following the lifetime of Alexander the Great. Around 2000 years ago, however, it disappeared from the historical record. Copies of the message contained on its surface were made and passed from generation to generation over the centuries. As mentioned earlier, many translations of its contents have been made by famous occultists through the centuries. This version dates from 1620 and carries the title 'Glory of the World, or the Tablet from Heaven':

> It is true, without any error, and it is the sum of truth; that which is above is also that which is below, for the performance of the wonders of a certain one thing, and as all things arise from one Stone, so also they were generated from one common Substance, which includes the four elements created by God. And among other miracles the said Stone is born of the First Matter. The Sun is its Father, the Moon its Mother, the wind bears it in its womb, and it is nursed by the earth. Itself is the Father of the whole earth, and the whole potency thereof. If it be transmuted into earth, then the earth separates from the fire that which is most subtle from that which is hard, operating gently and with great artifice. Then the Stone ascends from earth to heaven, and again descends from heaven to earth, and receives the choicest influences of both heaven and earth. If you can perform this you have the glory of the world, and are able to put to flight all diseases, and to transmute all metals. It overcomes Mercury, which is subtle, and penetrates all hard and solid bodies. Hence it is compared with the world. Hence I am called Hermes, having the three parts of the whole world of philosophy.

For those who can penetrate its depths, the Emerald Tablet contains all the knowledge required for the creation of the philosopher's stone. It also offers an understanding of creation, our place in the 'scheme of things' and, ultimately, the secrets of life eternal. An ancient Sufi dictum provides another way of explaining the message of the tablet:

> Man is the microcosm, creation the macrocosm – the unity. All comes from One. By the joining of the power of contemplation

all can be attained. This essence must be separated from the body first, then combined with the body. This is the Work. Start with yourself, end with all. Before man, beyond man, transformation.

Perhaps, then, the philosopher's stone is ultimately not a physical object at all, but a powerful metaphor for man's eternal craving for meaning and understanding.

SEE ALSO: Alchemy; Fulcanelli; Hermeticism

PYTHAGORAS

If a triangle with two sides forming a right angle has squares drawn out from each of its sides, then the square opposite the right angle will have an area exactly equal to the areas of the squares on the other two sides added together. An easy example is a triangle with sides of 5, 4 and 3 cm. Square the longest side, and you get 25 cm². Now square 4 to get 16 cm² and 3 to get 9 cm² and add them together: 16 + 9 = 25. The Ancient Greek mathematician Pythagoras is credited with having discovered this fact, and generations of young maths students have been taught Pythagoras's theorem, as it is called. Although he is given the credit, the Babylonians in fact discovered the properties of the right-angled triangle hundreds of years before his time. Pythagoras is said to have claimed that he learned that it was advisable always to be truthful from the wise men of Babylon. Presumably they taught him mathematics as well.

Pythagoras was born around 580 BC on the island of Samos off the coast of modern Turkey but emigrated to Croton in southern Italy in or around 531 to escape the tyrant Polycrates. He commanded a great deal of respect for his knowledge, and a group of men and women joined him to form a religious society dedicated particularly to the god Apollo, who was believed to be a highly talented musician. Pythagoras became identified by some with Hyperborean Apollo ('Hyperborean' signifies 'beyond the north wind,' 'where the sun always shines'), and he is said, like the god, to have been adept on the lyre.

PYTHAGORAS

All that we know of Pythagoras's work comes to us second hand at best. We have no works directly written by him so we have to rely on what others tell us. Secrecy surrounded his organisation, though legends grew up around the group. What are we to make, for example, of the story that he believed in the transmigration of souls and as a consequence Pythagoreans decided to become vegetarians, since they did not want to eat any of their old friends who had been reborn as animals? The logic of the idea is obvious enough, but we cannot be sure whether the tale is true. Until the middle of the nineteenth century, a person who did not eat meat was termed a Pythagorean. It has been said that Pythagoras's followers also eschewed beans as a foodstuff, since they thought they contained the embryos of unborn people. If you open a bean pod and use your imagination, you can see how the idea came about.

The religion of the Pythagoreans was based on a desire to become purified and attain a higher state, among the gods. They practised abstinence, believing that the physical body was a tomb for the soul (itself a flawed immortal), which was destined to return repeatedly to earth after death, inhabiting a human, animal or plant – hence the dietary restrictions. After all, a leg of lamb may look good to eat, but that lamb could just contain another human soul! Purification, however, could release the soul from its corruptible prison in a mortal body and, unrestricted by earthly bonds, it would become truly immortal. One could facilitate this purification by gaining an understanding of how the world is ordered and fully complying with these natural laws.

It may not be wholly coincidental that Gautama Siddhartha, the Buddha, was born on the Nepalese–Indian border within years of Pythagoras in Greece and the latter had visited Egypt, which had trade links with India. Could it be that some of the Buddha's wisdom came to be incorporated in Pythagoras's teaching?

Perhaps inevitably, given their search for immortality, it seems that the Pythagorean religious practices had a great deal in common with mystery religions, cults whose initiates sought to ensure a happy afterlife. Pythagoreans are reported to have taken part in the Orphic mysteries, which were tied up with their religious convictions. The legendary Orpheus was not only a poet but also, significantly, a musician, who had descended into the underworld in an attempt to rescue his beloved wife, Euridice. Among the powers of Orpheus was the ability to tame wild animals by playing the lyre. Since

Pythagoreans knew that harmonious music was linked to numbers and mathematics, and they also believed that numbers were the basis for everything, their devotion to Orpheus is understandable. We can also see a connection between the Pythagorean belief in immortality and Orpheus's descent into and return from Hades. Another link with Pythagoras's philosophy is that his favoured god, Apollo, was reputed to have taught Orpheus his musical skills. According to some versions of the legend, Apollo was Orpheus's father.

Early mathematicians were very interested in divination by the use of numerology, and Pythagoras was no exception. Numbers could be used to tell fortunes, assess character and forecast the future. Today, however, most mathematicians regard this practice as nothing but pseudo-science. Pythagoras believed that everything in the world around us is based on numbers, and he is said to have been fascinated by the number ten, which is the sum of the first four integers, one, two, three and four. Ten was referred to as 'the sacred decad' and given the mystical name 'tetraktys'. Study was also made of so-called perfect numbers, those which are the sum of their divisors (for example: 6 = 1 + 2 + 3). Pythagoras is credited with the theory that everything can be expressed numerically. He realised that the main intervals in the musical scale are linked to numerical ratios. Although the name of Pythagoras is inevitably linked with geometry as a result of his famous theorem, it was another aspect of mathematics, arithmetic, which was important in many of his theories. His ideas influenced later philosophers such as Plato (born *c.* 427 BC).

More broadly, Pythagoreans believed that the soul was located in the brain, and also that the interaction of opposites held the world together. Examples of the Pythagorean table of opposites include male–female, left–right, straight–curved and one–many. This world-view runs totally counter to the Kabbalist notion that pairs are dangerous, linked to evil, while one represents God.

Some of the theories of the followers of Pythagoras have re-emerged in later religions. To give only some examples from heretical Christianity, we have Manichaeism, a belief first proposed by Mani, a third-century Persian who taught dualism and believed that the world arose out of the opposites darkness and light. The Zoroastrian religion clearly coloured Mani's thinking, for it saw the world as the scene of a constant struggle between the forces of good and evil. In the Middle Ages, influenced in their turn by these ideas, there arose groups known by various names such as Bogomils, Paulicians and Cathars that proved very serious challengers to the orthodox Christian churches, which fought to exterminate them with extreme ruthlessness and cruelty.

Their chief crime was to believe that the Devil had similar powers to God and that the world was controlled by the Evil One. For this reason, they believed in living virtuous, simple lives, praying, being truthful, fasting and working hard and treating women as equals, but they looked upon the corrupt Church as part of the Devil's realm. They tried to live as they thought Christ would wish. Without the seed of the philosophy of Pythagoras, they might never have existed.

Uncertainty about what precisely the Pythagoreans believed is compounded by the fact that some of his followers peddled their own ideas as those of Pythagoras to give them more weight and authority. However, it is believed that by around 500 BC the Pythagoreans had arrived at the conclusion that the world is a sphere, which they believed to be at the centre of the universe – a view that was still prevalent two millennia later. Their study of the way in which nature works developed into a religion which gained great political influence for a time in Italy, although the Pythagoreans tried to distance themselves from political activism at least until after their leader's death.

Pythagoras was forced to leave Croton when political unrest erupted, and he lived out his life at Metapontum on the Gulf of Taranto, Italy. After his death (*c.* 500 BC), his followers kept faith with his ideas, but they suffered persecution, indulged in internal squabbles and were forced to disperse. The fame of Pythagoras has persisted throughout the ages and his image (or at least his imagined portrait) has appeared in philosophical works, on ancient coins and on modern postage stamps. His influence on early history was incalculable, which is ironic if all can be explained by numbers!

SEE ALSO: Divination; Kabbalah; Numerology

REMOTE VIEWING

Humans are generally believed to have five senses: hearing, sight, smell, touch and taste. There are those who believe that it is also possible to 'see' things which exist or are happening which the normal senses could not be expected to detect, that there is a type of sixth sense. This is often known as remote viewing (RV). It allows a person to know what is happening inside high-security buildings, under the earth or sea, or even on other planets. It is supposed to be a controlled use of the powers of extrasensory perception in which specific techniques are applied in order to view particular objects or happenings.

Cynics will dismiss the idea out of hand. In the twenty-first century, we are conditioned by our education and by convention to accept only what we experience in our everyday lives and what we are taught is the truth. Unorthodox beliefs are not encouraged by society; those who think 'outside the box' may well be dangerous cranks. We are programmed to reject the suggestion that there may exist a reality with which our five senses are unfamiliar. Yet millions accept that Christ rose from the dead, that God spoke to Moses from the burning bush, and still others that the Prophet Muhammad once made a journey to the heavens and back, and other such miraculous happenings. These events are hardly experiences which can be thought of as normal, yet many believe in their truth.

Max Weber (1864–1920), a leading German sociologist, argued that in modern times we have lost our sense of mystery and magic.

We no longer believe in any reality that goes beyond our mundane experience. He thought that this applied particularly to the Western world as opposed to the East, largely as a result of the different prevailing religions in those areas. In Western civilisation today, magic is generally thought of simply as the tricks performed by stage or television entertainers, and the spiritual realm is connected simply with ghosts. These are much easier concepts to grasp than the idea that a person might have the psychic powers to experience extraordinary phenomena. The ability to remotely view is a gift claimed by a few but rejected as an impossibility by the vast majority. Yet even governments have been persuaded that there might be something of value in the concept.

For around 20 years, the intelligence services in the USA funded research into gathering information by such unconventional means, variously termed clairvoyance, RV or psychic spying. Had this been entirely successful, it could have developed to a stage where Iraq's 'weapons of mass destruction' might have been proved a fantasy, and billions of dollars and thousands of lives might have been saved as a result.

Joseph McMoneagle has been called the most renowned remote viewer in the United States. In 1979, the US Army gave him map coordinates and instructed him to report what his RV ability showed him. Focusing on the target in a deep meditative state, he began to see buildings and the sea. Then, having been shown a photograph of the site, he could make out welding being carried out in a building, and over a short time it became obvious that the Soviet Union was carrying out repairs to and construction of submarines there. While many in authority were understandably sceptical about the information McMoneagle provided, a few months later satellite photographs confirmed the authenticity of his vision. He has since gone on to use his special powers to perform such services as tracing missing persons. It is not unknown for police forces in various parts of the world to ask people who claim the gift of RV, dowsing or other extrasensory powers to assist them in investigating intractable cases.

The famous 'spoon-bender' Uri Geller has claimed that information from a remote viewer in the USA led to the discovery of Saddam Hussein's hiding place after Iraq was invaded and his regime overthrown. Geller claims to have worked for the Central Intelligence Agency during the Cold War and still to have contacts able and apparently willing to pass on such intriguing claims to him.

Remote viewing is closely related to telepathy, which is mind-to-mind communication. When the communication is mind-to-object, this is termed telecognition. Many of us have seen demonstrations of telepathy in which two persons, remote from each other and apparently using only their special powers, are able to transmit information about playing cards or words in books, for instance, chosen at random by an audience. We may believe that this is genuine RV or alternatively dismiss it as a clever trick. Yet when it is demonstrated that a remote viewer can detect an object hidden by a totally unconnected party in a distant place and describe that object accurately, our natural scepticism may be disturbed.

In a 2005 article in *Mind Power News*, Dr Leanna Standish of Bastyr University in Seattle admitted that she could not explain why telepathy, or 'distant neural signalling', fails in some cases but works in others. She does, however, believe, on the evidence of experiments she has conducted, that the phenomenon exists.

Many people who are owned by cats will have noticed that their pets seem to detect that their humans are planning to go on holiday even before suitcases are packed or transportation boxes taken from storage for a trip to the cattery. Disturbed and moody behaviour marks the pet's disapproval. It may well be more than coincidence or an innate ability to read human body language. Animals seem to have certain abilities which may be dismissed as instinct, but which might just be telepathic ability of a kind which most humans cannot access.

The human mind normally seems to run along channels which do not allow access to the occult. If it is freed from its usual constraints, however, it can experience things outside the normal. This is termed a psychedelic experience, and there are ways in which those who wish to participate in such matters might attempt to alter their mind state, by sensory deprivation, for instance, or by the use of drugs. It may be that outside our own perception of reality there is another place that certain people can reach. From that vantage point, they can perceive objects and occurrences remote from their physical being.

As this book was being written, the BBC reported that in 2002, during the build-up to the invasion of Iraq, the British Ministry of Defence commissioned trials of remote viewing. Volunteers were given sealed envelopes and their success in 'reading' the images contained within the envelopes was measured. It seems that 28 per cent of those tested gave a reasonably close account of the contents, but that this was not considered sufficient to make further investigations worthwhile. It seems that the defence of the nation will not be conducted by remote viewing, and a spokesperson for the MoD said, 'The study concluded that remote viewing theories had little value to the MoD and was taken no further.'

ROMAN MYSTERY CULTS

The Roman authorities generally had a fairly relaxed attitude towards the wide variety of religions practised throughout their empire. Provided that people obeyed the laws and paid their taxes, they were generally free to worship in their own way. The Romans even made special arrangements to accommodate the Jews. It was only when religion led to dissidence – as in the time of the Jewish Revolts, or when troublesome Christians refused to acknowledge and sacrifice to the 'genius of the emperor' or fought among themselves or against non-believers – that the state came down hard and persecution arose.

As the Empire expanded, the importation of 'foreign' religion became less controversial as old Republican values declined, non-Italians became senators and emperors were no longer made in Rome. However, seriously odd characters such as the emperor Elagabalus (r. AD 218–22), who was of Syrian origin and who imported a sacred stone into Rome with disastrous consequences for himself and his mother, found that tolerance was not absolute. After establishing worship of the Syrian god Baal, Elagabalus participated in homosexual orgies, cross-dressed and was eventually murdered by the Praetorian Guard. Mother and son were dumped into the River Tiber after being dragged through the streets by the mob, an indignity commonly inflicted on the corpses of criminals in the capital city. The stone seems to have been returned to Emesa in Syria. It was better to pay token respect, at least, to the traditional gods and to keep your own particular religion separate, so that no offence was caused.

Mystery religions (sometimes referred to simply as mysteries) spread from the East and from Greece throughout the Roman Empire, offering to reward adherents with immortality. Secret initiation ceremonies made new converts feel special; being made party to hidden truths about which the man in the street knew little or nothing lent the believer a sense of superiority. Orthodox Graeco-Roman religion, on the other hand, had the defect of not promising a happy afterlife to its adherents. The prospect of a heavenly reward was a major factor in the spread of Christianity, which was itself a mystery religion, having its own initiation rites, incantations, prayers, ceremonies and particular beliefs.

Mithraism was a widespread mystery cult that was particularly popular among the Roman military, merchants and high-ranking officials, who were very influential. Mithraic temples, often subterranean, were built in imitation of the cave in which, symbolising the triumph of life over death and good over evil, the god Mithras had caught and killed a divine bull. Some of these temples still exist, gloomy and totally unlike other ancient temples in that the rites were carried out indoors rather than outside, which was not the case in most places of worship. Benches lined the walls of the long narrow room, and a depiction of the bull being killed by Mithras, generally wearing a Phrygian cap, perhaps to symbolise his Eastern origins, was on the wall opposite the entrance. Other deities related to Mithraism, the protectors of the seven grades of initiates into the mysteries, might also be portrayed.

Mithras was originally a god worshipped in Persia (modern Iran); he reached a peak of popularity in the Roman Empire in the third century AD, and his cult was open only to men. It involved wearing special clothing and undergoing a kind of baptism, perhaps involving bull's blood. The religion had developed from Zoroastrianism, and, although his worship took place in dark temples, Mithras came to be thought of as a solar deity. The Romans sometimes identified him with Sol Invictus, 'the Unconquerable Sun', and celebrated his birthday on 25 December, when the sun begins its return to strength. It is no coincidence that this should also be chosen as the date on which Christ's birth would be celebrated, as the early Christians adopted several aspects of pagan worship and incorporated them into their own religion. Mithras was a god who came to earth, had a miraculous birth, was a saviour, had disciples, was buried and rose from the dead, and promised immortality to those who believed in him, among other similarities with Jesus. How much of this is coincidental is debatable.

Perhaps the best known of the ancient mystery cults was centred on the Greek city of Eleusis, which lies about 14 miles west of Athens. The original Hall of Initiation used in the Eleusinian mysteries, the Telestrion, was erected before 1000 BC, suggesting that this cult must pre-date most, if not all, of the mysteries adhered to in Roman times. For centuries, Eleusis belonged to its powerful neighbour, and the Athenians built the Eleusinion, a temple below the Acropolis. Worshippers would process, carrying cultic objects, from the temple to Eleusis, celebrating their mysteries. Since it was a religion based on secret knowledge, little is known of what took place, but it seems that the legends involving Persephone and Demeter were central to the cult. Demeter was the goddess of grain – a seed which has the appearance of a dead thing, from which life nonetheless arises – and was associated with death and happy rebirth.

The Roman emperor Hadrian was initiated into the Eleusinian mysteries in AD 128. It is also known that the great Marcus Aurelius and his worthless son and successor Commodus (portrayed in the film *Gladiator*) were both initiated in AD 176. Interestingly, it appears that Nero was refused the honour. While visiting the sacred precinct at Eleusis, Nero heard a priest warn that all unpurified sinners must leave or risk the punishment of the gods. The emperor, who was responsible for the violent deaths of both his mother and his wife, exited!

Another major cult was that of Bacchus, the Latin name for Dionysus, a nature God especially associated with wine and ecstasy. Legend had it that the men of Athens had dishonoured the cult of the god and were punished with impotence. Pentheus, King of Thebes, was, it is said, torn to pieces for attempting to spy on the activities of the bacchantes as they were conducting their orgiastic rites. Stories had it that it was women, in flagrant defiance of normal custom, who left their homes and loved ones and joined in the orgies attendant on the drunken dancing and revelry, receiving occult powers as they did so. Dionysus was said to possess the gift of prophecy, and in Thrace an oracle spoke under his influence, while in Phocis he had a shrine where the sick went to be healed. Plutarch tells us that the priests at Delphi put him nearly on a par with the great Apollo.

In 186 BC, the Roman Senate decreed that private worship of Bacchus was unacceptable; it was officially suppressed and Bacchic sanctuaries were destroyed. However, the bacchanalian rituals remained popular, especially in southern Italy, where many of the inhabitants were of Greek origin. The Romans identified their traditional god Liber Pater, a fertility god with a cult centre on the Aventine Hill, with Bacchus. As the Greek Dionysus, Bacchus had descended into the underworld and returned. By the second century AD, not only was he the god of wine but he had also become associated with a life after death. Followers of Bacchus believed that he was important to their hopes of an afterlife, and by this time they numbered in the thousands. Sarcophagi began to be decorated with scenes of Bacchus as the lord of life and as an agricultural deity.

Only five years before the Bacchic sanctuaries were outlawed, the sacred black stone of the goddess Cybele, also known as Magna Mater, or 'the Great Mother', was placed in a temple on the Palatine Hill. There were other shrines to her in Rome, and though her worship was at first viewed with suspicion by some Romans, the Emperor Claudius supported it, and it became an official part of the state religion. Her cult was of Anatolian origin. She was the mother of all things, a goddess of fertility and of nature, and she was accompanied by lions. She could, like the Egyptian goddess Sekhmet, both cause and cure sickness. Cult followers were able to reach a point of such ecstasy that they could no longer feel pain, and in that state they were gifted with the ability to prophesy. It has been argued that the adoration of the Virgin Mary has much in common with that of Magna Mater and that the form of Christianity called Gnosticism incorporated elements of her cult.

Another mystery cult originating in Greece was Orphism, and it too particularly appealed to the Greeks of southern Italy. Orpheus had descended into the underworld to try to rescue his dead wife, the nymph Euridice, in which he was almost successful, having charmed the god Hades with his music, at which he was accomplished. (Roman art depicting Orpheus playing music in order to tame wild animals can still be seen.) However, he looked back before he reached the light, which he had been warned not to do, and Euridice was lost forever. Yet he had shown that it was possible to go to death and return to life. The myth of Dionysus, who had also returned from Hades, was also significant in Orphism. The cult was concerned with the conflict of good and evil, with death and resurrection, and with proper retribution for the wicked in the underworld. The good, on the other hand, might hope to go after death to the Isles of the Blessed. An initiate's chances of experiencing this happy outcome would be enhanced by refraining from killing and eating animals. Followers of the prescribed regime of self-denial believed that while the physical body was evil, the soul could be divine.

Worship of the Egyptian goddess Isis, wife of Osiris, god of the dead, was another foreign import which spread widely among the Romans during the first century AD. This too was a mystery religion, requiring devotees to undergo initiation. The goddess was usually accompanied at these ceremonies by Anubis (the jackal-headed god of the underworld), Harpocrates (the Roman name for Horus, god of the sky) and Serapis (a compound deity combining aspects of the powerful gods Osiris and Apis). Harpocrates and Serapis, together with Isis, symbolised creative power. Isis was identified with Aphrodite by many Greeks, though others may have associated her with Demeter. Her special interests included marriage and fertility, and depictions of her with her baby son are incredibly similar to Christian images of the Virgin and Child. Isis, often recognisable by the special knot in the shape of the ankh, the hieroglyph for 'life', holding her robe together, and by the crescent moon or horns on her crown, could grant life eternal to the initiates of her mystery.

SEE ALSO: Gnosticism

ROSICRUCIANISM

The Rosicrucian Order was most likely founded at the start of the seventeenth century, although it claimed much earlier origins. It was an esoteric society formed with the intention of bringing about a change in European civilisation, of creating a more perfect human society based on hermetic values and alchemical teachings. The Rosicrucians were a Christian order but they had more occult leanings and were rather more mystical than traditional Christian societies. They were also an intellectual group, obsessed as much with the arts and sciences as with religion and philosophy.

The Rosicrucian Manifestos, the canon of Rosicrucian texts, are comprised of three works. The first was published in 1614, and is called the *Fama Fraternitatis*. Printed first as an appendix to another text, in Kassel in Germany, it was later published in its own right. It was circulated throughout Europe and was intended to proclaim the existence of the Rosicrucians to the intellectual elite of the Western world. This first document tells of a mysterious character named Father C.R. (referred to in later texts as Father C.R.C.) and explains his initiation into arcane knowledge and the establishment of a secret order known as the Fraternity of the Rose Cross.

The second document of the Manifestos, known as the *Confessio Fraternitatis*, appeared the following year, again in Germany. Published as a pamphlet throughout Europe, it declared that a secret brotherhood of alchemists existed who intended to bring about a reformation of mankind, a process which it claimed had already begun, a new age having been signalled by certain natural phenomena, one of which was the appearance of new stars in the night sky.

Finally, the work which forms the last leg of the famed tripod of the Rosicrucian Manifestos is *The Chymical Wedding of Christian Rosenkreutz* (published 1616), a text that tells a strange and complex alchemical story featuring the supposed founder of the Rosicrucians.

According to the Manifestos, Rosenkreutz, the Father C.R. of the *Fama Fraternitatis*, was a German born in the fourteenth century who travelled to the Middle East and learned of an important and sacred tradition of knowledge. He is said to have founded the 'Fraternity of the Rose Cross' upon his return to Europe. The prime mission of the fraternity seems to have been to cure the sick, and to this end all the members were devoted. This gift of healing was seen in the order as coming directly from God and was held in the highest esteem. Intriguingly, the Manifestos state that Rosenkreutz wished that knowledge of the fraternity should remain secret for 100 years. Perhaps this is just a convenient fabrication, for 130 years after the date given for the death of Christian Rosenkreutz, the Manifestos were made public and the silence was broken.

The symbol of the Rosicrucians, enshrined in their very name, was the Rose (or Rosy) Cross, usually represented as a traditional cross with a rose at its centre. It was a powerful icon, rich in alchemical symbolism, that seems primarily to have represented salvation to the Rosicrucians.

What is intriguing is that in the Rosicrucian Manifestos we find reference to new stars appearing, the presence of which seems to symbolise the beginning of a new age. One of these stars appeared in the constellation of Cygnus, the swan:

> . . . yea, the Lord God hath already sent before certain messengers, which should testify his will, to wit, some new stars, which do appear and are seen in the firmament in Serpentario and Cygno, which signify and give themselves known to everyone, that they are powerful Signacula of great weighty matters.

Cygnus is also commonly known as the Northern Cross, and is one of the most recognisable constellations in the northern hemisphere. As

Cygnus, it is seen as a swan with outstretched wings, swimming in the middle of the luminescent stream of the Milky Way. The swan has often been used as a symbol for the agony and death of Christ on the Cross, so it is interesting that the Northern Cross should be associated with Cygnus and especially that a new star in Cygnus should act as a sign to the Rosicrucians that their order should begin and a new age be ushered in. Therefore the question arises, is the symbol of the Rose Cross linked closely here with the Northern Cross of the constellation Cygnus? Did the Rosicrucians see the Northern Cross in the sky as the true Rosy Cross and is this why the appearance of a new star in its midst was so significant? While there is not enough evidence as yet to reach a conclusion, it is worth noting that there is an abundance of red and orange stars in Cygnus. In fact, this region of the heavens contains more red and orange stars than any other part of the night sky and Agnes Mary Clerke, the Victorian astronomer, wrote that this region of the sky contained 'perhaps the most lovely effect of colour in the heavens'. Could it be that Cygnus was the Rosy Cross of the secret society?

Whatever their origins, the Rosicrucians became one of the most talked about esoteric institutions in Europe, and even today their influence is still felt. At the time the Rosicrucian Manifestos were printed, many thought that the group was a fiction, a ghost order created by a handful of individuals as a hoax, nothing more than a charade. However, this didn't stop the Rosicrucians becoming a sensation. By 1622, some 400 books and documents had been published discussing the contents of the Manifestos.

Today, Rosicrucianism still exists, though whether its lineage can truly be traced back to the original founders is debated. According to certain documents released between 1618 and 1710, the Rosicrucians fled Europe during this period for the Middle East, where Christian Rosenkreutz first found his sacred knowledge. Later, to fill this void, many Rosicrucian societies sprang up declaring that they were true offshoots of the original order. While these groups were certainly inspired by the works of the Rosicrucians c.1614, it is unknown whether any of them are actually direct descendants of the original society. That we may never know the answer is hardly surprising when we consider the secrecy surrounding the order; the founding Rosicrucians – who, according to the Manifestos, numbered no more than eight at the outset – referred to themselves and their order as 'the College of Invisibles'.

However authentic they may be, the modern Rosicrucians follow the philosophy outlined in the Manifestos and later documents and still uphold the values of the original order, attempting to add more esoteric teachings to the lessons of Christ and to bring about a more altruistic and caring society that is based on hermetic teachings as well as those found in the Bible. Whether Christian Rosenkreutz was real or imagined, the legacy left to us in his name lives on today.

SEE ALSO: Alchemy; *Chymical Wedding, The*

ST GERMAIN, COUNT OF

This mysterious gentleman has long been the subject of so many legends that it is virtually impossible to separate fact from fiction or to be certain of the details of his birth or death. He is thought to have been, among many other things, an alchemist, an inventor and scientist, a composer and violinist, a courtier and also an occultist.

Rumour had it that his mother was the widow of King Charles II of Spain or that his father was an exiled Transylvanian prince. The truth may be more mundane, as he was not given to revealing much about his background. He is recorded to have been in London in 1743 and in Edinburgh three years later, when he was temporarily detained on suspicion of being a Jacobite spy. St Germain was well enough connected to meet famous and influential men such as Jean-Jacques Rousseau and Horace Walpole. The latter was of the opinion that he was mad. Walpole also described something of the confusion surrounding St Germain: 'The other day they seized an odd man who goes by the name of the Count of St. Germain . . . he sings and plays on the violin wonderfully, is mad and not very sensible.' Walpole relates that he was perhaps a priest, a fiddler or a great noble, hailing from Spain, or Poland or Italy. The famous libertine Casanova believed that St Germain was really a violinist named Catalini.

He returned to France and made himself very popular with some friends by giving gifts of precious diamonds. He claimed to have the ability, which he was prepared to have put to the test, to make fabulous dyes, which would produce colours of tremendous depth and quality. St Germain rubbed shoulders with the King of France, Louis XV, and his mistress Madame de Pompadour, and was a popular guest, though he never ate in public, preferring instead to make witty conversation. His youthful appearance, despite the great age he hinted at, he put down to a diet containing a large percentage of oatmeal and to an abstemious lifestyle. St Germain did nothing to discourage the rumour that he was hundreds of years old, and indeed he fuelled it by displaying a tremendous knowledge of history.

A coup in Russia set the redoubtable Catherine the Great on the throne on 9 July 1762, at which time St Germain was alleged to have been in St Petersburg. He was later credited with having masterminded the conspiracy. After disappearing from the public eye for several years, he claimed the title Count Tsarogy while in Bavaria. Then, in Germany, he went under the name Chevalier Welldone, making a living selling wines and liqueurs while diversifying into chemical processes. He claimed to be able to transmute base metal into gold. He admitted, when asked, that he was once a Freemason, though, extraordinarily for one claiming so many talents, abilities and knowledge, he stated that he had forgotten their signs. It was at this time that he actually made a comparison between himself and God, a little like John Lennon's famous 'bigger than Jesus' gaffe a couple of centuries later. Adulation can easily go to the head.

The death of this confidence trickster, if that is all he was, is thought to have occurred in 1784. At that time, he was a guest of Prince Karl of Hesse-Kassel, Governor of Schleswig-Holstein. The prince had Masonic interests and was an occultist, and as a consequence of their shared interests, the two men studied chemistry and made medicines available to the poor, though whether these were truly efficacious is unknown. Prince Karl referred to St Germain as the greatest philosopher who ever lived. The prince was absent when his friend died, but a doctor was present. Astonishingly, since his death is supposed to have been witnessed, he was a representative at a Freemasons' gathering in 1785, there were purported sightings of him in 1835 and 1867, and theosophists (those believing in the wisdom of the divine and the 'eternal truth') claimed to have met him as late as 1926 and 1930.

Theosophists have named St Germain a Mahatma, one who has the power to influence the spiritual growth of others and consequently to benefit civilisations. Whatever view we may take of such matters, it illustrates the great impact St Germain made during his lifetime, although, of course, it is not entirely easy to speak of his 'lifetime' since there are those who believe that he possessed the elixir of life, or that he was the immortal Wandering Jew. If this were true, it would explain how he has been able to appear from time to time over a period of centuries.

There are new-age believers who credit him with the design of the Great Seal of the United States of America and claim that he inspired the Declaration of Independence and the US Constitution. He may well have been a master of ventriloquism and have had the ability to charm snakes, both gifts he has been credited with which are not exactly unique, but what are we to make of his supposed powers of telepathy, teleportation and levitation, or his facility for walking through walls?

His talents seem to have been almost limitless if we are to believe the stories told of him. Casanova apparently gave him a silver coin, which, a few moments later, St Germain returned to its owner transmuted into gold. He could, it was said, fuse a group of small diamonds into one large and consequently more valuable stone. Louis XV owned a flawed diamond which the Count made perfect, which was no doubt one very good reason why he was in favour with the French monarch.

Much ink has been expended on speculation about St Germain. The mystic Max Heindel wrote that the Count was the latest incarnation of Christian Rozenkreutz, founder of the Rosicrucian Order, who was himself said to be a reincarnation of the biblical Lazarus. Rosenkreutz had founded the fraternity after having imbibed secret wisdom from Arab sources. Alice A. Bailey, in *The Externalisation of the Hierarchy*, argued that St Germain is a 'Lord of Civilization', influencing his devotees to bring about the Age of Aquarius. She prophesies that sometime after the year 2025, Jesus, St Germain and other 'Masters' will return to earth with their disciples. Students of the religious movement I AM are taught that Jesus talks to them and that one of his messages is that St Germain has continued what he began two millennia ago. I AM students believe that both Jesus and St Germain are 'Ascended Masters' and have become immortal.

Finally, for those seeking a tangible link with the Count of St Germain, the recipe for his elixir, which he left us: it is an infusion of elderflower, fennel and senna pods, which you do not need to be a pharmacist to recognise is a pretty efficient laxative.

SEE ALSO: Alchemy; Rosicrucianism

SATANISM

'**S**atanism' is an umbrella term for a number of belief systems, many of them ancient, some of them relatively modern; however the word always has the same connotation: that the believer worships and reveres Satan himself. The stereotypical image we have of a satanist is of someone who has totally debased himself, who has abandoned all good and chosen to live by a code of evil – the complete opposite of everything that is wholesome and benevolent. Satanists feature regularly in the media, and the image is usually of sadistic child-killers, of people who prey on the rest of society and have no compunction or conscience whatsoever – people who have given themselves utterly to a god of darkness and evil. However, as we will see, this stereotype is very far from the truth about satanism.

In religions where the chief deity really is Satan, it must be stated that this is very rarely the same Satan that we find in Christian literature. One of the earliest written accounts of Satan is in the Avesta, a collection of Zoroastrian texts, where he is known as Ahriman. These works are thought to have had a profound influence on the development of Judaism. In the Avesta and in the early Judaeo-Christian tradition, Satan is not simply the embodiment of evil but rather an entity that God created to act in opposition to him. In other words, rather than being purely evil, he represents free choice and the potential to choose an alternative path. In Christianity and Judaism, this idea seems to have been corrupted, and Satan has come to be seen as a fallen angel; in this way, the inconvenience of the existence of a deity in opposition to God is removed at a stroke.

A lot of groups branded satanists are not what we might expect and have been misunderstood, while others actually do worship Satan and set him above all other gods, though, as we will see, even this is not what it might seem. Standing firmly in the camp of the former are the Setians, who loathe the misconception that they worship Satan. In fact, they worship the Ancient Egyptian god Set, also known as Seth, whom they consider to be the prime god in their pantheon. Though they acknowledge that Seth's name is behind the word 'Satan', they speak of a very different god to the Satan of the Bible, referring instead to the Seth we know through the texts of Ancient Egypt, who, while a dark and powerful god, was not seen as an evil god by the Egyptians – at least, not until much later, when Osiris became the chief god of Egypt and Seth was viewed as his murderer.

Setianism is a religion which follows the so-called left-hand path, the alternative route to spiritual enlightenment that does not preclude the initiate from using some of the darker forces in the universe, unlike many of the religions that follow the right-hand path, such as Christianity and Islam. The left-hand path is followed by those religions and belief systems that focus on the individualism of the believer; rather than preaching that the practitioner should become one with the universe or a higher god (as, for example, Buddhism or Taoism do), this alternative view teaches that true salvation lies in developing the individuality and encouraging separateness from nature. Rather than destroying the ego, as some right-hand-path religions teach, it should be nourished and developed. Of course, many have argued that such distinctions are merely academic and have no place in real life, that, for example, if the concept of yin and yang (or whatever we want to call it) demonstrates that without balance nothing at all would exist, then what is needed to reach enlightenment and spiritual satisfaction is not a left- or right-hand path but a mixture of the two.

A modern religion that demonstrates the principles of the left-hand path more than adequately is the Church of Satan, a religion that has at its core a set of beliefs that are in complete opposition to right-hand-path faiths such as Christianity and Confucianism. The Church of Satan was formed in 1966 by Anton Szandor LaVey, a former circus performer and musician. In 1969, he wrote *The Satanic Bible*, the book on which the canon of the Church of Satan is based. At its core stand the 'Nine Satanic Statements', which demonstrate quite clearly how opposed to the right-hand path this religion is:

1. Satan represents indulgence instead of abstinence!
2. Satan represents vital existence instead of spiritual pipe dreams!
3. Satan represents undefiled wisdom instead of hypocritical self-deceit!
4. Satan represents kindness to those who deserve it instead of love wasted on ingrates!
5. Satan represents vengeance instead of turning the other cheek!
6. Satan represents responsibility to the responsible instead of concern for psychic vampires!
7. Satan represents man as just another animal, sometimes better, more often worse than those that walk on all-fours, who, because of his 'divine spiritual and intellectual development', has become the most vicious animal of all!
8. Satan represents all of the so-called sins, as they all lead to physical, mental, or emotional gratification!
9. Satan has been the best friend the Church has ever had, as He has kept it in business all these years!

According to LaVey, quoted from the Church of Satan's own documents, this is what he hoped to achieve in the founding of this new Church:

> We blended a formula of nine parts social respectability to one part outrage. We established a *Church* of Satan – something that would smash all concepts of what a 'church' was supposed to be. This was a temple of indulgence to openly defy the temples of abstinence that had been built up until then. We didn't want it to be an unforgiving, unwelcoming place, but a place where you could go to have fun.

Rather than fitting the stereotypical image, the Church of Satan preaches that all life is sacred, especially those of children and animals, and that nothing should be done that would harm another individual. We find this from their own website, in an address to younger readers:

If you have read our books, you know that Satanism isn't about taking drugs, and it isn't about harming animals or children. Unlike many religions and philosophies, Satanism respects and exalts life. Children and animals are the purest expressions of that life force, and as such are held sacred and precious in the eyes of the Satanist. Besides, it is very un-Satanic to take any creature's life against its will. It is equally un-Satanic to cloud your brain and impair your judgment with mind-altering substances. A real magician has no need of those kinds of things, as he should be able to bring about changes in consciousness by the very power of his Will and imagination.

Therefore, while on the face of it the Church of Satan might seem an evil institution, the truth appears to be rather different, and not at all what we might expect. Furthermore, here we have a group set up simply to oppose the restrictive religious traditions of Christianity, Judaism, Islam and other right-hand-path religions and to explore what it means to be individual and to worship that uniqueness. In fact, it must be said that if we did not have such a history of dominance of these right-hand-path faiths in the West, then it is very likely that the Church of Satan would not have been born. Returning once again to this idea of cosmic balance, one could say that it is in fact a necessity – that we cannot have one without the other. Whenever one religion tries to repress people, others will spring up which preach the opposite.

That is not to say that there are not satanists out there who practise everything that we abhor and are repelled by and would live up to our preconceptions of what satanism is. They certainly do exist and might well match our idea of what a devil-worshipper would be like, but, thankfully, they seem to be a very small minority. Furthermore, we must not forget that most evil in the world is done not in the name of Satan, but in the names of other gods and principles that set themselves far above Satan and satanism, yet cause just as much harm and destruction, if not more, than Satan could ever contrive.

SEE ALSO: Fallen Angels; Taoism

SHAMANISM

Shamanism has existed, and still exists, across many cultures around the world and, along with animism, can claim to be the most ancient form of religion. There is some evidence that even Neanderthals may have had their shamans, and the rock art of early *Homo sapiens* has been interpreted as being associated with shamanistic ritual. Bronze Age carvings on cave walls in Sweden show winged human figures that may represent shamans travelling to the spirit world.

A shaman performs the important task of linking those people who live in the everyday world with the spiritual realms, which only those with special knowledge and powers can access. 'Shaman' ('one who knows') is derived from a Siberian word which the Tungus people use to describe a person connected with mystical spiritual acts, and the term has come to be applied to those who perform such rituals across the continents. The religion of the Tungus was shamanistic until they came under the rule of the Soviet Russians.

In their article 'The Quest for the Shaman', Miranda and Stephen Aldhouse-Green state that people in shamanistic societies 'perceive the world as a three-tiered cosmos: the underworld, "middle-earth" (where humans and animals live), and an upper world, the abode of the spirits'.

While the work of the shaman will usually be thought to be generally beneficial by his tribe or village, the spells which he casts can sometimes be malevolent. His special knowledge of the spirit world, which is believed to influence the lives of mortals, allows a shaman to counteract the forces of evil; but if a shaman is given cause to dislike another person, he can harness the spirits in order to have his revenge and illustrate his power. Though a shaman can see and communicate with the spirits, he only has the power to influence a limited number of them.

Devotees of old cowboy movies cannot have failed to have seen the Native American medicine man on the screen. In real life, these medicine men (or women) were able to perform services including not only healing ailments both physical and mental, and counteracting malevolent spells and influences, but also securing good hunting. A knowledge of herbal medicine went with the job, and it was necessary to have a sufficiently imposing presence to convince a patient that a 'cure' would be effective. Modern orthodox doctors of medicine are well acquainted with the benefits of a good 'bedside manner', which gives the patient confidence in both the physician and the cure. The art of homeopathy seems to work for many people but it is difficult to explain scientifically. An important factor is the relationship between practitioner and patient; faith in the efficacy of the cure appears to be important, although when an animal benefits from such treatment, it is much more difficult to explain.

Further north from the plains of America, the Inuit peoples may be found. Shamanism played an important role in their culture – in their beliefs, in their medicine and in their folk tales. It is generally thought that their beliefs are more likely to be tied in the mists of time with those of the Siberian native peoples rather than with those of the rest of North America. On the other side of the world, Native Australians have from time immemorial employed shamanism to influence the natural world. Often their rituals involve invoking the memory of their ancestors, who are frequently thought of as animals or birds. They employ singing and dancing in telling stories of the Creation.

Shamanism is often linked to totemism, a belief system involving relationships between a person or group and some object, sometimes an animal or plant, which symbolises that kinship. In some cultures, for example among the Ojibwa of North America, people having the same totem are regarded as belonging to the same family and are therefore forbidden to marry.

Some of the great religions are believed to have arisen from shamanism, including Zoroastrianism, Buddhism and Taoism. What these and many other religions have as a basis is a belief in, or adoration of, a god, accompanied by prayers and grateful offerings to that deity. A shaman provides a focus for these activities in societies which have no great temples and a belief in spirits rather than gods. One of the less spectacular ways in which a shaman may communicate with the spirits is through dreams. Messages may be transmitted to the shaman while he sleeps; he can then pass them on to individuals or to his group, whose lives may be altered by these spiritual revelations. It may be recalled that dreams and their interpretation played a major part in the biblical Joseph's rise to power in Egypt, the land of magical ritual in the ancient world. The Sem priests of Egypt themselves practised shamanism, according to Greg Reeder in his 1994 article 'A Rite of Passage: The Enigmatic Tekenu in Ancient Egyptian Funerary Ritual'. The Sem priests officiated at royal funerals and claimed to be able to go into trances to communicate with the deceased. In Egyptian art, they can be recognised by the leopard skins which they wear over their shoulders. Their distinctive dress marks their very high status; indeed, Sem priest was often a position held by the son of the pharaoh.

Shamans, whatever part of the globe they inhabit, seem generally to have several things in common. The world they have the power to access is a spiritual one, and predictions and prophecies can be transmitted via the shaman. Their healing powers are supernatural. They are able to achieve a state of ecstasy, sometimes assisted by rhythmic chanting or drumming, often through the ingestion of drugs by various means. In Central and South America, a brew of the leaves of the ayahuasca vine, a powerful psychotropic compound, is made. The shaman's senses are enhanced, and he can descend into the underworld or rise into the sky. It has been suggested, though never properly explained, that the famous Nazca Lines (huge stone outlines of birds, animals, insects and plants created in the Peruvian desert, some of which are believed to be over 2,000 years old), which can be clearly perceived only from the air, might be what shamans, perhaps drugged on extracts from the trichocereus cactus, would have seen during their 'flights'.

Although there is a wide variation in practices which qualify for the description 'shamanism', there are similarities as well. Shamans are healers, communicators with the spirits, curers of sickness, advisers in times of need and magicians with very special powers.

SEE ALSO: Animism; Divination; Taoism

TAOISM

Tao translates as 'way' and is one of the world's oldest philosophical and spiritual traditions. It can also mean 'word', 'truth' and 'reason', suggesting to us that Taoism is a study of all that is, not just of one way of living and thinking.

Taoism developed in Ancient China, and its roots lie in the depths of Chinese history, although it is impossible to identify its precise origins. Taoism probably took hold in China because it had something to offer the common man. Two other great religions were prevalent in pre-Communist China, Buddhism and Confucianism, yet it was Taoism that spoke to the majority of the Chinese population, due to its simple message rooted in the natural world.

Although what we would recognise today as Taoist ideas existed long ago in antiquity, it was through the work of Lao Tzu, a Chinese philosopher of the sixth century BC, that the Taoist school of thought really came together. Lao Tzu wrote the Tao Te Ching, which translates as 'the Book of the Way'. Although it is a short work, the breadth of ideas present is astounding, and it demonstrates that at the time it was written there was a very developed and profound philosophy in existence that attempted to understand how the universe operated and exactly how man fitted into the scheme of things. A small taste of what the Tao Te Ching contains follows:

> The Tao doesn't take sides;
> it gives birth to both good and evil.
> The Master doesn't take sides;

she welcomes both saints and sinners.

The Tao is like a bellows:
it is empty yet infinitely capable.
The more you use it, the more it produces;
the more you talk of it, the less you understand.

Hold on to the centre.

Though the Tao Te Ching is attributed to Lao Tzu, known also as 'the Old Philosopher', many scholars believe that he simply compiled the text from a multitude of Taoist principles and sayings that were already in existence in his lifetime. This is indeed a distinct possibility, especially because, as scholars have shown, many of the ideas contained within the Tao Te Ching are so complex that they must have taken centuries to develop. Yet even if we assume that Lao Tzu did not write the text himself, by the very act of collecting these philosophies together in one volume he catalysed the movement and turned what were perhaps myriad ideologies into one cohesive whole.

Some early Chinese writers tell us that Confucius, half a century Lao Tzu's junior, once went to visit the Old Philosopher to seek his counsel. Sze-Ma Ch'ien, a writer and historian born in the second century BC, tells us that the two great sages could not understand each other and that both left the meeting disappointed. He writes that afterwards Confucius described Lao Tzu in this fashion:

> I know that the birds can fly, I know that the fishes can swim, I know that the wild animals can run. For the running, one could make nooses; for the swimming, one could make nets; for the flying, one could make arrows. As to the dragon I cannot know how he can bestride wind and clouds when he rises heavenward. Today I saw Lao-Tzu. Is he perhaps the dragon?

Nature and her cycles are a dominant theme in Taoism, and much of the wisdom imparted is phrased in terms that describe the natural world and the creatures and plants that populate the earth, comparing aspects of the human condition with situations that occur in the natural world. Constant change and the ceaseless rhythm of the natural cycles are important notions in Taoism.

Taoism also teaches that life should be about stripping away what is not needed and returning to a simpler existence, a philosophy in stark contrast with the modern world we live in, where the current prevalent view seems to be that consumerism and the accumulation of material goods is the right path to take.

What is clear when studying the Tao is that 'the way' is often illustrated in negative terms, so that rather than being offered a description of exactly what the Tao is, we are left with an idea of what it is not. It is the sum of all things and therefore untouchable and ultimately unknowable. This is a recurrent idea in Taoism, and its teachings speak of meditating to connect with the void within, the vacuum where nothing exists. Also, the aim of meditation in Taoism is often to remove the individual from the world that surrounds him or her, to strip away all of the material world until only the self remains.

One famous saying that might be said to sum up Taoism is: 'The Tao that can be put into words is not the Everlasting Tao.' This reinforces the idea that the Tao cannot adequately be expressed in words, that no attempt to define it will ever come close to the reality of it. There is also an echo here of something that seems to be hinted at in the Taoist scriptures: that the Tao itself cannot in fact ever be known by the human mind, that it is utterly beyond our comprehension, yet, nevertheless, we should not cease to try.

What must also be understood about Taoism and the Ancient Chinese viewpoint on the world is that they differed radically from the philosophical and religious thinking of the West. In the Western mind, and especially in Christianity, there existed the belief that humankind was separate from nature and, worse still, that humans were superior and all of nature had been created solely for their benefit. Taoism teaches that far from being separate from the natural world, humankind is merely one small part of it. So, in the Taoist belief system, salvation (if we can use the word in this context) can be achieved only through union with the natural world, rather than by breaking away from it. There is a Chinese folk saying that a farmer, or someone who works the land, does not need to study Taoism because he is already a part of the landscape, already in tune with nature. It is only those of us who are out of step with nature and the seasons who need to embrace Taoism in order to find the way again and to fall once more into step with the natural rhythms of the world.

The idea of going with the flow, of being non-assertive and passive and flowing where the Tao takes you is also one of the core tenets of

Taoism. However, this does not mean that one should just lie down and accept fate – far from it. Taoism teaches the individual to turn to nature and learn the ways of all things, rather like looking to see which way the grain in a piece of wood runs before choosing how best to shape it. In other words, forceful actions that go against the grain of nature will not be of any benefit at all and indeed will come to ruin. This principle was called by Lao Tzu '*wu wei*', which we might translate as 'non-action'. Perhaps a closer equivalent would be 'to act without acting'. According to Tao, to act without causing a single ripple in the world is the most fruitful action.

We cannot discuss Tao without briefly mentioning chi. To the Chinese, chi is both energy and breath, and without chi, there could be no Tao. It is the thread which runs through the universe and connects everything; without chi, nothing would exist. In contrast to the Western concept that energy is a part of matter, the Taoist mode of thought would have us accept that chi is separate from matter and exists as an energy force all by itself. Linked to Taoism are many of the martial and meditative arts, like Chi Kung, Tai Chi Chuan and Wudangquan, disciplines which also teach the existence of chi and make extensive use of knowledge of this energy. Many modern forms of these arts originated in Taoist temples before spreading and being adopted by everyday practitioners.

A philosophy with a lineage as ancient and distinguished as the Tao is bound to attract its fair share of celebrated devotees, and Taoism has always been of interest to occultists. Aleister Crowley himself claimed to have spent ten years of his life working on his own translation of the Tao Te Ching. It is unsurprising that his version puts a different slant on the text, and it offers intriguing insights into the nature both of Tao and Crowley; ultimately what we see is the philosophy of Lao Tzu coloured by the tinted lens of Crowley's own unique take on life. An excerpt from Chapter 28 is typical of his unique and sometimes perceptive translation:

> Balance thy male strength with thy female weakness and thou shalt attract all things, as the ocean absorbeth all rivers; for thou shalt formulate the excellence of the Child eternal, simple, and perfect.
>
> Knowing the light, remain in the Dark. Manifest not thy Glory, but thine obscurity. Clothed in this Child-excellence eternal, thou hast attained the Return of the First State.

Knowing splendour of Fame, cling to Obloquy and Infamy; then shalt thou remain as in the Valley to which flow all waters, the lodestone to fascinate all men. Yea, they shall hail in thee this Excellence, eternal, simple and perfect, of the Child.

The raw material, wrought into form, produceth vessels. So the sage King formulateth his Wholeness in divers Offices; and his Law is without violence or constraint.

With the rise of China and the East as an economic superpower, we are potentially on the verge of a very important world shift. For the last thousand years, the trinity of Abrahamic religions – Christianity, Islam and Judaism – have held sway over most of the world, dominating its affairs. Now we are on the threshold of a sea change. Will Confucianism and Taoism come to be the dominant religions for the next thousand years? It certainly seems possible as the cultures that promoted a Jerusalem-centric view on religion begin to lose their dominance.

Some might fear such a radical shift. However, just one look at the last thousand years shows us that while the big three Abrahamic religions have preached love and tolerance, in fact we have had a millennium of war and suffering. Could a world-encompassing faith based on Taoism, with its emphasis on holistic modes of being, reliance on self-empowerment rather than the sermons of holy men and a foundation built on alternative medicine, meditation and therapeutic martial arts such as Tai Chi Chuan offer us a more peaceful and balanced future than the current world system? When put that way, it seems very desirable indeed and a delightful proposition.

SEE ALSO: Crowley, Aleister; Meditation

TAROT

The Tarot deck is a set of cards used for divination and fortune telling. It has a long history and has assumed an air of mystery over the years. Most people would now associate the Tarot deck with occult practices, although its beginnings seem to have been considerably more mundane.

The deck consists of seventy-eight cards in total and is divided into two subsections: the major arcana, which comprises 22 trump, or key, cards; and the minor arcana, which contains the remaining 56 cards, often called pips. It is the major arcana that contains the most familiar imagery of the Tarot. These trump cards include the Hanged Man, Death, the Devil and the High Priestess.

No one knows where the Tarot originated or who was responsible for creating the famous deck of cards that is today used for divination. The most popular theory is that the deck dates back to Ancient Egypt and that the god Thoth was responsible for its creation. Another common idea is that the Tarot is rooted in the ideas and philosophical concepts present in the Kabbalah and has its origins in Hebrew culture. What we do know for certain is that this deck of cards was being used in Italy in the fifteenth century, where it was fashionable for wealthy aristocrats to commission their own sets of the cards, employing famous miniaturist painters of the period. It seems that at this time the cards were used in a popular game as well as for divination.

Playing cards had been in existence in Europe since the fourteenth century, and decks varied in the number of cards they contained. To create the Tarot, a standard deck of forty cards (ten each of four suits) was supplemented with twenty-one trump cards plus a fool, or joker, and four court cards – page, knight, queen and king – of each suit. This completed the seventy-eight-card Tarot deck that is still in use today. The first reference we have to the existence of the Tarot cards is from a sermon given in Italy by a Franciscan friar sometime between 1450 and 1470, in which strong criticism is levelled at the cards and at games of chance in general. This friar even went so far as to suggest that the deck of cards had been invented by the Devil himself and that he had named the trump cards personally. We know that his sermon refers specifically to the Tarot because a detailed description of its trump cards is given.

The earliest complete sets of Tarot cards to have survived are all Italian and appear to date to sometime between 1420 and 1450. These decks are known as Tarocchi and were originally used as normal playing cards. The first evidence we have of their use in divination comes from 1781, when Antoine Court de Gébelin wrote a detailed account of the cards, speculating on their history and recording for posterity how they were used to foretell the future. Gébelin, an occultist as well as a Freemason, was convinced that the cards had originated in Egypt, where they had been used as a method of initiation by the Egyptian priesthood. It was Gébelin who first put forward the idea that the major arcana of the Tarot was an abbreviated visual representation of the Book of Thoth, a legendary book attributed to the god, which, he believed, had survived the destruction of the great Library of Alexandria and had somehow become encapsulated within the Tarot.

After Gébelin, other writers took up the themes he had developed and attempted to prove that the Tarot did in fact originate in Egypt. A French writer, Paul Boiteau d'Ambly, put forward the idea that it was the Gypsies who had brought the Tarot from Egypt into Europe. Gypsies were known to practise divination, so their association with the Tarot is understandable, although it is not at all clear whether they brought the cards into Europe or simply picked up the use of the Tarot once they arrived there.

The famous occultist Aleister Crowley seems to have believed Gébelin's claims, because he too thought that the Tarot was closely linked to the Book of Thoth and even created, with the help of the artist Frieda Harris, his own Book of Thoth Tarot.

The Tarot deck most widely used today is known as the Rider-Waite deck and was first published in 1910 by the Rider Company. The designs were drawn by the artist Pamela Coleman Smith at the instigation of A.E. Waite, a prominent member of the esoteric society the Hermetic Order of the Golden Dawn.

Like the I Ching, the Tarot, rather than telling the future outright, seems to help the person seeking divination make choices and examine more closely what is going on in their life at the time of the reading; thus it helps to point to a route through difficult or trying circumstances. Like the I Ching, the Tarot is ambiguous, allowing room for interpretation, yet both can be surprisingly accurate. This accuracy often convinces people that the person offering the Tarot reading is somehow in possession of supernatural powers. It is a testament to whoever designed the cards, wherever they originated, that the deck is so well balanced that it can help to provide useful answers concerning the future. However long ago the cards were devised, it is clear that people will continue to use them for centuries to come.

SEE ALSO: Crowley, Aleister; Hermetic Order of the Golden Dawn; I Ching; Kabbalah

VAMPIRES

Legends of vampires seem always to be in vogue and are a perennial subject for films and TV series. What is it that fascinates us so much about vampires that we feel so strongly the need to keep the myths alive? And what is it about these stories that they never go out of fashion?

Stories of the mythical vampire grew up in Eastern Europe and are to be found in Slavic legends of the Middle Ages, where it is related that certain people were susceptible to becoming vampires when they died. Typical traits that could lead to vampirism included being buried without the correct rituals, living a wicked life or practising witchcraft. Even committing suicide left an individual vulnerable.

Additionally, there was a wealth of signs and conditions relating to a person's birth indicating a risk of becoming a vampire. A child might be born with a tail or teeth, be conceived on a certain day, or there might be some other irregularity of birth, such as being born with a caul, the part of the amniotic sac that is sometimes still attached to the infant at birth. Furthermore, if a woman was spotted by a vampire while she was pregnant, or if she did not consume salt during the term of her pregnancy, then her child was said to be destined to become a vampire.

When someone died and turned into a vampire, he would return at night to the world of the living, and there he would feast on the blood of local people or even their cattle and livestock. Such tales of vampires were popularised throughout Europe before they became fashionable in Britain through the Victorian gothic novel, which imported vampires and their ilk from the Continent and unleashed them on an unsuspecting audience.

It was in the 1700s in continental Europe that literature featuring vampires first sprang up, inspired by a series of bizarre vampire-hunts in what is now Serbia. The first incident to cause widespread panic was the claim that a peasant named Peter Plogojovitz, who died in 1725, was a vampire and that even after his death he was responsible for the murders of several of his former fellow villagers. Some even claimed, just before breathing their last, that they had been visited at night by the dead Plogojovitz and that he had attempted to throttle them.

What followed was the exhumation of Plogojovitz's body. On examination, it was concluded that he bore all the signs of being a vampire: the contemporary report says that he had shed his old nails and grown new ones and that his hair had also grown while in the ground. Traces of blood around his mouth provided further damning evidence. The corpse was therefore staked through the heart and burned, as was customary in such cases, and it is reported that this caused more fresh blood to be expelled from the mouth, evidently yet further proof of poor Plogojovitz's blood-sucking ways. It is worth mentioning here that nowadays the process of decomposition is more clearly understood, especially such phenomena as the pulling away and contraction of the skin, so that it often appears as if hair and even teeth are growing. Furthermore, another supposed telltale sign of vampirism was darkening of the skin (interestingly the opposite of the pallor attributed to the much later Count Dracula and the vampires of the cinema age), and it is now realised that ruddiness of the complexion is a common feature of decomposition.

A second well-publicised case occurred in Serbia a year later, in 1726. This time, a man named Arnold Paole died after breaking his neck in a fall from a haywagon, and he was subsequently blamed for the deaths of four others, who all reported during their last illnesses that he had been returning from his grave to plague them. A local soldier who had experience in these matters advised the villagers to open Paole's grave and, as in the case of Plogojovitz, they pronounced that the corpse was in fact subject to vampirism, and so they staked the cadaver – which process was said to cause a great deal of groaning and bleeding – and burnt the remains. They also repeated the same procedure on the corpses of all four of his victims. However, this was not the end of the story. Five years later, a second outbreak of vampirism occurred, and this time seventeen people were said to be victims of vampires in the village. It was not Paole himself who was blamed this time, but the meat of the cattle whose blood he was said to have feasted on five years before. The first woman to die in this fresh outbreak had eaten beef from one of the beasts.

So much fear was generated by the case that the local administration were minded to conduct an official investigation into the matter, and the final report is signed by no fewer than five serving officers of the army of Charles VI of Austria, three of them medical officers. Upon arriving at the scene, they began to exhume the bodies of the victims. Having examined them, they decided that they were killed by a vampire. This is from the official report conducted by the chief military surgeon on the scene, Johannes Fluchinger:

> There was a woman by the name of Miliza (60 years old), who had died after a three-month sickness and had been buried 90-some days earlier. In the chest, much liquid blood was found; and the other viscera were, like those mentioned before, in a good condition. During her dissection, all the haiduks who were standing around marvelled greatly at her plumpness and perfect body, uniformly stating that they had known the woman well, from her youth, and that she had, throughout her life, looked and been very lean and dried up, and they emphasised that she had come to this surprising plumpness in the grave. They also said that it was she who started the vampires this time, because she had eaten of the flesh of those sheep that had been killed by the previous vampires.

These events caused a flurry of interest and trepidation across Europe during the subsequent decades, and a real vampire craze spread, spawning literature featuring vampires who came back from the dead to meet with their victims. Even at this early stage, in the eighteenth century, an erotic element crept into the tales, a theme that was to remain firmly coupled with the stories of vampires in the centuries that followed. Poems such as *The Bride of Corinth* by Goethe and Gottfried August Burger's *Lenore* tell the stories of dead lovers who return from their coffins to take their spouses to the grave. This is an excerpt from *Lenore*:

'Ah! where is the chamber, William dear,
And William, where is the bed?'
'Far, far from here: still, narrow, and cool;
Plank and bottom and lid.'
'Hast room for me?'– 'For me and thee;
Up, up to the saddle right speedily!
The wedding-guests are gathered and met,
And the door of the chamber is open set.'

Maybe it was the climate of fear created by the real-life vampire cases that caused these poems to become a sensation. *Lenore* in particular was read and translated all over Europe and inspired a rash of vampire fiction in English.

The work that sealed the popularity of vampires forever has to be Bram Stoker's *Dracula*, which was published in 1897. Stoker is reported to have spent some seven or eight years researching the novel, studying Eastern European folklore and history before composing the story, which is told through a series of letters and diary entries.

Stoker brought out a resonant element of the myths that had not been emphasised in literature before: the idea that vampirism was a disease that could be passed on to the victim, that the person who was bitten by a vampire could become infected. He took the name of his villain from a real historical character, Vlad Draculea, better known as the cruel Vlad the Impaler, who was the fifteenth-century Prince of Wallachia (now a part of modern-day Romania). In Stoker's novel, Count Dracula hatches a plan to infect London's population with vampirism and so spread his dark cult across the world. The popular image we have of vampires today comes largely from Stoker and the legion of novels and films his book spawned.

Although the vampire is best known as a figure of Eastern European folklore, it is worth noting that there are references to these mythical creatures in Ancient Greece, for example in the story of Lamia, the first Queen of Libya, whose children were murdered by the goddess Hera. Lamia lost her mind and turned through grief into a monster. Later, this story was corrupted, resulting in legends of a whole host of creatures called lamiae, which travelled the world drinking the blood of infants, as well as appearing in the guise of beautiful women and seducing men before eating their flesh.

Even in Ancient Egypt, we have the story of the goddess Sekhmet, born of the god Ra, who was sent to earth to exact his vengeance on humanity. Sekhmet took the form of a great lion and wreaked havoc on humankind, slaughtering all she came across and drinking their blood. Even Ra grew afraid of her huge appetite, and so, in an attempt to subdue her, 7,000 barrels of beer were mixed with red ochre to fool the goddess. Sekhmet, thinking the barrels were full of blood, drank the huge quantity of beer and became intoxicated, and the destruction ended.

So it would seem that the being who feasts on the blood of the living is a theme that has been around as long as there have been people to tell stories. Perhaps the idea of the vampire is a primeval fear, an age-old terror, one that arose because people did not understand well enough the fragile boundary that separates the living from the dead; thus vampires were not only conceived in the imagination but thought actually to exist and prey on the living.

VOODOO

Contrary to popular belief, voodoo has little or nothing to do with satanic rituals, and its association with so-called zombies has been overplayed in the popular media. Also known as vodou, vodoun or vudu, this traditional belief system seems to have originated in Benin, spreading to Senegal and other parts of West Africa soon afterwards. In 1996, voodoo became the official state religion of Benin (where it is called Vodoun), and it is estimated that some 35 million Africans practise this multi-faceted faith system today.

If it wasn't for voodoo's later association, via the Caribbean, with dark occultic practices, it would have no place in this book, being a straightforward religion rather than an aspect of the occult. Voodoo has also had a pretty bad press over the past few decades: movies such as *The Believers*, *The Serpent and the Rainbow*, *The Skeleton Key* and the James Bond adventure *Live and Let Die* have painted a picture of demonic possession, black arts, zombie control and satanic-style rituals that have left an impression of voodoo as an occult practice.

The popular idea of the so-called voodoo doll is a further example of how modern creative media can manipulate the real facts. The scenario of the doll as a mannikin representing the intended victim of magic, with pins and other objects used to elicit a real response on the individual, is a common one in the media. Today, the idea has caught on to such an extent that ranges of voodoo dolls are even marketed as toys, with examples such as the Bad Boyfriend doll and the Ex-Husband doll. You can even buy a doll specially designed so that you can affix a photo of your boss 'to get revenge'!

The reality is that dolls within voodoo are not malevolent. Cloth figurines are often used as messengers to the spirit world, when they are left, for example, at the entrance to graveyards, with notes written to the dead attached to them. In Louisiana, 'voodoo poppets' (a small figure or doll representing a person) were used in healing rituals and in some cases made as images of the sacred spirits of the religion.

Voodoo began as the common religion of two West African tribes known as the Mina and Ewe, who believed in a dual cosmological principle of the divine. Their god and creator was known as Nana Buluku, whose twin children, Lisa, a god of the sun, and Mawu, the goddess of the moon, both had sons and daughters known as Voduns. These Voduns, or Loa, are the spirits responsible for the day-to-day running of the physical world, and they are closely linked with nature, each having a special affinity with particular plants or animals. They control the mundane order of things, whilst the creator-god sits apart. However, it is not this original religion of voodoo that has shaped our ideas and misconceptions; it is from the Caribbean and southern United States that the modern notion of voodoo as a dark force has sprung. It would seem that voodoo as practised in the Caribbean, most notably on the island of Haiti, is a modified form of the original religion of West Africa, retained by African slaves who found themselves amongst a predominantly Catholic community.

In the voodoo religion, the universe is seen as a single entity, and the actions of every individual are seen as having consequences throughout the universe. The priests can be male or female, and they act as healers, using a combination of traditional medicine and ritual to treat their followers. During religious ceremonies, there may be ritual sacrifice of an animal, which is then cooked and eaten by the participants, although it is intended as nourishment for the spirits. Another common feature is dancing to a ritual drumbeat with musical accompaniment and singing. The link between the living and the dead is very significant, and the reverence of ancestors is given great importance. The Catholic All Saints Day and All Souls Day are used to celebrate the spirits of a family's ancestors.

Each human is regarded as having two elements: the ti-bon-ange (little good or guardian angel), which can be considered as similar to a good conscience; and the gros-bon-ange (big good angel), equivalent to the Christian concept of the soul. During ritual dancing, it is thought that a Loa may enter a participant, whose gros-bon-ange would then temporarily leave their body.

It is from the American South, specifically New Orleans, that the spelling 'voodoo' seems to have originated. 'Vodou' is the more proper spelling of the original West African religion.

A commonly held belief about voodoo is that it incorporates a form of satanism. This is a misconception arising from the presence of references to both voodoo and Satan within some Southern blues and folk songs written at the turn of the twentieth century. These songs often mixed voodoo and Christian ideas for several different reasons. For example, voodoo as practised in the Caribbean and the American South had assimilated much of the Catholicism originally brought to the region by the Spanish invaders. In many cases, particular Vodun deities had become identified with Catholic saints, each with a specific attribute. Also, it was through such references that many of the social ills of the day could be described, using the metaphor of Satan to explain problems such as endemic racism and lowly social status.

Lurid tales of zombies under the domination of evil voodoo priests are commonly told. The voodoo explanation of a zombie would be that it was a person whose ti-bon-ange had been removed and who was now under the influence of a malign spirit. Other explanations for stories about zombies, have suggested that drugs could be used to induce a death-like coma before reviving the victim and keeping them sedated and compliant, but little evidence exists that this has ever actually happened. It could be that a vulnerable person who believed that their spirit had been taken might be controlled by a rogue practitioner of voodoo. However, reputable priests (hougans) and priestesses (mambos) can reasonably point out the lack of documentary evidence for the existence of zombies in any form and argue that these myths are part of a collection of ill-informed misconceptions about their faith.

In the Caribbean especially, several traditions similar to voodoo have existed alongside it for many generations. Amongst these are hoodoo and the Cuban variant called Santería, or 'Way of the Saints', which has assimilated to a greater degree the Catholic worship of saints, many of the Santería gods and goddesses being based on Catholic saints themselves. For example, the thunder spirit Chango is associated with St Barbara, who is believed to protect those who pray to her from lightning. It is argued that Santería is based on a fundamentally different original religious ideal from voodoo, another West African belief system known as Lukumi, which was prevalent among the Yoruba tribe.

SEE ALSO: Angelology; Animism

WICCA

The neopagan religion of Wicca is a relatively new phenomenon, despite laying claim to roots that go back centuries, if not millennia. There is a popular misconception that Wicca is one and the same as witchcraft, but this is not true. While Wicca is based on the ancient traditions of witchcraft, and the two share similar themes and beliefs, they are not synonymous. It is possible to be a Wiccan without being a witch and vice versa. Wicca is an officially recognised religion, and a modern one at that, while witchcraft is a tradition, a very old tradition, for sure, but never a religion. Witchcraft has, over the centuries, attracted negative connotations, but Wicca is a wholesome and very peace-loving religion, promoting nature and the worship of all things in the natural world, including the yearly cycles such as the equinoxes and solstices.

Gerald Gardner is often considered to be the architect of Wicca, and the religion owes a great deal to his writings and work. In 1951, in the UK, the Witchcraft Act was finally repealed. With its roots in the fifteenth century and passed as an act in 1541, it stated that:

> It shall be Felony to practise, or cause to be practised Conjuration, Witchcraft, Enchantment or Sorcery, to get Money; or to consume any Person in his Body, Members or Goods; or to provoke any Person to unlawful Love; or for the Despight of Christ, or Lucre of Money, to pull down any Cross; or to declare where Goods stolen be.

The Witchcraft Act was amended in 1735, but remained in force, remarkably, until 1951, with the last person successfully convicted under it charged in 1944. After 1951, no longer in fear of persecution, many people practising witchcraft, Gardner included, felt that the times were changing and that they could openly discuss and promote their activities and beliefs.

It was through an esoteric society known as the Rosicrucian Order Crotona Fellowship, a group based in Christchurch in southern England, that Gardner became initiated into witchcraft. While he was a member of the Crotona Fellowship, Gardner was introduced to the New Forest coven, a group of witches who met regularly in the area. Gardner claimed that the High Priestess of this group, Dorothy Clutterbuck, initiated him into the arts of witchcraft in a ceremony at her house. Some have asserted that Gardner made up the whole scenario, including the existence of this Clutterbuck, but Doreen Valiente, the woman who would become Gardner's own High Priestess, claimed she had evidence that this woman had existed and had in fact initiated Gardner. Valiente proved this by identifying Clutterbuck and finding her birth, marriage and death certificates.

Gardner had already published two works of fiction prior to the abolition of the Witchcraft Act in 1951, but after this date he no longer felt the need to hide behind a pseudonym or to fictionalise his beliefs. In 1954, he wrote *Witchcraft Today*, a book that is considered to represent the birth of Wicca. In his groundbreaking book, Gardner described his meetings with the High Priestess of the New Forest coven, Dorothy Clutterbuck (never actually named in the book but described by Gardner as 'Old Dorothy'), and documented in great detail the rituals that the coven enacted in the forest. Never before had such details been made available to the general public, and Gardner explained that the New Forest coven had been in existence for decades and was in possession of beliefs, practices and rituals that went back centuries, the remnants of a craft that Gardner called 'the Old Religion'.

An intriguing element of Gardner's revelations is his description of rituals that took place outdoors and involved nudity – termed 'sky-clad' within the Wicca religion. Later, members of covens said to have been in existence before Gardner popularised Wicca and witchcraft argued that this was not a necessary part of witchcraft and that they had always performed the rituals in robes, not naked. It turned out that Gardner had a propensity for naturism, and it has been suggested that it was this predilection that led him to add this new element to the growing religion of Wicca, much to the chagrin of witches who claimed they had been practising for far longer than the newcomer Gardner.

Gardner makes it clear in the introduction to *Witchcraft Today* that he was not able to tell the whole story, but he revealed enough for the general public to gain an insight into the world of witchcraft:

> I have been told by witches in England: 'Write and tell people we are not perverts. We are decent people, we only want to be left alone, but there are certain secrets that you mustn't give away.' So after some argument as to exactly what I must not reveal, I am permitted to tell much that has never before been made public concerning their beliefs, their rituals and their reasons for what they do, also to emphasise that neither their present beliefs, rituals nor practices are harmful.

As Wicca gained a hold on the public's imagination, Gardner became a celebrity in his own right, and he appeared to revel in the limelight. Many new covens were created following the publication of Gardner's book, and it served to ignite a reawakening of witchcraft in the UK, although critics claim that what was actually created was a fantasy of witchcraft. There is no doubt that what Gardner helped create was an amalgamation of many traditions. The religion which grew up in the wake of *Witchcraft Today* was called Wicca (Gardner himself actually spelled this with one 'c', 'Wica'), and it was known later as Gardnerian Wicca to distinguish it from the alternative forms that evolved as Wicca become increasingly popular.

One thing that is not widely known is that Gardner almost single-handedly created the rituals that were to become the foundation of the religion of Wicca. Some elements were authentic, having been taught to him by Clutterbuck and the New Forest coven, but many were completely new or borrowed from other works and traditions. For example, Gardner was an honorary member of the Ordo Templi Orientis and knew Aleister Crowley, whom he met on more than one occasion. Many believe that it was in fact Crowley who inspired Gardner to establish Wicca as a new religion. It has been shown that parts of Gardner's Wiccan initiation rituals were taken from ceremonies that originated in the Ordo Templi Orientis, in particular Crowley's own Gnostic Mass.

Gardner was not alone; helping him to formulate the doctrine of Wicca was Doreen Valiente, someone who would prove invaluable to Gardner. Together they created the blueprint for what would become the religion of Wicca. At the heart of Wicca is belief in a fertility Goddess and her consort, a Horned God. Gardner believed that these were the ancient gods of Great Britain and that they had been worshipped long ago in antiquity by the ancestors of the British. Wiccans often referred to them as the Lady and the Lord, and they are seen to represent the opposing yet interacting forces of the universe through which all creation is born. It is the Goddess who is generally seen as the most powerful deity in Wicca, because she is able to give birth and hence is seen as the creator of the universe, the Great Mother.

Although the names of these two gods are a secret revealed only to initiates, it has been suggested that the Goddess is Aradia (a name popularised by Charles Leland's 1899 book *Aradia, or the Gospel of the Witches*, in which Aradia is the daughter of Diana who instructs mortals in the arts of witchcraft) and that the Horned God is Cernunnos, a deity originally worshipped by the Celts, though it must be said that the Wiccan version of Cernunnos tends to include many elements that are found in Pan, the Greek god of nature, who is also horned.

Each group or particular coven tends to worship not only these two but also other gods that have been added to the pantheon and are peculiar to that group's activities and beliefs, such as Hecate or Brigid, for example. Wiccans use many ceremonial objects in their rituals, and these often include an altar, a Book of Shadows (a book that originated with Gardner and contains Wiccan rituals), brooms, candles, pentagrams (the ancient symbol of the five-pointed star), crystals and incense, amongst others. Eight Sabbats (Samhain, Yule, Imbolc, Ostara, Beltane, Midsummer, Lughnasadh and Mabon) are celebrated by Wiccans throughout the year, and these comprise the two solstices, the two equinoxes and four cross-quarter days.

The religion's code of morality is summed up by the Wiccan Rede, a saying of unknown origin: 'An it harm none, do what thou wilt.' ('An' in this case means 'if'.) This phrase bears a remarkable similarity to Aleister Crowley's Law of Thelema, which states: 'Do what thou wilt shall be the whole of the Law.' The Wiccan Rede first appears in the form shown here in Gardner's book *The Old Laws*, and if we remember that Gardner used some of Crowley's work when setting out the Wiccan initiation rites, the similarities between the two phrases may not surprise us.

One of the leading voices of Wicca as it grew throughout the late twentieth century was Doreen Valiente, Gardner's High Priestess. She was to split from him in the late '50s following a difference of opinion. Valiente went on to found her own coven, as well as writing several well-respected books on witchcraft, and she became acknowledged as a luminary of the movement and advocate of its cause. Her books include *Where Witchcraft Lives* and *The Rebirth of Witchcraft*.

It is widely acknowledged amongst Wiccans that their religion is a burgeoning and fast-changing one. Wiccans themselves will be the first to admit that much of what is practised today is not identical to the rituals of 50, 40 or even 30 years ago. We are witnessing the birth of a new religion, one that is still finding its feet, still adapting its rituals and still shaping its core belief system.

Critics of Wicca argue that it is a religion created from a vacuum, that what really inspired its birth was a group of people interested in esoteric matters and willing to concoct a new religion from a wealth of other sources and ideologies. Gardner himself admitted that the rituals of the New Forest coven were fragmentary and that in order to make sense of them, they had to be grafted onto other material from different sources, such as Crowley's Ordo Templi Orientis rituals. In answer to these criticisms, Wiccans acknowledge that their religion is a fledgling one but argue that what has been created is something positive and wholesome, and that at the very least it embodies many of the traditions, morals and practices of the Old Religion, or witchcraft.

In spite of his faults, one thing that Gardner did do was cast off the old chains that had dogged witchcraft for so long, revealing that, rather than adhering to the stereotype of the devil-worshipper, witches were actually peace-loving individuals who venerated nature and the natural rhythms of the world. And so it is that Wicca has come today to be seen as a religion preaching tolerance, love and harmony with nature.

SEE ALSO: Crowley, Aleister; Ordo Templi Orientis; Pentagram

YOGA

The practice of yoga is first recorded in a large collection of sacred Hindu texts called the Vedas, which originated in Ancient India. This set of scriptures is often cited by scholars as the oldest in existence, although no date can be conclusively affixed to them. The foundations for the teachings of yoga come from a distinct section of the Vedas known as the Vedanta, which literally means 'the end of knowledge' or 'the ultimate knowledge' ('Veda' itself meaning 'knowledge') and seems to imply that this section of the scriptures contains the very essence of what the Vedas are about. The Vedanta contain more mystical themes and deal with meditation and personal spiritual growth. Nowadays, the term 'Vedanta' refers not just to these sections of the Vedas but also to the school of philosophy that was born from the study of these scriptures.

One of the most important texts on yoga, and certainly the most well known, is the Bhagavad Gita, part of the great epic the Mahabharata, thought to have been composed sometime between 500 and 50 BC. However, even this broad dating is controversial, as it has been pointed out, based on planetary positions recorded in the text, that it might be as old as 5500 BC. Whatever the final dating, many who study these texts would argue that some of the concepts outlined in the Bhagavad Gita, and in the larger Mahabharata, have their origins in ancient history.

The aim of yoga was never simply to develop a regime to rejuvenate the body alone; the purpose of yoga was to purify and cleanse the body so that unification of the self or the spirit, the *jiva*, with the divine, the all-encompassing consciousness of the universe, the Brahman, would be possible. It was thought that only by training both body and mind at the same time could such a union occur. The Sanskrit word 'yoga' itself actually means 'to unite', 'to yoke'. Someone who practises yoga is known as a yogi, although this term is usually reserved for a master or someone who has devoted himself to living life by yogic principles.

We see from the text of the Bhagavad Gita that, as in Taoism, to reach the divine the seeker must detach himself from the physical universe and emancipate himself from all earthly desires:

> One who performs his duty without attachment, surrendering the results unto the Supreme Lord, is unaffected by sinful action, as the lotus leaf is untouched by water.
>
> The yogis, abandoning attachment, act with body, mind, intelligence and even with the senses, only for the purpose of purification.
>
> The steadily devoted soul attains unadulterated peace because he offers the result of all activities to Me; whereas a person who is not in union with the Divine, who is greedy for the fruits of his labour, becomes entangled.

Yoga at its heart works on the principle that all matter is energy and that movement is the key to refining the body and the mind. It recognises – as scientists have only begun to acknowledge in the last couple of centuries – that most matter is not solid, that atoms are filled largely with empty space and that it is the movement of particles within these atoms that creates the illusion of solidity. This idea that the cells of our body operate at a certain vibrational level is utilised in yoga techniques.

It is impossible to split yoga into its constituent parts, as it is a holistic process, that is, it nourishes both the mind and the body. In fact, according to the philosophy that gave birth to yoga, one is not separate from the other and neither can live without the other. However, if we were to look artificially at just the purely physical effects of yoga, the results are surprising to say the least. In the West, yoga is sometimes taught simply as a physical discipline, and the effects even of this limited form of yoga can be very beneficial, making the body supple and stronger and helping to relax and calm the participant. The list of ailments that yoga has been shown to aid is extremely long, and it is clear that it is both a gentle and a powerful method of improving one's health.

The physical element of yoga involves maintaining a series of positions known as *asanas*. These movements are only one part of classical yoga, or raja yoga, and the asanas are thought of as just one of eight 'limbs' of yoga, the other seven being: *yamas* (restraints or moral obligations), *niyamas* (devotions), *pranayama* (breath control), *pratyahara* (withdrawing the senses), *dharana* (concentration), *dhyana* (meditation) and *samadhi* (self-realisation).

One of the most important figures responsible for introducing yoga to the West was Swami Sivananda, who was born in 1887 and who established the Divine Life Society in the 1930s with the aim of spreading knowledge of the Vedanta and yoga. He trained many remarkable minds, amongst them Swami Vishnu Devananda, whom Swami Sivananda sent to the West to disseminate the remarkable body of knowledge of which they were the guardians. The story goes that Swami Sivananda one day placed ten rupees in the palm of Swami Vishnu's hand and told him to enlighten the people of the West, simply saying, 'People are waiting.'

Swami Vishnu adapted yoga to the needs of Westerners, having observed them for many years, and from this work he developed a set of five basic principles that today are at the core of yoga as it is known in the West. These are: proper relaxation, proper exercise, proper breathing, a proper diet and, finally, proper thinking and meditation.

If further evidence is needed that yoga is a magical practice, a way of elevating the spirit, it is worth mentioning that Aleister Crowley devoted much of his later life to yoga, believing that it led to a higher spiritual enlightenment, and he even used it to replace ritual magic in his own life. During his final years, he proposed that magical ritual was merely a process of initiation into spiritual matters which would lead in turn to yoga. In other words, yoga would replace ritual, as the initiate progressed on his or her personal spiritual journey.

What must be understood about yoga is that although in the West it is viewed primarily as a physical discipline, in its true form it is a method of obtaining spiritual enlightenment and in fact a complete guide to living – and practised as it was intended by the ancients, it can benefit in a great way not just the body but also the mind.

SEE ALSO: Crowley, Aleister; Meditation; Taoism

BIBLIOGRAPHY

Aldhouse-Green, Miranda and Stephen, 'The Quest for the Shaman', in *Minerva* (September/October 2006)

Baigent, Michael, and Leigh, Richard, *The Elixir and the Stone* (Viking, London, 1997)

Bailey, Alice A., *The Externalisation of the Hierarchy* (Lucis Publishing Co., New York, 1983)

Baker, Robert A., *They Call It Hypnosis* (Prometheus Books; Buffalo, New York; 1990)

Becker, Udo, *The Continuum Encyclopedia of Symbols* (Continuum, New York, 1997)

Beitchman, Philip, *Alchemy of the Word: Cabala of the Renaissance* (State University of New York Press, Albany, 1998)

Bentley, G.E., Jr., *The Stranger from Paradise: A Biography of William Blake* (Yale University Press, New Haven, 2001)

Bradbury, Will (ed.), *Into the Unknown* (Reader's Digest Association, New York, 1981)

Brookesmith, Peter, *Cult and Occult* (Orbis Publishing Limited, London, 1985)

Buckland, Raymond, *An Illustrated Guide to Magical and Spiritual Symbolism* (New Age Books, Delhi, 2005)

Budge, E.A. Wallis, *Egyptian Magic* (Kegan Paul, Trench, Trübner & Co. Ltd, London, 1901)

Budge, E.A. Wallis, *The Egyptian Heaven and Hell* (Kegan Paul, Trench, Trübner & Co. Ltd, London, 1905)

BIBLIOGRAPHY

Burton, Richard, *The Arabian Nights Entertainments* (The Modern Library, New York, 1997)

Carus, Paul, *The Teachings of Lao-Tzu: The Tao Te Ching* (Rider, London, 1999)

Cavendish, Richard, *The Black Arts* (G.P. Putnam's Sons, New York, 1967)

Charles, R.H., *The Book of Enoch* (Society for Promoting Christian Knowledge, London, 1917)

Church, Alfred John, and Brodribb, William Jackson, *The Annals by Tacitus* (Washington Square Press, New York, 1964)

Clifton, Chas S., 'A Goddess Arrives: The Novels of Dion Fortune and the Development of Gardnerian Witchcraft', in *Gnosis* 9 (1988)

Copenhaver, Brian, *Hermetica: The Greek Corpus Hermeticum and the Latin Asclepius* (Cambridge University Press, New York, 1992)

Crowley, Aleister, *The Book of the Law* (S. Weiser, York Beach, 1997)

Crowley, Aleister, *The Confessions of Aleister Crowley* (Routledge, London, 1979)

Crowley, Aleister, *Diary of a Drug Fiend* (S. Weiser, York Beach, 1970)

Crowley, Aleister, *Magick Theory and Practice* (Peter Smith Pub. Inc.; Gloucester, Massachusetts; 1940)

Crowley, Aleister, *The Tao Teh King: A New Translation* (Thelema Publications, Kings Beach, 1976)

Crowley, Aleister, and Mathers, Samuel Liddell MacGregor, *The Goetia: The Lesser Key of Solomon the King* (Weiser Books, Boston, 1995)

Dan, Joseph, *Kabbalah: A Very Short Introduction* (Oxford University Press, Oxford, 2006)

Dee, John, *The Diaries of John Dee*, ed. Edward Fenton (Day Books, Charlbury, 1998)

Douglas, Alfred, *The Tarot: The Origins, Meaning and Uses of the Cards* (Taplinger, New York, 1972)

Drury, Nevill, 'Seers and Healers: The Ancient Tradition of Shamanism,' in John Matthews (ed.), *The World Atlas of Divination* (Headline, London, 1992)

Drury, Nevill, and Skinner, Stephen, *The Search for Abraxas* (Spearman, London, 1972)

Dundes, Alan, *The Evil Eye: A Folklore Casebook* (Garland Publishing, Inc., New York, 1981)

Elworthy, Frederick Thomas, *The Evil Eye: The Classic Account of an Ancient Superstition* (Dover Publications; Mineola, NY; 2004)

Faulkner, R.O. (trans.), *The Egyptian Book of the Dead: The Book of Going Forth by Day* (Chronicle Books, San Francisco, 1994)

Fortune, Dion, *The Mystical Qabala* (Williams & Norgate, London, 1935)

Fortune, Dion, *Psychic Self-Defence* (Aquarian Press; Wellingborough, Northamptonshire; 1988)

Fortune, Dion, *The Sea Priestess* (Inner Light, Alpine, 1938)

Fortune, Dion, *The Winged Bull* (Williams & Norgate, London, 1935)

Frazer, Sir James, *The Golden Bough* (Penguin Books, London, 1996)

Freke, Timothy, and Gandy, Peter, *Jesus and the Goddess* (Thorsons, London, 2002)

Fulcanelli, *Le Mystère des Cathédrales*, trans. M. Sworder (Brotherhood of Life, Albuquerque, 1984)

Gardiner, Philip, *Gnosis: The Secret of Solomon's Temple Revealed* (Radikal Phase Publishing; Underwood, Nottinghamshire; 2005)

Gardner, Gerald, *Witchcraft Today* (Arrow Books Ltd, Tiptree, 1970)

Gilbert, Adrian G., *Magi: The Quest for a Sacred Tradition* (Bloomsbury, London, 1996)

Gordon, Stuart, *The Paranormal: An Illustrated Encyclopaedia* (BCA, London, 1992)

Graham, O.J., *The Six-Pointed Star: Its Origin and Usage* (New Puritan Library, 1984)

Hall, Manly P., *The Secret Teachings of All Ages* (Philosophical Research Society, Los Angeles, 1977)

Harris, Melvin, *Sorry, You've Been Duped!* (Weidenfeld & Nicolson, London, 1986)

Hudson, Thomas Jay, *The Law of Psychic Phenomena* (Kessinger Publishing; Whitefish, Montana; 1998)

Hudson, Wilson M. (ed.), *The Healer of Los Olmas and Other Mexican Lore*, Publications of the Texas Folklore Society No. XXIV (Southern Methodist University Press, Texas, 1951)

Hulse, David Allen, *The Key of It All: An Encyclopedic Guide to the Sacred Languages and Magical Systems of the World* (Llewellyn, St Paul, 1994)

Iverson, Jeffrey, *More Lives Than One? The Evidence of the Remarkable Bloxham Tapes* (Pan Books, London, 1977)

Izutsu, Toshihiko, *Sufism and Taoism: A Comparative Study of Key Philosophical Concepts* (University of California Press, Berkeley, 1983)

BIBLIOGRAPHY

Jones, Prudence, 'Shapes in the Stars: Patterns of Western Astrology', in John Matthews (ed.), *The World Atlas of Divination* (Headline, London, 1992)

Jones, Richard, *Haunted Castles of Britain and Ireland* (New Holland Publishers, London, 2003)

Jung, Carl, *The Collected Works of Carl Jung* (Routledge and Kegan Paul, London, 1953)

Karcher, Stephen, *The Illustrated Encyclopedia of Divination* (Element Books, Dorset, 1997)

Karcher, Stephen, *Ta Chuan: The Great Treatise* (Carroll & Brown, London, 2000)

Kieckhefer, Richard, *Magic in the Middle Ages* (Cambridge University Press, Cambridge, 1989)

Knight, Christopher, and Lomas, Robert, *The Hiram Key: Pharaohs, Freemasons and the Discovery of the Secret Scrolls of Jesus* (Century, London, 1996)

LaVey, Anton Szandor, *The Satanic Bible* (Avon, New York, 1969)

Lemesurier, Peter, *Nostradamus: The Illustrated Prophecies* (O Books, Oakland, 2003)

Lincoln, Henry, *The Holy Place: Decoding the Mystery of Rennes-Le-Château* (Arris Publishing Ltd, Gloucestershire, 2005)

Lindsay, Jack, *The Origins of Alchemy in Graeco-Roman Egypt* (Barnes and Noble, New York, 1970)

Luck, Georg, *Arcana Mundi: Magic and the Occult in the Greek and Roman Worlds – A Collection of Ancient Texts* (John Hopkins University Press, Baltimore, 1985)

Macdevitt, W.A., *'De Bello Gallico' & Other Commentaries of Caius Julius Caesar* (Everyman's Library, London, 1915)

McLean, Adam, *The Alchemical Mandala: A Survey of the Mandala in the Western Esoteric Traditions* (Phanes Press, Grand Rapids, 1989)

McLean, Adam, and Green, Deirdre, *Commentary on the Chymical Wedding* (Magnum Opus Hermetic Sourceworks, Edinburgh, 1984)

Malinowski, Bronislaw, *Coral Gardens and their Magic: The Language of Magic and Gardening* (George Allen & Unwin Ltd, London, 1966)

Malinowski, Bronislaw, *Sex, Culture and Myth* (Hart Davies, London, 1963)Maple, Eric, *Witchcraft: The Story of Man's Quest for Supernatural Power* (Octopus Books, London, 1973)

Meyer, Marvin W., and Smith, Richard, *Ancient Christian Magic: Coptic Texts of Ritual Power* (Princeton University Press, Princeton, 1999)

Motyer, J.A., 'Curse', in J.D. Douglas (ed.), *The New Bible Dictionary* (Inter-Varsity Press, London, 1975)

Murray, Margaret A., *The God of the Witches* (Sampson Low, Marston & Co., London, 1931)

Murray, Margaret A., *The Witch-Cult in Western Europe* (Clarendon, Oxford, 1921)

Nataf, André, *The Wordsworth Dictionary of the Occult* (Wordsworth Editions Ltd, Hertfordshire, 1994)

Nordh, Katarina, *Aspects of Ancient Egyptian Curses and Blessings: Conceptual Background and Transmission* (Acta Universitatis Upsaliensis Boreas, Upsala, 1996)

Pagels, Elaine, *The Gnostic Gospels* (Vintage Books, New York, 1981)

Patrizzi, Francesco, and Stanley, Thomas (trans.), *The Chaldaean Oracles as Set Down by Julianas* (Heptangle, New Jersey, 1989)

Pavlov, Ivan, *Experimental Psychology* (Philosophical Library, New York, 1957)

Picknett, Lynn, and Prince, Clive, *The Templar Revelation: Secret Guardians of the True Identity of Christ* (Bantam Press, London, 1997)

Reeder, Greg, 'A Rite of Passage: The Enigmatic Tekenu in Ancient Egyptian Funerary Ritual', in *KMT: A Modern Journal of Ancient Egypt*, Vol. 5, No. 3 (1994)

Ritner, Robert K., *The Mechanics of Ancient Egyptian Magical Practice,* Studies in Oriental Civilisation 54 (The Oriental Institute of the University of Chicago, Chicago, 1993)

Ritner, Robert K., 'The religious, social and legal parameters of traditional Egyptian magic', in M. Meyer and P. Mirecki (eds), *Ancient Magic and Ritual Power* (E.J. Brill; New York, Leiden; 1995)

Rix, Robert, 'William Blake and the Radical Swedenborgians', in *Esoterica*, Vol. V (2003)

Roberts, Royston M., *Serendipity: Accidental Discoveries in Science* (Wiley, Hoboken, 1989)

Smith, Richard Furnald, *Prelude to Science: An Exploration of Magic and Divination* (Charles Scribner's Sons, New York, 1975)

Snow, Dr Chet B., and Wambach, Dr Helen, *Mass Dreams of the Future* (McGraw-Hill, New York, 1989)

BIBLIOGRAPHY

Spanos, Nicholas P., and Chaves, John, *Hypnosis: The Cognitive-Behavioral Perspective* (Prometheus Books; Buffalo, New York; 1989)

Spanos, Nicholas, Burgess, Cheryl and Burgess, Melissa, 'Past-life identities, UFO abductions, and Satanic ritual abuse: The social construction of memories', in *International Journal of Clinical and Experimental Hypnosis* 42 (1994)

Spence, Lewis, *An Encyclopaedia of Occultism* (G. Routledge, London, 1920)

Stevenson, Dr Ian, *Twenty Cases Suggestive of Reincarnation* (University of Virginia Press, 1980)

Stoker, Bram, *Dracula* (Little, Brown; London, 2006)

Valiente, Doreen, *Where Witchcraft Lives* (Aquarian Press, Wellingborough, 1962)

Waite, A.E., *The Pictorial Key to the Tarot: Being Fragments of a Secret Tradition under the Veil of Divination* (Rider, London, 1911)

Walls, A.F., 'Gnosticism', in J.D. Douglas (ed.), *The New Bible Dictionary* (Inter-Varsity Press, London, 1975)

Wei, Henry, *The Authentic I Ching* (Newcastle Publishing, North Hollywood, 1987)

Wilson, Colin, *Beyond the Occult* (Caxton Publishing Group, London, 2002)

Yudelove, Steven, *The Tao and the Tree of Life* (Llewellyn, St Paul, 1996)